Company Accounts – A Guide

Company Accounts – A Guide

by

DAVID FANNING and

MAURICE PENDLEBURY

London
GEORGE ALLEN & UNWIN
Boston   Sydney

George Allen & Unwin (Publishers) Ltd,
40 Museum Street, London WC1A 1LU, UK

George Allen & Unwin (Publishers) Ltd,
Park Lane, Hemel Hempstead, Herts HP2 4TE, UK

Allen & Unwin, Inc.,
9 Winchester Terrace, Winchester, Mass. 01890, USA

George Allen & Unwin Australia Pty Ltd,
8 Napier Street, North Sydney, NSW 2060, Australia

First published in 1984
Second impression 1985

British Library Cataloguing in Publication Data

Fanning, David
    Company accounts.
    1. Corporations – Great Britain – Accounting
    2. Financial statements – Great Britain
    I. Title   II. Pendlebury, Maurice
    657′.95′0941   HF5686.C7
    ISBN 0-04-332092-9
    ISBN 0-04-332093-7 Pbk

Library of Congress Cataloging in Publication Data

Fanning, David.
    Company accounts.
    Bibliography: p.
    Includes index.
    1. Corporation reports. 2. Financial statements.
I. Pendlebury, M. W. II. Title.
HG4028.B2F36   1984   657′.33   84-349
ISBN 0-04-332092-9
ISBN 0-04-332093-7 (pbk.)

Set in 10 on 12 point Times by Fotographics (Bedford) Ltd
and printed in Great Britain by Mackays of Chatham

Contents

Preface   *page*   vii
1   The purpose and format of company reports   1

Part One: PUBLISHED FINANCIAL STATEMENTS

2	The profit and loss account	15
3	The balance sheet	38
4	The funds flow statement	58
5	The value added statement	68
6	The directors' report	72
7	The chairman's statement	77
8	Other reports and statements	81
9	The auditor's report	92

Part Two: INTERPRETATION AND ASSESSMENT

10	Financial statement analysis and comparison	101
11	Profitability and performance	107
12	Efficiency and effectiveness	127
13	Liquidity and stability	135
14	Capital structure and financial risk	142
15	The use of financial ratios	151

Part Three: APPENDICES

A	Financial Review of The BOC Group plc for the year ended 30 September 1982	163
B	Sources of comparative statistics and data	217
	Further Reading	219
	Index	221

Preface

This book provides a thorough and analytical discussion of the nature and format of published company annual reports and accounts and a full introduction to the analysis and interpretation of financial statements. It takes notice of the effects and impacts of recent legislation and regulations, particularly the Companies Act 1981, and all published statements of standard accounting practice, thereby providing a relevant and up-to-date guide to this important area.

We have designed the book to be most useful to students preparing for the examinations of the accountancy bodies, to accountancy practitioners and others anxious to analyse published financial statements, to a wide range of students preparing for the examinations of other professional bodies, and to undergraduate students entering upon a course of studies in accountancy and business.

In Part One, we provide an analytical description of the nature and role of company annual reports and accounts and a detailed discussion of the impact of British legislation and regulation and of professional practices and recommendations. In Part Two, we provide a detailed analysis of the principal and subsidiary financial statements of a leading British company, interpreting and assessing that company's performance by means of a wide range of financial ratios. The appendices include the complete text of that company's 1981-82 financial statements, which were amongst the first sets of British accounts to be prepared in accordance with the Companies Act 1981 and its provisions. The book provides a rounded appreciation of the issues involved and the techniques employed in interpreting company accounts.

We are grateful to the directors of The BOC Group plc for permission to reproduce and extract from that company's annual report for the year ended 30 September 1982.

As teachers and researchers, we are deeply appreciative of the considerable assistance given by successive generations of undergraduate students who have permitted us to try out our ideas and refine our teaching practices with their cooperation. Our colleagues in the Department of Business Administration and Accountancy at the University of Wales Institute of Science and Technology in Cardiff have demonstrated continued support and interest. Our editor, Nicholas Brealey, and his advisers have played a significant role in the preparation of this book, and we are obliged to our secretaries – Stevie Burges, Kath Hollister and Margaret Pritchard – for their unfailing goodwill and dedication in the task of turning a number of drafts into a cohesive finished typescript.

Cardiff   David Fanning
July 1983   Maurice Pendlebury

1 The Purpose and Format of Company Reports

The nature of the modern corporation is such that a wide range of people are affected by and properly interested in its activities and influences. In fairly broad terms, those parties may be categorized as follows: investors, whether equity or preference shareholders; creditors and lenders, whether debenture or mortgage holders or trade suppliers or bank officials; employees and their representatives; government officials and administrators, whether tax collectors or statisticians; members of the local, regional and national communities within which the corporation operates. Each of those parties has a clear right, whether defined by law or otherwise, to have reasonable access to certain levels of information about the company's activities and prospects. This chapter is concerned with setting the scene by discussing the accountability and stewardship aspects of a company's reporting practices and by outlining some of the legal and professional background for those practices.

The considerable increase in the legislative requirements impinging on the activities of limited companies has led to a widening of the range of information that a company has to provide by law. The even greater increase in the ethical and professional requirements imposed by accountants, stock market administrators and others has brought about a burgeoning succession of standards and pronouncements with which the modern corporation is obliged to comply. As will be discussed in Part One, the extent and complexity of company legislation and regulation are daunting. The volume of legislation alone – encompassing five successive Companies Acts from 1948 to 1981 – comprises 781 clauses, 34 schedules and 839 pages. Additionally, the greater part of the 1948 consolidating act comprises statute law that was first enacted more than a century or so ago. That law has remained practically unchanged despite changes in legislative policy and in the nature of companies, and even despite the considerable impact of giving effect to European Community directives in the 1980 and 1981 acts. In particular, the Companies Act 1981 has altered radically the bases on which and the ways in which companies' reports and accounts are to be prepared.

Accountability and Stewardship

The very substantial protection afforded to company directors and managers by the concept of limited liability and the considerable separation in recent years between the ownership of a company (which rests solely with its shareholders) and its day-to-day control (which rests largely with its corporate executives and full-time directors) have forced a proper concern that those responsible for the financial and trading activities of a company should report conscientiously and honestly on the affairs of the company and its current and prospective status.

Shareholders assign to a board of directors the duties and obligations of running their company from year to year, while retaining the legal duties and obligations of owning shares in a company. Those directors will include some who act in a part-time or non-executive capacity; in effect, the affairs of the company will be under the routine control of a handful of executives. That being the case, there has to be adequate provision for those executives to report on their stewardship of what are frequently very considerable assets and their management of very substantial operations.

Without delving too deeply into company law, the legal control and ownership of a limited company reside in the shareholders in general meeting. For many companies, that may involve nothing more than the directors and their immediate families. For one of the 3,000 or so quoted public companies in Britain, that general meeting could potentially involve some 40,000 or 50,000 separate shareholders. In practice, it has to be said, company general meetings rarely attract more than 100 or 200 actual participants. Nevertheless, as the steward of an estate is responsible to its owner, so the directors of a company are responsible to its shareholders.

In general terms, that accountability is served by reporting to the shareholders on the sales and other activities of the company during a stated period (usually a twelve-month fiscal or calendar year, supplemented by half-yearly reports) and on the profits (or losses) generated by those activities. Such reports will take the form of a financial statement (the trading and profit and loss account) reporting the money value of those activities and their results, and a further statement (the balance sheet) reporting the position in money terms of the company at the year-end and revealing the impact of the previous year's activities on the company's asset and liability characteristics. Additionally, those financial statements will be supported by a qualitative report by the directors, amplifying the statements and reporting certain additional information (see Chapter 6). Conventionally, the directors will make further statements, whether by choice or by constraint of legal or regulatory measures, revealing the flow of funds through the company (see Chapter 4) and the value added by the year's activities (see Chapter 5). For the larger companies, those statements will be accompanied by a chairman's review of the past year and his expectations for the future (see Chapter 7) and by other informational reports on additional relevant aspects of the company's activities and affairs (see Chapter 8).

Where legally or institutionally necessary, the directors' reports and statements will be accompanied by a certificate from the company's auditors (whose qualifications are prescribed by law) attesting the reasonable reliability and apparent truth and fairness of the company's financial statements. The nature and implications of the auditor's opinion are discussed more fully in Chapter 9; it has to be recognized that an 'unqualified' auditor's report (that is, one in which no reservations are expressed on the grounds of uncertainty or disagreement) is not the equivalent of a guarantee that the company's affairs are wholly sound and its future secure.

Every company registered in the United Kingdom, whether public (quoted or unquoted) or private, and no matter what its size, has to have an annual audit under the Companies Acts. Notwithstanding that fact, the law says little about the statutory duties of an auditor. How an audit should be conducted and what an auditor should do to ensure that he has displayed reasonable care and skill are not spelled out in any part of the relevant statutes. The various professional bodies, however, have laid down certain minimal standards to be complied with by auditors. All those who rely on financial statements, whether as shareholders, creditors, regulators or similarly interested parties, are closely affected by an auditor's work and a proper appreciation of the nature and scope of an audit is essential to a full understanding of the purpose and characteristics of company accounts.

Regulation and Supervision

Company annual reports and accounts are the statements by which government departments, stock exchanges, professional associations, pressure groups and special interest bodies measure the extent of compliance with or departure from statutory and regulatory requirements, professional and institutional recommendations, ethical and best practice standards, and social and environmental considerations of propriety and best behaviour.

Chapters 2–9 describe and discuss the impacts on various aspects of company reporting of British legislation and regulation and European directives and guidelines and of professional standards and recommendations as they affect particular statements and reports, but it will be of value to outline here the major constituents of each of the above general processes of regulation and supervision.

Statutory requirements

The main body of statutes prescribing the nature and activities of limited companies comprises the five extant Companies Acts. The principal act is the Companies Act 1948, which consolidated and extended statute law at that time. Subsequent acts – those of 1967, 1976, 1980 and 1981 – have supplemented, rather than replaced, provisions of the 1948 statute. The

1981 act, however, introduced new disclosure and presentation rules (largely as a result of European Community initiatives and directives); amongst those requirements, discussed more fully in the following chapters, the annual report and accounts must contain four basic components: a directors' report; a profit and loss account; a balance sheet; an auditor's report.

The provisions of the 1981 act increase considerably the amount of information to be disclosed and alter significantly the ways in which information is to be disclosed in published accounts. The relevant chapters in Part One detail the revised requirements, but there are some notable departures from previous practice that may be commented upon here. The directors' report is now subject to audit, in so far as it must be consistent with the financial accounts. In addition, the directors are required to give clearer information on such matters as employment practices, directors' interests and research and development activities. The content of the profit and loss account has been considerably enhanced, in particular by the inclusion of information on the cost of sales and the costs of distribution and administration. Some of those items may be combined with others where they are not significant or they may be disclosed by way of notes to the account rather than by being shown on the 'face' of the account. The format and content of the balance sheet have been drastically altered by the Companies Act 1981, and the classification of information has been widened markedly by the introduction of a number of minimum categories under which information must be provided on the 'face' of the balance sheet.

The auditor's report will state whether or not the accounts give a true and fair view of the company's affairs at the end of the period and of its profit or loss for that period. In addition, it will aver compliance with approved auditing standards and report any disagreement as to the proper treatment of anything stated in the accounts. In usual terms, this will arise from any significant departure from standards of accounting practice. Doubt may also be expressed in cases where there is any material unresolved litigation or other contingent liability or where there is any doubt about the continuation of the company as a going concern. In the cases of certain small companies, the auditor's report may mention reliance on management assurances rather than on specific audit evidence.

The 1981 act permits the preparation and filing of 'modified' accounts by certain small and medium-sized private companies, as discussed in Part One, to be accompanied by special directors' statements and a special form of audit report.

New requirements have been introduced to cover the statutory publication of company accounts. By law, registered companies are required to file copies of audited accounts with the Registrar of Companies and there are various penalties for non-compliance or tardiness in that regard. In addition, the 1981 act introduced provisions to allow publication in full or in part in a newspaper and by distribution to employees of an abridged or simplified version (see Chapter 8).

The requirements of the 1981 act are particularly notable in that, for the first time, a number of basic accounting principles are written into the law. For the most part, these give statutory backing to matters that are the subjects of statements of standard accounting practice, although there continues to be statutory provision for reliance on 'generally accepted accounting principles'. These basic rules are discussed more fully in the relevant chapters in Part One.

However, the Department of Trade has drawn attention to what it sees as the clear distinction to be drawn betwen compliance with the law and adherence to accounting standards. In the Department's view, it would be misleading to interpret recent cases as implying that accounting standards have the force of law. They may be 'material evidence on questions as to accounting principles and practices' but they have no formal status in law. The Department of Trade is concerned to emphasize that where there is any conflict between the statutory requirements on the form and content of company accounts and the overriding requirement that accounts should give a true and fair view, the presentation of a true and fair view in the accounts is to be achieved by the provision of additional information in the balance sheet or the profit and loss account or the notes to the accounts. The Department of Trade emphasizes that it sees

> nothing inconsistent between the law . . . and the disclosure and other requirements elaborated by Accounting Standards by way of guidance statements and indicators of best practice. It does, however, consider it axiomatic that any emphasis on substance over form must not be at the expense of compliance with the law.

In other words, specific statutory reporting requirements may not be departed from in order to conform to accounting standards. Subsection (2) of Section 1 of the 1981 act does, however, permit departure from those statutory requirements in situations where compliance with the law would mean that accounts did not show a true and fair view. (Where departure does occur, full particulars must be given together with reasons for that departure and an explanation of the effect of such departure.) Departure would clearly not be permissible, on the other hand, where two different approaches show a true and fair view and where the preferred approach (whether for reasons of clarity or otherwise) results in a presentation that breaches specific statutory requirements as to form or content.

Proponents of accounting standards have sought for a number of years to achieve statutory recognition for accounting standards, with Statements of Standard Accounting Practice having legal endorsement and being enforceable through the executive or the courts. The nature of the standard-setting body (see below) as a private sector agency outside the control of Parliament would render such a step objectionable. In the profession's view, judicial enforcement is neither practicable nor desirable. Nevertheless, a number of quasi-judicial regulatory bodies (such as the Council of the Stock Exchange or the ruling council of Lloyd's) have sought to make adherence to accounting standards necessary conditions for continued membership by firms and individuals.

It is expected that extant company legislation will be consolidated in either one single act or a series of related acts on individual aspects of company behaviour and regulation, and the Law Commission has appointed a leading expert to draft the consolidating measure or measures. Such a procedure will, of course, simply reproduce existing statute law in a consolidated form; by parliamentary practice, consolidation bills do not amend existing law. There is a limited power under the 1981 act for the statute law on companies to be changed by Order in Council but that is designed only to facilitate the production of a satisfactory consolidation bill.

Professional and institutional recommendations

These may conveniently be considered in two categories: the recommendations and standards of the accountancy and auditing professions, and the requirements and provisions of certain professional associations and regulatory agencies, such as the Council of the Stock Exchange. Certain aspects of these will be examined further in the relevant chapters in Part One, but it will be valuable to outline the principal features here.

Practising accountants and auditors are required to adhere to accounting and auditing standards promulgated by their professional bodies and to follow the ethical guidelines and recommendations of those bodies. In addition, companies are expected to conform with accounting standards in the preparation of their financial statements and accounts.

Accounting and auditing standards are produced by the Accounting Standards Committee and the Auditing Practices Committee of the Consultative Committee of Accountancy Bodies, which is a joint representative committee of the principal validating accountancy bodies in the United Kingdom. Those committees produce a series of papers giving guidance and instruction on various aspects of the treatment and presentation of a company's financial statements.

In general, the committees issue a series of discussion papers on topics that they consider of significance, take advice and comment from interested parties on those discussion papers, prepare and issue exposure drafts of proposed accounting standards, and formally promulgate Statements of Standard Accounting Practice (conventionally known as SSAPs). These SSAPs are endorsed by the governing councils of the constituent professional accountancy associations and their provisions made binding on members. The process has often been criticized as unsatisfactory, and there have been a number of instances in which vested interests have been seen to be able to influence the tenor of a particular statement or even its postponement.

Extant statements cover such topics as current cost accounting, group accounts, accounting for depreciation, statements of the source and application of funds, the valuation of stocks and work in progress, accounting for and reporting post balance sheet events, accounting for deferred taxation, accounting for contingencies, and so on.

In addition to those formally promulgated standards, the professional bodies issue guidelines and recommendations to their members, covering many matters not yet enshrined in SSAPs and items ancillary to matters on which accounting standards have been adopted.

As an example of the endorsement of accounting standards by non-accountancy associations, the Council of the Stock Exchange requires listed companies (that is, those public companies whose shares can be traded in the Stock Exchange's markets) to agree to maintain certain minimum standards and to provide basic information on their activities and status. In particular, companies would have to explain any departure from generally accepted accounting principles or non-compliance with accounting standards. Additionally, listed companies are required to provide many items of information not required by law or accounting standard. Participant companies are required to sign a form of general undertaking or listing agreement under which they promise to adhere to generally accepted accounting principles and to provide detailed and regular information on their activities and status and any significant changes therein.

Other supervisory and regulatory bodies adopt the same stance as the Council of the Stock Exchange, requiring their participants and members to conform to best practice in the matter of information disclosure and the form and content of financial statements and reports.

Social and environmental considerations
With the growth in recent years of pressure groups, such as those concerned with environmental issues, racial and ethnic minorities, disabled or disadvantaged groups, and political ideologies, there has developed an increased attention to companies' published accounts as a source of information on those companies' social and environmental impacts. Equally, many companies have availed themselves of the opportunity to include with their financial statements detailed information designed to rebut or forestall criticism or pressure on social and environmental grounds.

Legal requirements on the disclosure of information on matters relating to employment, health and safety at work, training, and the employment of disabled people, for example, have been considerably extended in recent years and have forced the wider disclosure of many employee-related matters. In 1975, the forerunner to the present Accounting Standards

Committee produced a discussion document in which it advocated the production of an enhanced series of reports and statements. The committee's proposals received a mixed reception, but a number of its more beneficial suggestions have been widely adopted, as discussed in Chapter 8.

In addition, the activities of chemical companies, mineral extraction companies and the like have come in for closer scrutiny by lobbyists and campaigners. That increased scrutiny has, almost invariably, resulted in enhanced or widened disclosure of relevant financial and non-financial information.

There has been a marked tendency in the past decade or so to move away from the traditional solely financial orientation of company reports and to introduce a wider degree of disclosure in respect of all the resources used in a company's business, including human and environmental resources. This method of presenting information has been labelled 'social accounting' or 'social reporting' and it has attracted a certain amount of support amongst both academics and accountancy practitioners. Nonetheless, it has been eschewed by many companies on the grounds of cost and complexity and by others on the grounds of irrelevance or inapplicability. Some companies have presented so-called social reports, as discussed in Chapter 8, but the area of social accounting has been largely ignored by both companies and practitioners.

Format

There are two related considerations in respect of the format of published accounts and reports: the actual format of the accounts themselves, that is their content and structure as ordained by law or best practice, and the format of the document in which they are published, that is its characteristics and usual form. In broad terms, the first of these considerations applies to virtually all companies, while the second varies markedly from company to company.

Content and structure of financial statements

In accordance with the Companies Act 1981, balance sheets and profit and loss accounts must be presented in conformity with one of the prescribed formats. Two alternative formats are permitted for the balance sheet, allowing either a horizontal or a vertical presentation of specified minimum levels of information. Four alternative formats are permitted for the profit and loss account, allowing for either a horizontal or a vertical presentation and for either an 'operational' or an 'expenditure' basis of calculation. These alternative formats are described and discussed in Chapters 2 and 3, and pro forma examples presented in illustration.

Once a particular format has been selected, it should be adopted consistently in subsequent periods unless there are 'special reasons' for not doing so. In each case, comparative figures for preceding periods must be in a compatible format.

For any given format, as will be seen from Chapters 2 and 3, the order in which the items are listed and the headings and sub-headings describing them are strictly delineated. Subject to those statutory requirements, items may be shown in greater detail than laid down, new headings may be introduced, items may be combined where they are not individually material, certain items may be shown in the notes rather than on the face of the account, and arrangements and headings may be adapted where the special nature of a company's business requires it.

The formats and structures detailed in the 1981 act are major departures from those commonly followed by companies and accountants in former years and, in many ways, make the analysis and interpretation of company accounts that much easier and more pertinent. The discussion in the following chapters of this book, and in particular in Chapters 10–15, follows the post-1981 formats and requirements and draws on the published report and accounts of The BOC Group plc for the year to 30 September 1982. At the time of writing, the BOC document was the first example available of a major company's accounts prepared in accordance with the 1981 act. It is worth recording the fact that The BOC Group and its directors have consistently been in the forefront of their peers and competitors in the matter of information provision and disclosure. The authors of this book are particularly pleased to be able to acknowledge here the very marked contribution that the company and its executives have made to financial reporting in the United Kingdom. The full text of the company's Financial Review is reproduced in Appendix A and numerous examples from its reports and accounts appear in the following chapters.

Published reports and accounts
Leaving aside the statutory definition of the 'publication' of company accounts (which covers the delivery of certified copies of the financial statements and the auditor's report to the Registrar of Companies and the transmission of copies to the shareholders of limited companies), the conventional view of a company annual report and set of accounts is a glossy booklet, generally of A4 size, illustrated with photographs of the company's directors and some of its activities, containing a chairman's statement and other promotional or publicity material, and supplemented by a closely printed section carrying complex and detailed financial data.

Many financial commentators and analysts have a rough and ready rule of thumb: the glossier the report and the weightier its contents, the more at risk is the company. Needless to say, that rule is patently not universally applicable!

Against that kind of cavalier assessment, it has to be recorded that shareholders need and are entitled to full and relevant information on their companies and so the annual report and accounts offer a unique opportunity of providing not only the statutory legal and financial information and notices but also important corporate reports, statements and background information. Against that has to be weighed the very considerable costs of designing, printing, producing and distributing each annual report to very large numbers of shareholders. The Imperial Group plc, for example, saved more than £100,000 in one year by using lighter-weight paper for its report and accounts, by omitting photographs and other multi-coloured and glossy material, and by despatching the reports in plastic wrappers instead of manilla envelopes.

For the greater majority of companies, the annual report and accounts document is little more than the bare provision of statutory information and a brief statement from the chairman or the directors. For the 3,000 or so companies listed on the Stock Exchange, the yearly document is generally more informative.

Faced with ever-increasing costs associated with the identification and reproduction of the many items of information now required to be included in company accounts and reports, a number of companies and their directors have advanced the proposal that shareholders do not require and often do not want the full set of financial statements and supporting notes. Instead, it is argued, there should be a simplified form of financial statement that could be sent to all shareholders, with the fuller document being available on request to those shareholders who asked for it.

Equally, there exists the general practice of making simplified or extracted financial statements available to employees and their representatives. In most cases, those employee reports are highlighted paragraphs or inserted pages in the normal employee newspaper or bulletin. In some instances, employee reports are prepared specifically and issued separately.

Both these areas of reporting, to shareholders and to employees, are crucially important. Of their nature, both those publics are relatively unsophisticated in the interpretation and manipulation of accounting and financial data and there are significant dangers in presenting them with a considerably simplified set of accounts. Some aspects of these matters are discussed in Chapter 8, but it is clear that the safeguards embodied in various statutes and professional recommendations cannot lightly be abandoned in the cause of 'readability' or 'relevance'.

It will continue to be essential for full, detailed and wide-ranging statements to be available to analysts and commentators, over and above their availability to shareholders and their public availability at the Companies Registration Offices.

Conclusion

As W. T. Baxter has said (in Lee, 1981), the original purpose of company reports is still fundamental and

... even if reports help decision in only an indirect way, we have no cause to feel apologetic about them. They are important. Their original task ... was to provide evidence that the accounting records have been kept properly, and to show what has happened to the owners' wealth. This they still do. They are the culmination of complex and exacting work. Much of it may have become routine, yet it is essential for business survival.

What accounting reports and financial statements give, then, are items of background information. They provide a framework against which may be judged the stewardship of a company's directors and managers and its viability and health.

The purpose of this book is to describe and analyse the characteristics and components of company financial statements and to provide guidance on the use and interpretation of financial reports and their contents. As such, the book is not directly concerned with the debate about the nature and purpose of accounting standards – other than to explain their impact and demonstrate their use. However, there are a number of points about accounting standards that might usefully be mentioned here.

In the view of most preparers and users of financial reports, accounting standards are necessary and will continue to be necessary. In so far as they narrow the choice of alternative accounting treatments, they serve to make financial reports more comparable. There is a danger that statements of standard accounting practice could be seen as 'benchmarks' against which deviations may be measured; the better assessment of such statements sees them as statements of accounting principles (hopefully, firm and definitive affirmations rather than weak and permissively conditional suggestions), which should be used in financial statements and departure from which should be allowed only in exceptional circumstances.

If the sole use of a set of financial statements were related to a single enterprise in isolation, then there might be no need for accounting standards. Such is rarely the case, however. Financial statements are designed to be used by a wide range of participants who need a very high degree of consistency and comparability between the financial reports of all enterprises. At the very least, accounting standards are designed to narrow the choices available to preparers, thereby making the users' task that much easier.

There is, in addition, the undefined statutory requirement that financial statements of limited companies should give a true and fair view of a company's activities and financial position. To that extent, accounting standards seek to ensure that comparable financial statements share a common aim.

Accounting standards are not accepted by all parties in the financial reporting network, and there are significant political, organizational and managerial motives to militate against a universal endorsement of accounting standards. Nonetheless, their formulation and promulgation represent perhaps the most sensible way to achieve comparability and consistency.

Clearly, the world of company reports and accounts is a dynamic one, susceptible to frequent and varying pressures and influences as the needs of users change, as the requirements of government and the professions change, and as the expectations of shareholders and employees change. There is a considerable amount of work to be done still on identifying pertinent informational needs, formulating regulatory and supervisory provisions, and codifying appropriate reporting structures and formats.

Part One:

Published Financial Statements

2 The Profit and Loss Account

In essence, the profit and loss account (often known as the income statement) summarizes the results of the company's activities during the financial period under review. It reports income, operating expenses, non-operating income and expenses, extraordinary income and expenses, taxation charges, proposed and paid dividends, transfers to and from reserves. It has a particular attraction for most users of accounts, in that it reports a 'bottom line' figure – the profit or loss for the financial year – which can be used as a shorthand performance measure.

Profit and loss accounts need considerable scrutiny and careful attention, however, if they are not to be misleading. To a very large degree, the altered formats introduced by the 1981 act will serve to reveal much more information and to enhance decision-making based on analysis of profit and loss statements.

This chapter will proceed by examining the alternative formats permitted by the 1981 act and by describing and discussing the various items to be included on the face of the account or in the notes thereto. Alternative treatments will be illustrated with examples from post-1981 accounts. As appropriate, the provisions and requirements of SSAPs and professional recommendations will be linked with the legal requirements imposed by the latest act.

Formats

Schedule 1 to the 1981 act (which replaces Schedule 8 to the 1948 act) introduced the concept of prescribed formats for financial statements. While it had been common practice in European countries for a number of years, the introduction of standardized formats to the United Kingdom represented a significant departure from previous practice. There are advantages and disadvantages associated with standardization of format. On the one hand, it encourages greater consistency of treatment between one financial period and another and facilitates comparison between the results of one year and another. It also ensures that different companies follow much the same disclosure practices, both as to the nature of the items disclosed and as to the extent of the information disclosed. On the other hand, the prescription of standard formats removes some of the otherwise welcome flexibility that companies had adopted in presenting their results, allowing them to present their individual accounts in what they considered the most appropriate way. By and large, however, such considerations applied with more force to balance sheets than to profit and loss accounts. On the whole, the introduction of standardized formats and enhanced minimum levels of disclosure is to be welcomed.

Four alternative formats are now permitted for a company's profit and loss account. Exhibits 2.1–2.4 reproduce (with the permission of the Controller of Her Majesty's Stationery Office) the four alternative profit and loss account formats.

Formats 1 and 2 are vertical arrangements, while formats 3 and 4 are double-sided or horizontal arrangements. The essential difference between the alternative formats is in the nature of their classification of the presented information. Formats 1 and 3 classify income and operating expenses by function, whereas formats 2 and 4 classify information by type of income and expense.

That difference can be shown summarily as follows. Formats 1 and 3 will require analyses of operating expenses to be shown as follows:

- cost of sales,
- distribution costs,
- administrative expenses,

leading to the identification of operating income perhaps more easily than other alternative arrangements. Formats 2 and 4 will require operating expenses to be analysed as follows:

Exhibit 2.1   *Profit and Loss Account – Format 1*

1	Turnover
2	Cost of sales
3	Gross profit or loss
4	Distribution costs
5	Administrative expenses
6	Other operating income
7	Income from shares in group companies
8	Income from shares in related companies
9	Income from other fixed asset investments
10	Other interest receivable and similar income
11	Amounts written off investments
12	Interest payable and similar charges
13	Tax on profit or loss on ordinary activities
14	Profit or loss on ordinary activities after taxation
15	Extraordinary income
16	Extraordinary charges
17	Extraordinary profit or loss
18	Tax on extraordinary profit or loss
19	Other taxes not shown under the above items
20	Profit or loss for the financial year

- change in stocks of finished goods and in work in progress,
- own work capitalized,
- raw materials and consumables,
- other external charges,
- staff costs,
- depreciation and other amounts written off tangible and intangible fixed assets,
- exceptional amounts written off current assets,
- other operating charges,

and would make the calculation of cost of sales and gross profit less easy than under alternative formats. In the case of many companies, gross profit is a significant performance measure and its calculation under formats 2 and 4 would be possible only if substantial further information were provided in respect of such items as depreciation, employment costs and other operating charges.

Companies and their advisers will be able to adopt the format that they

Exhibit 2.2   *Profit and Loss Account – Format 2*

1	Turnover
2	Change in stocks of finished goods and in work in progress
3	Own work capitalized
4	Other operating income
5	(a) Raw materials and consumables
	(b) Other external charges
6	Staff costs:
	(a) wages and salaries
	(b) social security costs
	(c) other pension costs
7	(a) Depreciation and other amounts written off tangible and intangible fixed assets
	(b) Exceptional amounts written off current assets
8	Other operating charges
9	Income from shares in group companies
10	Income from shares in related companies
11	Income from other fixed asset investments
12	Other interest receivable and similar income
13	Amounts written off investments
14	Interest payable and similar charges
15	Tax on profit or loss on ordinary activities
16	Profit or loss on ordinary activities after taxation
17	Extraordinary income
18	Extraordinary charges
19	Extraordinary profit or loss
20	Tax on extraordinary profit or loss
21	Other taxes not shown under the above items
22	Profit or loss for the financial year

consider most appropriate, but it is considered that the vertical formats have rather more to commend them than their horizontal counterparts.

Before turning to an examination of the various permitted components of the alternative formats, it is necessary to set out the rules by which modification or extension of the permitted formats is allowed. As can be seen from Exhibits 3.1 and 3.2 (in Chapter 3), items to appear in statutory balance sheets and profit and loss accounts are denoted by either letters (A, B, C, etc.), or Roman numerals (I, II, etc.) or Arabic numbers (1, 2, 3, etc.). Every balance sheet and profit and loss account must show the items denoted by letters or Roman numerals in the respective formats. Those items must be shown in the order and under the headings and sub-headings given (unless the amounts are nil in both the relevant period and the immediately preceding one). Items denoted by Arabic numbers may be combined on the face of the accounts if the amounts involved are not material to an assessment of the company's profit or loss for the relevant period or if such a combination would facilitate that assessment. In the latter circumstance, the individual amounts must be disclosed separately in the notes to the account.

The act specifically requires only three items to be shown on the face of the profit and loss account:

- the amount of the company's profit or loss on ordinary activities, before taxation;
- the amount of any transfers to or withdrawals from the company's reserves, both completed and proposed;
- the aggregate amount of any dividends paid and proposed.

Exhibit 2.3   *Profit and Loss Account – Format 3*

A Charges	B Income
1 Cost of sales	1 Turnover
2 Distribution costs	2 Other operating income
3 Administrative expenses	3 Income from shares in group companies
4 Amounts written off investments	4 Income from shares in related companies
5 Interest payable and similar charges	5 Income from other fixed asset investments
6 Tax on profit or loss on ordinary activities	6 Other interest receivable and similar income
7 Profit or loss on ordinary activities after taxation	7 Profit or loss on ordinary activities after taxation
8 Extraordinary charges	8 Extraordinary income
9 Tax on extraordinary profit or loss	9 Profit or loss for the financial year
10 Other taxes not shown under the above items	
11 Profit or loss for the financial year	

Exhibit 2.4   *Profit and Loss Account – Format 4*

A Charges	B Income
1 Reduction in stocks of finished goods and in work in progress	1 Turnover
2 (a) Raw materials and consumables	2 Increase in stocks of finished goods and in work in progress
(b) Other external charges	3 Own work capitalized
3 Staff costs:	4 Other operating income
(a) wages and salaries	5 Income from shares in group companies
(b) social security costs	6 Income from shares in related companies
(c) other pension costs	7 Income from other fixed asset investments
4 (a) Depreciation and other amounts written off tangible and intangible fixed assets	8 Other interest receivable and similar income
(b) Exceptional amounts written off current assets	9 Profit or loss on ordinary activities after taxation
5 Other operating charges	10 Extraordinary income
6 Amounts written off investments	11 Profit or loss for the financial year
7 Interest payable and similar charges	
8 Tax on profit or loss on ordinary activities	
9 Profit or loss on ordinary activities after taxation	
10 Extraordinary charges	
11 Tax on extraordinary profit or loss	
12 Other taxes not shown under the above items	
13 Profit or loss for the financial year	

All items listed in the prescribed formats are prefixed by Arabic numbers, which allows a company's directors to adapt the arrangement and headings of those items as most appropriate to the company's affairs. There is also the flexibility mentioned above – that of combining those items on the face of the account. That flexibility must be used sensibly, however. It is unlikely that directors would be justified in combining all the items making up 'profit or loss on ordinary activities' and showing one number on the face of the account with the individual items of 'turnover', 'cost of sales', operating expenses and so on relegated to the notes to the account. Equally, however, it would appear sensible to report 'extraordinary items less tax' as one entry on the face of the profit and loss account and show in the notes such items as 'extraordinary income', 'extraordinary charges', 'extraordinary profit or loss', and 'tax on extraordinary profit or loss'.

Greater detail may be given than prescribed by the permitted formats and directors have the flexibility to introduce new items or headings for matters not otherwise covered.

The format chosen may not be varied from period to period, unless there are special reasons for such change; those reasons must be disclosed in the notes to the account. The account must report corresponding amounts for the immediately preceding period, adjusted as necessary to ensure comparability.

Exhibit 2.5   *The BOC Group plc – Consolidated profit and loss account (year ended 30 September 1982)*

	1982	1981
	£ million	(£ million)
Turnover	1,534.2	1,521.7
Cost of sales	(920.4)	(882.6)
Gross profit	613.8	639.1
Distribution costs	(164.3)	(164.1)
Administrative expenses	(292.3)	(325.3)
Research and development	(24.9)	(19.2)
Share of profits of related companies	9.7	7.6
Income from other fixed asset investments	1.2	1.0
Operating profit	143.2	139.1
Realized stock holding gains	17.6	18.2
Trading profit	160.8	157.3
Interest payable (net)	(65.3)	(65.7)
Interest capitalized	7.1	3.5
Profit on ordinary activities before tax	102.6	95.1
Tax on profit on ordinary activities	(27.6)	(37.6)
Profit on ordinary activities after tax	75.0	57.5
Minority interests	(10.5)	(11.2)
Earnings	64.5	46.3
Extraordinary items	6.1	0.6
Profit for the financial year	70.6	46.9
Dividends	(19.5)	(16.9)
Transfer to reserves	51.1	30.0

Note: This is a modified extract from the company's published profit and loss account; the full version can be seen in Appendix A.

As examples of adaptations of permitted formats, attention can be drawn to the consolidated profit and loss account of The BOC Group plc (extracted in Exhibit 2.5) and to that of Fleet Holdings plc (extracted in Exhibit 2.6). Neither of these accounts is a complete replication of the 1981 act's permitted formats, although each contains the required minimum items discussed above. The BOC account is atypical in that it contains information prepared on the modified historical cost basis. Under that convention, the group's tangible fixed assets have been stated at either replacement cost or economic value, whichever was the lower, and depreciation charged accordingly. The Fleet Holdings account is atypical in that it contains no comparable figures for a preceding period and is for a period covering only some nine months. That circumstance is due to the fact that the company was incorporated on 24 September 1981 and had taken over the share capitals of certain public companies from their parent company – a process known as 'demerger'.

Exhibit 2.6   *Fleet Holdings plc – consolidated profit and loss account (period from 24 September 1981 to 30 June 1982)*

	(£ thousand)
Turnover	217,787
Cost of sales	(142,931)
Gross profit	74,856
Distribution costs	(37,289)
Administration expenses	(35,150)
	2,417
Income from shares in related companies	21
Income from other fixed asset investments	312
Other interest receivable and similar income	2,436
Interest payable and similar charges	(2,254)
Profit from ordinary activities before taxation	2,932
Taxation on profit from ordinary activities	(182)
Profit from ordinary activities after taxation	2,750
Extraordinary item	(306)
Profit for the period	2,444
Dividend proposed	(602)
Profit retained for the period	1,842

Note: This is a slightly modified extract from the company's published profit and loss account; references to notes to the account have been omitted, as has information on earnings per ordinary share; the layout has been marginally altered.

Nonetheless, these two extracted accounts illustrate the points made above and will form the basis for the ensuing discussion of usual profit and loss account components.

Contents

The following sections describe and discuss the various items to be included either on the face of the profit and loss account or in the notes thereto. Reference is made as appropriate to three complementary sets of requirements: the statutory requirements contained in the Companies Acts; the professional requirements contained in SSAPs and accountancy bodies' recommendations; the supervisory requirements imposed on public listed companies by the Council of the Stock Exchange. These will be considered in an 'incremental' manner – that is, the second and third categories of requirement will be described and discussed only where they augment or extend the statutory requirements laid down by the Companies Acts.

Turnover

All formats given in the first schedule to the 1981 act require the disclosure of turnover, which is defined as the amounts derived from the provision of goods and services falling within the company's ordinary activities, after deduction of trade discounts, value added tax, and any other taxes based on the amounts so derived. In the case of consolidated financial statements, turnover should exclude intra-group transactions. It is important, especially in regard to long-term contract work, that the reported turnover should bear a proper relationship to the profit shown for the period.

Turnover must be stated (by way of a note to the account) in respect of each substantially different class of business carried on by the company or group, although class of business is not defined by the relevant acts. In general terms, the practice is to differentiate between activities on the basis of consequential horizontal diversification, where activities are undertaken in distinctly different areas of industry and commerce. The BOC Group plc reports its 1982 turnover by business as follows, for example:

	(£ million)
Industrial gases and cryogenic plant	695.8
Health care	243.6
Carbon, graphite and carbide	134.5
Welding	269.9
Other businesses	162.8
Continuing businesses	1,506.6
Discontinued businesses	27.6
	1,534.2

whereas Fleet Holdings plc reports its nine-month turnover simply as:

	(£ thousand)
Newspapers	174,474
Magazines	43,313
	217,787

Additionally, the acts require the notes to disclose the amount of turnover in respect of each geographical market that, in the directors' opinion, differs from any other market served by the company or group. It is open to directors to withhold this information in circumstances where disclosure would be prejudicial to the interests of the company, but the fact of such withholding must be stated in the notes.

As can be seen from Appendix A, the BOC accounts report turnover both by country of origin and by country of destination. That information is given in note 1 to the financial statements, which also reports profit and capital figures by region. Fleet Holdings reports by reference to two broad geographical areas: United Kingdom (£208,036,000) and United States (£9,751,000).

Where overseas operations represent more than 10.0 per cent of a company's turnover, the Stock Exchange listing agreement requires that companies produce geographical analyses of significant turnovers, generally continent by continent. If more than half a company's overseas operations relate to just one continent, the listing agreement requires a further analysis within that continent, by country or region, for example.

Cost of sales

Formats 1 and 3 require the disclosure of cost of sales as a separate item. Cost of sales will normally include all direct elements of the cost of ordinary activities, and companies will no longer be permitted to exclude production overheads. Typically, the elements of cost included will be as follows:

- opening stocks and work in progress,
- direct materials,
- other external charges,
- direct labour,
- fixed and variable production overheads,
- depreciation or diminution in value of productive assets,
- research and development costs,

and adjustments will be made for own work capitalized and for closing stocks and work in progress. 'Own work capitalized' includes the value of direct materials and labour and appropriate overhead costs capitalized in connection with the company's own construction of tangible fixed assets. Where those cost elements are shown elsewhere in the profit and loss account, they would be shown gross of adjustments in respect of own work capitalizations.

Distribution costs

Under Formats 1 and 3, distribution costs are required to be shown separately. Broadly, such costs include all costs of holding goods for sale, promotional, advertising and selling costs, and costs of transferring goods to customers. The following elements of cost will be included:

- sales salaries, commissions and bonuses and related employment costs (including social security and pension costs),
- advertising and promotion costs,
- warehousing costs,
- transportation costs (including depreciation on vehicles),
- sales outlet costs (including depreciation and maintenance costs),
- sales discounts.

Administrative expenses
Similarly required to be disclosed separately under Formats 1 and 3, these expenses include all other operational costs than those associated with the production and distribution of goods and services (which are required to be shown separately as mentioned above). Typically, administrative expenses will include the following:

- administrative staff salaries, bonuses, etc., and related employment costs (including social security and pension costs); this item will include directors' executive salaries and related employment costs,
- administration buildings costs (including depreciation and maintenance),
- professional fees,
- amounts written off in respect of bad debts.

While the BOC financial statements show a total for administrative expenses on the face of the profit and loss account (see page 176), indicating that such expenses totalled £292.3 million in the year ended 30 September 1982, only aggregated expense categories are reported at different places in the notes to the financial statements:

Directors' emoluments (note 9(b) on page 196)		
– fees as directors	67,000	
– management remuneration	1,898,700	
– payments to past directors & dependants	68,300	
		2,034,000
Employment costs (note 10(b) on page 197)		
– wages and salaries	381,900,000	
– social security costs	39,600,000	
– other pension costs	25,300,000	
		446,800,000

Depreciation and maintenance costs are not reported separately as between administration buildings and other buildings (see note 11 on page 199, where all classes of fixed assets are reported). Professional fees are not generally reported separately, other than the statutory requirement to report the total fees paid to auditors (see note 8 on page 194) – a total of £1.4 million in the year 1981–2. Amounts written off in respect of bad debts are not revealed in the published financial statements.

Based on the published accounts, it is clearly not possible to reconcile the reported administrative expenses total of £292.3 million with any of the other reported aggregated heads of expenditure. It might have been better, in this instance as in some others, if the profit and loss account entry had been supported by an explanatory note indicating the various components separately.

Depreciation

The mechanics of determining and accounting for depreciation charges and provisions are not discussed here, being somewhat outside the scope of the book, but it is pertinent to mention the statutory and regulatory requirements in respect of the profit and loss account treatment of depreciation. The four 1981 act formats require the disclosure of depreciation provisions either in a note to the financial statements (under formats 1 and 3) or on the face of the account (under formats 2 and 4). The provisions of Schedule 1 to the 1981 act are fully consistent with the requirements of SSAP 12 ('Accounting for depreciation'), stating that the historical cost or revalued book cost of fixed assets less any estimated residual value should be written off systematically over the useful 'economic life' of the assets. Under the 1981 act's schedule, total depreciation charges in respect of a revalued asset may be included in the profit and loss account (or the notes) in two parts – one representing the depreciation charge on the historical cost and the other representing the depreciation charge based on the revaluation surplus.

In its statements (see note 11(d) on page 200), BOC presents the following analysis:

	(£ million)
Depreciation on original cost	80.6
Additional depreciation on revaluations	42.0
	122.6

Of that total, depreciation on leased assets amounted to £5.6 million in 1981–2.

Revaluation of assets

This topic is discussed in more detail in Chapter 3, but it is pertinent to highlight here some of the main requirements of Schedule 1 to the 1981 act.

Any profit or loss arising from revaluation must be dealt with in a separate revaluation reserve. Only profits realized at the balance sheet date may be included in the profit and loss account. It is not permitted to adopt a 'portfolio' approach to the valuation of assets, as for example by revaluing all assets by some index of movement in retail prices; the amount of the value of each asset must be determined separately.

In note 11(c) on page 199, the BOC financial statements report the basis of revaluations, detailing the different treatments of plant and machinery, for example, and property. Note 11(a) on page 198 reveals that fixed asset revaluations during the year to 30 September 1982 totalled £52.3 million:

	(£ million)
Land and buildings	(6.5)
Plant, machinery and vehicles	48.6
Cylinders	10.7
Construction in progress	(0.5)
	52.3

Other operating income

This income is required to be disclosed separately under all four formats. Included in this category are all other incomes associated with a company's ordinary activities – with the exception of interest receivable and investment income, which are required to be disclosed separately. However, if income from investments or interest receivable is not material, it is permissible for it to be included under this heading. Examples of such other operating income might be:

• rental income from surplus premises or facilities,
• sales income from canteen or recreational facilities,

and it can be seen that, for most companies, such income is unlikely to be significant.

Income from shares in group companies

The 1981 act requires this item to be included separately under all four formats. The amount disclosed should include all dividends – received and receivable – from subsidiary companies and from fellow subsidiaries when a company holds shares in a group company. Generally, the 1981 act did not alter the requirement to produce group financial statements (provided for in section 150 of the 1948 act); the definitions of 'group', 'holding company' and 'subsidiary' were laid down in the 1948 act and have been adopted in SSAP 14 ('Group accounts'). Under the terms of the 1981 act, consolidated financial statements must combine the financial information given in the separate statements of the holding company and its subsidiaries, as if the group of companies was a single corporate entity.

In addition to the dividends referred to above, the 1981 act rules that this item should include also the group's share of the earnings of unconsolidated subsidiaries where they have been accounted for on the 'equity method' and any dividends received or receivable from other unconsolidated subsidiaries. It may be appropriate here to outline briefly what is meant by the equity method of accounting. It is defined in SSAP 14 as follows:

> ... the investment in a company is shown in the consolidated balance sheet at: (i) the cost of the investment; and (ii) the investing company's or group's share of the post-acquisition retained profits and reserves of the company; (iii) less any amounts written off in respect of (i) and (ii) above; and ... the investing company accounts separately in its profit and loss account for its share of the profits before tax, taxation and extraordinary items of the company.

The equity method differs from the normal consolidation process in that the group's share of the net assets of the subject company is included in the investment account of the group company and the share of operating profit or loss and taxation is given separately in the group's profit and loss account. Under the normal consolidation process, a subject company's assets, liabilities, turnover and other profit and loss data are included in the group company's totals, and the interest of minority shareholders in the subject company's net assets is shown as a separate item.

In general terms, the equity method should be used only when subsidiaries are not consolidated for one of two reasons – either the subsidiary engages in dissimilar activities to those of the group or the degree of control by the group is not effective (even though the 'related' or 'associated' company definition applies – see below). Additionally, the equity method can be used appropriately when investments in companies meet the criteria for either 'related' or 'associated' company status.

Income from shares in related companies
Again, this class of income is required to be shown separately under all four formats. The 1981 act defines 'related' companies in much the same terms as the amended SSAP 1 ('Accounting for associated companies'), whose principal difference from the original version is its introduction of the notion of 'significant influence'.

The 1981 act definition indicates that a 'related' company is any corporate body (other than another group company) in which an investing company holds, on a long-term basis, a qualifying capital interest for the purpose of securing for the investing company a contribution to its own activities by virtue of the exercise of any influence or control that arises from that qualifying capital interest. A qualifying capital interest is defined as an interest in a class of equity share capital of the subject company, such that the interest carries voting rights. A corporate body or subject company will be assumed to be a 'related' company if the group company holds 20.0 per cent or more of the issued equity shares of the subject company, with the exclusion of any shares not carrying voting rights.

The amounts to be included under this heading should include all those required by SSAP 1, but there are several problems connected with the treatment of related and/or associated companies. It is appropriate to discuss those problems here.

The revised SSAP 1 differs from the original version in three important respects. Firstly, as mentioned above, the new standard places considerable emphasis on the question of 'significant influence'. Formerly, it was sufficient to follow a criterion simply based on the '20.0 per cent rule'. Now, a company has to demonstrate that significant influence is not exercised if its holding is more than 20.0 per cent and it does not wish to treat a subject company as an associated company; conversely, if its holding is less than 20.0 per cent and it does wish to treat the company as an associated company, then it has to demonstrate that significant influence can be exercised. For the most part, where a holding is greater than 20.0 per cent it is presumed that significant influence can be exercised. Secondly, the definition of 'company' has been extended to encompass any enterprise that comes within the catchment area of the accounting standards, including consortia and joint ventures. Thirdly, the revised SSAP 1 alters the disclosure requirements, in particular requiring the disclosure of any element of goodwill included in the cost of an investment in an associated company and the disclosure of loans to or from associated companies and, if material, the disclosure of normal trading balances with associates.

The 1981 act and SSAP 1 do not fit snugly together in all respects, and a number of problems arise. Firstly, the definition in the act is somewhat wider than that in the revised standard; the revised SSAP 1 permits the treatment of related companies as associated companies, provided that the notes to any accounts state that there are no other related companies besides those treated as associated companies.

The second problem is more acute. Take, for example, the following hypothetical situation. G is a holding company with two subsidiary companies, A and B. A owns 15.0 per cent of the equity share capital of E, a corporate body; B owns 12.0 per cent of the equity share capital of E. Under the provisions of the standard, and assuming significant influence is exercised, E would qualify as an associated company. Under the rules of the 1981 act, however, it would not be classed as a related company and would not qualify to be accounted for by the equity method permitted in the act's Schedule 1 (see above). It is permitted, however, to be brought into the accounts of the group under the dispensations of what may be labelled the 'true and fair override' provided in the 1981 act: if statements drawn up under the provisions of the 1948 and 1981 acts do not give a true and fair view, then the necessary additional information must be given.

One of the particular difficulties illustrated by these discrepancies between statutory provisions and accounting standards is that accounting standards have no formal status in law but may be regarded as 'material evidence on questions as to accounting principles and practices', as stated in a 1982 statement from the Department of Trade on the relationship between the statutory requirements on the form and content of group accounts and the requirement that accounts should give a true and fair view. As an example of the problems inherent in the relationships between law and best practice, readers are referred to the prosecution brought by the Department of Trade in 1981 against a director of a major British company, Argyll Foods plc.*

In addition to the financial information required to be disclosed by the 1981 act and the provisions of SSAP 1, the Listing Agreement of the Stock Exchange enjoins the disclosure of information on the principal country of operation of 'related' or 'associated' companies, particulars of their issued share and loan capital and the percentage of each class of loan capital attributable to a group company's interest, either direct or indirect.

The notes to BOC's financial statements present outline information on related companies and other investments. As shown in note 13 (pages 202 and 203), the company reports the name, domicile and share capital of related companies and the extent of BOC holdings in those companies' equities. It is interesting to see that (note 14 on page 203) BOC did not consolidate two related companies on the equity basis because 'significant commercial and financial influence did not exist'.

Other investment income

All formats call for the separate disclosure of income from other fixed asset investments and other interest receivable and similar income. Income from listed investments must be shown in a supplementary statement to the profit and loss account; 'listed' investments are those that are quoted on a recognized stock exchange, and they would normally be regarded as current asset items (unless they are held on a long-term basis for purposes of trade) and therefore included in the category of 'other interest receivable and similar income'.

Interest payable and similar charges

Similarly required to be disclosed separately under all four formats, this heading should include:

- interest charged and payable on borrowings,
- imputed interest element of financing leases and cognate obligations,
- amounts amortized on discounts or premiums on bills, debentures, etc.,
- commitment and procurement fees on loan arrangements and credit facilities,

* See, for example, David Balfour, 'The Argyll Foods case', *The Accountant's Magazine*, September 1981, pp. 308–9.

and the 1981 act requires an analysis of other interest and similar charges to show separately the aggregate interest on bank loans and overdrafts and loans wholly repayable within five years (whether by instalments or not), and the aggregate interest on any other loans. In that way, interest on short-term loans is separated from interest on medium- and long-term loans.

The capitalization of interest on borrowings to finance assets in course of construction causes a slight problem. Under the terms of the 1981 act, the amount of any interest so capitalized must be disclosed, and the Listing Agreement of the Stock Exchange requires listed companies to disclose the amount of any interest capitalized during an accounting period and the treatment of any related tax relief.

Profit or loss on ordinary activities before taxation
Unlike any of the foregoing items, a company's profit or loss on ordinary activities before taxation must be shown on the face of the profit and loss account. The figure reported must represent the balance of all the previously mentioned items, including exceptional items (see below), that relate to the ordinary activities of the company, but excluding taxation and extraordinary items (see below).

Exceptional items
Generally, these represent the effect of any transactions or occurrences that fall within the ordinary activities of the company but are exceptional by virtue either of their size or their incidence. Such items would include:

• research and development expenditure,
• write-offs in respect of current assets, such as stock or abnormal bad debts,
• provisions for losses on contracts,
• income grants,
• tax provision adjustments.

Prior to the 1981 act, the disclosure of such exceptional items had been covered by the requirements of SSAP 6 ('Extraordinary items and prior year adjustments'), which dealt also with those items considered 'extraordinary' and described below. Previously, such exceptional items had been discussed elsewhere in the annual report, rather than in or near the profit and loss account. The BOC financial statements show research and development expenditures separately on the face of the profit and loss account (see page 176); £24.9 million was spent (or written off) in the year to 30 September 1982, as against £19.2 million in the previous year.

Taxation
The treatment of taxation in the profit and loss account is governed both by the provisions of the 1981 act and by the requirements of SSAP 8 ('The

treatment of taxation under the imputation system in the accounts of companies') and SSAP 15 ('Accounting for deferred taxation'). In addition, other standards contain matters pertinent to the treatment of taxation in the course of their statements on other topics.

The profit and loss account formats prescribed under the 1981 act require the disclosure of three essential taxation items:

- tax on profit or loss on ordinary activities;
- tax on extraordinary profit or loss;
- other taxes not shown under the above items.

Tax on profit or loss on ordinary activities
The disclosure of charges or provisions under this heading should take account of the following items:

- corporation tax on the profits for the period,
- double taxation relief,
- deferred taxation,
- overseas taxation,
- irrecoverable advance corporation tax,
- income tax,
- related companies' corporation tax and deferred taxation,
- changes to taxation provisions for prior periods.

These items would not include taxation relating to extraordinary items, which would be shown separately in the category 'tax on extraordinary profit or loss', discussed below.

The basis on which corporation tax has been computed and the amount of the charge have to be disclosed. In the case of Fleet Holdings plc, the notes to the financial statements include the following statement:

There is no charge for corporation tax on the group's profit for the period as the profit is offset by tax losses brought forward.

The BOC accounts report a charge of £6.0 million (at the rate of 52.0 per cent on taxable profit) in respect of corporation tax for the period ending 30 September 1982.

Double taxation relief is gained on the part of income that originates overseas and on which foreign tax has been paid. In the case of BOC, a relief of £6.0 million was available for 1981–2, making the amount payable nil.

Deferred taxation is defined variously by different authorities. In terms of SSAP 15, deferred taxation is taxation attributable to 'timing differences', differences between profits calculated for financial statement purposes and those calculated for taxation purposes. Items of income and expenditure are included in taxation computations in periods different from those in which they were or will be included in financial statements. These timing differences are created in four major ways:

- short-term timing differences, arising from the use of different bases for taxation and reporting statements (i.e. receipts and payments basis for taxation and accruals basis for financial accounts);
- accelerated capital allowances, arising from the initial excess of capital allowances over the corresponding depreciation charges;
- fixed asset revaluation, arising from differences between asset values and original costs;
- fixed asset disposal, arising from taxation liability on 'profits' from fixed asset disposal.

Adjustments to the deferred taxation balance can arise also from changes in the rate of tax.

Overseas taxation should be disclosed separately and the amount reported should include all overseas taxation charged in the financial statements of the overseas branch or company, whether relieved or not.

Advance corporation tax is payable at the rate of the basic income tax rate on dividends distributed or to be distributed to shareholders.

The remaining items of taxation charged on the profit or loss on ordinary activities are either straightforward or outwith the concern of this book. We recommend readers to a more specialized treatment of company taxation for further details; see, for example, Ashton (1983), or *Tolley's Corporation Tax*.

As examples of the reported tax on ordinary activities' profit or loss, Fleet Holdings reports as follows:

	(£ thousand)
Tax credits on franked investment income	93
Overseas taxation	78
Related companies taxation	11
	182

and The BOC Group reports its 1982 taxation computation as shown in Note 4 to the financial statements, summarized as:

	(£ million)
Payable in the United Kingdom:	
Advance Corporation Tax	8.2
Corporation Tax at 52%	6.0
Double taxation relief	(6.0)
Other provisions	0.9
	9.1
Payable overseas:	7.5
Provision for deferred taxation (overseas)	7.4
Tax charge arising in related companies	3.6
	27.6

Tax on extraordinary profit or loss

The amount disclosed under this heading will have been excluded from the taxation computations discussed above, but will have been calculated by reference to the same underlying principles. Extraordinary items are described below.

Extraordinary items

There is no statutory definition of what constitutes an 'extraordinary item', but it can be characterized as one that does not arise in the course of the company's ordinary activities. SSAP 6 ('Extraordinary items and prior year adjustments') defines extraordinary items as those that derive from events or transactions outside the company's ordinary activities and that are both material and not expected or unlikely to recur frequently or regularly. What is extraordinary for one company, therefore, may be ordinary for another; in general, extraordinary items occur rarely.

Fleet Holdings reports one extraordinary item: the cost of closing a journal entitled *Financial Weekly*, charged in the profit and loss account at £306,000. The BOC accounts report (Note 5 to the financial statements) an extraordinary gain of £6.1 million after tax.

Prior year items

The effect of any items in the profit and loss account that relate to the preceding period must be disclosed. SSAP 6 requires that such items must be dealt with in the profit and loss account of the period in which they are recognized; they should be shown separately if considered material. SSAP 6 restricts such prior year adjustments to the results of changes in accounting policies and the correction of fundamental errors.

Dividends

The 1981 act, as had usually been the case earlier, requires the separate disclosure of the aggregate amount of dividends paid or proposed to be paid. The straightforward requirement disguises an area of considerable confusion and complexity – the determination of 'distributable profits'. There are also the difficulties of calculating a company's 'realized' and 'unrealized' profits and losses. The definition of which profits are distributable was introduced by the Companies Act 1980.

Realized profits are those that are determined in accordance with generally accepted accounting principles at the time of preparation of the financial statements in question. Generally, this means that profits determined in accordance with the prudence concept set out in SSAP 2 ('Disclosure of accounting policies') are considered to be 'realized'. Profits should not be anticipated and should be recognized in the profit and loss account when realized in cash or other assets (including a commitment to pay or other obligation). Losses are provided when an amount is known with certainty or is a best estimate in the light of the circumstances and available information. Unrealized profits and losses are determined by having regard to best accounting practices at the time, and generally may be taken to be those that cannot be regarded as 'realized'.

Basically, any company that wishes to make a distribution must have profits available for that purpose. They are the accumulated realized profits that have not previously been either distributed or capitalized, less any accumulated realized losses that have not been previously written off. In addition, a public company (as defined in the 1980 act) must satisfy two further conditions: the amount of its net assets at the time of distribution must exceed the aggregate of its called-up share capital plus its undistributable reserves (any share premium account, any capital redemption reserve, any excess of accumulated unrealized profits over accumulated unrealized losses that have not been written off, any specifically undistributable reserve); and the amount of the distribution must not reduce the amount of its net assets below the aggregate of its called-up share capital plus its undistributable reserves.

The situation is complicated further when revalued assets and associated depreciation charges play a part in the net asset position of a company. Readers are referred to a textbook on advanced financial accounting for a fuller treatment; see, for example, Lewis, Pendrill and Simon (1981) or Samuels, Rickwood and Piper (1982).

Other profit and loss information
The 1981 act requires the disclosure of other information concerning the company's activities. In respect of employees and directors, the total average number of employees must be disclosed and that total should be broken down by the directors on the same basis as the organization of the company's activities. As mentioned earlier, staff costs must be disclosed under three separate headings, and full information must be given in respect of the emoluments of directors and senior employees.

Employees earning more than £30,000 per annum (as laid down in the Companies Act 1967 and amended by subsequent statutory instruments) must be classified in bands of £5,000. The emoluments of the directors must be reported, and separate disclosure must be made of the chairman's remuneration, and that of the highest-paid director (if he is not the chairman), and the number of directors in each successive £5,000 band. These additional items are not required to be disclosed where the company is not a member of a group of companies and the total of the director's remuneration does not exceed £60,000 per annum.

Information must be given in respect of directors' or past directors' pensions and in respect of any compensation paid to directors or past directors in respect of loss of office. Full details must be given of the interests of directors and their families in a company's or group company's shares and debentures, but these items are included in the directors' report (discussed in Chapter 6) in most cases. The BOC Group accounts (reproduced in Appendix A to this book) present director-related information as a supplement to the financial statements (Note 9 to the financial statements) and present employee-related information there also (Note 10 to the financial statements).

The act gives directors considerable flexibility in the manner in which they break down the employee statistics – by function (selling, producing, distributing, administering, and so on), or by activity (motor assembly, painting, oil exploration, and so on), or by job description (managers, foremen, clerical staff, salesmen, and so on). The BOC Group follows its earlier activity-based classification, whereas Fleet Holdings adopts a functional classification – production, editorial, sales and distribution, and administration. In addition, Fleet Holdings divides its reported staff costs between permanent and casual employees.

The aggregate remuneration of auditors must be disclosed by way of a note to the financial statements, such a total including both the fee and any related expenses. Fees for special services (accounting or management consulting, for example) should not be included in the reported amount.

Any amount charged to revenue in respect of the hire of plant and machinery (widely defined, so as to include such assets as motor vehicles or machine tools) must be disclosed in the notes to the financial statements.

Every profit and loss account is required to disclose details of movements in reserves that directly affect profit and loss account balances. SSAP 6 appears to require a profit and loss account to be followed immediately by a statement of retained profits and/or reserves.

Accounts must include, by way of note, details of the basis on which foreign currency amounts have been translated into sterling or the company's 'home' currency.

Profit and loss accounts must include comparative figures for the immediately preceding period, as has been mentioned earlier, or a statement of adjustments made to previous year's figures and the reasons for such adjustments.

A statement of accounting policies must be presented; the BOC Group's statement of accounting policies and definitions is reproduced on pages 181–185 of the accounts shown in Appendix A. Explanations must be given for any departures from preceding periods' accounting policies, and comparative data restated, and for any departures from statutory or presentational requirements.

Earnings per share

Under the provisions of the revised version of SSAP 3 ('Earnings per share'), listed companies quoted on a recognized stock exchange must show on the face of the profit and loss account a figure for earnings per share. That figure should be shown, if applicable, on both a 'basic' calculation (relating shareholders' attributable earnings to issued equity shares) and a 'fully diluted' calculation (relating attributable earnings to the full issued equity share base if all convertible options were exercised). The basis of calculation must be shown, and the figures of earnings and issued shares used must be given.

The accounts of Fleet Holdings include the following note:

> The calculation of earnings per ordinary share before extraordinary items is based on profits of £2,750,000 and on the number of ordinary shares in issue at the end of the period.

On that basis, with 60,220,000 issued ordinary shares, the basic earnings per share figure was calculated at 4.57 pence. The fully diluted figure is reported as follows:

> The fully diluted earnings per share assuming full conversion of the 8 per cent Convertible Unsecured Loan Stock into 39,426,590 shares is 2.97 pence.

The BOC Group calculations can be seen in Note 7 to the company's financial statements in Appendix A and are discussed in Chapter 11.

Exemptions and Modifications

The Companies Act of 1967 abolished the status of 'exempt private company' and for a number of years all limited companies were required to conform to the same basic auditing, disclosure and filing provisions, although differences in status (between 'public' and 'private', or 'parent' or 'subsidiary') led to differences in additional disclosure requirements. The 1981 act, however, permits reduced disclosure in the documents to be filed with the Registrar of Companies. Two points need to be emphasized: first, the implementation of reduced disclosure is permitted without being demanded; second, the permission extends only to those documents to be delivered to the Registrar and does not cover the documents to be delivered to members of the company in question. Members must receive full accounts, prepared wholly in accordance with all the act's requirements.

Two categories of limited company may opt to apply the exemptions from full public disclosure:

- medium-sized companies,
- small companies,

and the act lays down certain criteria for determining the category into which a company falls. It is perhaps best to consider first those companies that cannot be classified as either medium-sized or small. They are:

- public companies;
- member companies of a group of companies containing a public company;
- banking, insurance or shipping companies;
- member companies of a group of companies containing a banking, insurance or shipping company;
- member companies of a group of companies containing a non-British corporate body that may lawfully offer its securities to the public;
- member companies of a group of companies containing a non-British corporate body that is a recognized bank or insurance company.

If a company does not fall into any of those categories, it may be eligible to be considered either medium-sized or small, and those classifications depend entirely on size, as follows. Medium-sized companies are those that fulfil at least two out of the following three conditions in respect of the current financial period and the one immediately preceding it:

- turnover did not exceed £5.75 million;
- total assets did not exceed £2.8 million;
- average weekly number of employees did not exceed 250.

Similarly, the conditions for being considered a small company are as follows:

- turnover did not exceed £1.4 million;
- total assets did not exceed £700,000;
- average weekly number of employees did not exceed 50.

'Total assets' refers to the balance sheet total of fixed and current assets, as specified in the prescribed balance sheet formats, without deduction of any liabilities.

The exemptions for a medium-sized company are limited. It is permitted to omit only the following: turnover; costs of sales information; analyses of turnover and profit amongst different classes of business; and analyses of turnover amongst different markets. The whole of the balance sheet and the rest of the notes to the profit and loss account have to be given in full.

The exemptions for a small company are extensive. It is permitted to omit the following: the whole profit and loss account; the directors' report; particulars of the emoluments of directors and higher-paid employees; all those items in the balance sheet that are not identified with Roman numerals (see Chapter 3); considerable portions of the notes to the financial statements.

Both these categories of exempt company will have to file additional or expanded auditor's reports with those documents lodged with the Registrar of Companies; those reports are discussed in Chapter 9.

3 The Balance Sheet

Perhaps better described as a 'position' statement, the balance sheet reports the position at the close of business on a given day, detailing the values of assets and liabilities at the balance sheet date and offering considerable scope for the analysis of the relationships between the different classes of assets and liabilities. The bases on which assets and liabilities are valued are, of course, of crucial importance in any process of analysis and assessment.

This chapter proceeds by examining the alternative formats permitted under the 1981 act, by describing and discussing the various items to be included on the balance sheet or in the related notes, and by examining certain wider-ranging topics associated with particular balance sheet entries (such as depreciation and revaluation of assets).

Exhibit 3.1   *Balance sheet – format 1*

A	Called-up share capital not paid
B	Fixed assets
	I Intangible assets
	II Tangible assets
	III Investments
C	Current assets
	I Stocks
	II Debtors
	III Investments
	IV Cash at bank and in hand
D	Prepayments and accrued income
E	Creditors: amounts falling due within one year
F	Net current assets (liabilities)
G	Total assets less current liabilities
H	Creditors: amounts falling due after more than one year
I	Provisions for liabilities and charges
J	Accruals and deferred income
K	Capital and reserves
	I Called-up share capital
	II Share premium account
	III Revaluation reserve
	IV Other reserves
	V Profit and loss account

Formats

Schedule 1 to the 1981 act introduced two permitted formats for a company's balance sheet; these alternative formats are reproduced in Exhibits 3.1 and 3.2. The first format arranges the balance sheet items vertically (the practice most prevalent amongst United Kingdom companies), while the second format arranges those items horizontally (although the presentation does not necessarily have to be side by side).

Schedule 1 requires that headings that have been given Roman letters or numerals must be shown in the order and under the headings and sub-headings set out in the prescribed formats; no flexibility is permitted. The prescribed formats do, however, include a number of additional sub-headings, labelled with Arabic numerals, which enjoy greater flexibility. These additional sub-headings will be described in the appropriate sections below, and their arrangement and description are adaptable to meet the particular needs or nature of a company's business. They may be combined in circumstances where such a combination facilitates the better assessment of a company's affairs, but the fact of such combination must be stated and the details of such combined items must be disclosed in the notes to the financial statements.

Exhibit 3.2 *Balance sheet – format 2*

Assets	Liabilities
A Called-up share capital not paid	A Capital and reserves
B Fixed assets	I Called-up share capital
I Intangible assets	II Share premium account
II Tangible assets	III Revaluation reserve
III Investments	IV Other reserves
C Current assets	V Profit and loss account
I Stocks	B Provisions for liabilities and charges
II Debtors	C Creditors
III Investments	D Accruals and deferred income
IV Cash at bank and in hand	
D Prepayments and accrued income	

Note: 'Liabilities' may alternatively be shown below 'Assets' or be shown on a separate page.

Before turning to the detailed examination of the individual categories and their components, it is useful to consider two actual examples of balance sheets prepared under the provisions of the 1981 act. Exhibit 3.3 presents a modified extract from the balance sheet of The BOC Group plc as at 30 September 1982; the full version may be seen in Appendix A to this book. Similarly, Exhibit 3.4 presents a modified extract from the balance sheet of Fleet Holdings plc as at 30 June 1982. It can be seen immediately that the presentations are markedly different from those employed by British companies before the implementation of the 1981 act's provisions.

Exhibit 3.3   *The BOC Group plc – consolidated balance sheet (at 30 September 1982)*

	1982 (£ million)	1981 (£ million)
FIXED ASSETS		
Tangible assets	1,277.6	1,152.6
Investments	71.4	43.9
	1,349.0	1,196.5
CURRENT ASSETS		
Stocks	302.1	274.8
Debtors	288.2	310.3
Deposits at short call	31.4	14.3
Cash at bank and in hand	6.4	12.2
	628.1	611.6
CREDITORS: Amounts falling due within one year		
Borrowings and finance leases	(109.7)	(58.5)
Other	(290.0)	(306.7)
NET CURRENT ASSETS	228.4	246.4
TOTAL ASSETS LESS CURRENT LIABILITIES	1,577.4	1,442.9
CREDITORS: Amounts falling due after more than one year		
Borrowings and finance leases	(517.4)	(484.2)
Other	(15.8)	(15.2)
PROVISIONS FOR LIABILITIES AND CHARGES	(58.2)	(55.5)
	(591.4)	(554.9)
	986.0	888.0
CAPITAL AND RESERVES		
Called up share capital	85.4	84.8
Share premium account	45.6	44.3
Revaluation reserve	323.6	372.9
Other reserves	11.6	10.6
Profit and loss account	398.2	259.7
Related companies' reserves	18.6	14.7
	883.0	787.0
MINORITY SHAREHOLDERS' INTERESTS	103.0	101.0
	986.0	888.0

Exhibit 3.4 *Fleet Holdings plc – consolidated balance sheet (at 30 June 1982)*

	(£ thousand)
FIXED ASSETS	
Intangible assets	2,928
Tangible assets	45,211
Investments	201
	48,340
CURRENT ASSETS	
Stocks	4,996
Debtors	43,766
Cash at bank and in hand	10,115
	58,877
CREDITORS: AMOUNTS FALLING DUE WITHIN ONE YEAR	
Bank loans and overdrafts	3,794
Debenture loan – unsecured	589
Trade creditors	14,693
Bills of exchange	10,430
Amounts owed to related companies	10
Other creditors including taxation and social security	21,747
Proposed dividend	602
	51,865
NET CURRENT ASSETS	7,012
TOTAL ASSETS LESS CURRENT LIABILITIES	55,352
CREDITORS: AMOUNTS FALLING DUE AFTER MORE THAN ONE YEAR	(15,886)
PROVISIONS FOR LIABILITIES AND CHARGES	(2,177)
	37,289
CAPITAL AND RESERVES	
Called up share capital	12,044
Revaluation reserve	971
Other reserves	14,989
Profit and loss account	9,285
	37,289

The descriptions and discussions following will deal with the various items in this order:

- fixed assets;
- current assets;
- creditors;
- provisions for liabilities and charges;
- capital and reserves;
- minority shareholders.

Since the issue of historical cost vs. current cost is vital to an appreciation of the position of a company, the topic is considered in this chapter, although its ramifications have obvious impacts on matters considered in Chapter 2 and elsewhere.

Valuation Rules

The schedule to the 1981 act lays down certain rules for the valuation of balance sheet items. These general valuation rules are discussed here; the rules applicable to specific assets are discussed in the relevant sections below. For the greater part, the 1981 act's valuation rules are consistent with the valuation bases ordained in standard statements (SSAPs). Broadly, the rules distinguish between the historical cost convention and either the current cost accounting convention described in SSAP 16 ('Current cost accounting') or a mixture of historical and alternative valuations, as in the case of The BOC Group plc, which adopts a 'modified historical cost' convention.

The general rules may be summarized as follows. Under the historical cost convention, gross value shall be purchase price or production cost. Under the alternative conventions, gross value shall be either market value determined at the most recent valuation date or current cost. For example, tangible fixed assets shall be valued at market value or at current cost, stocks shall be valued at current cost, investments included in fixed assets shall be valued at market value or at a value determined by the directors on any basis considered appropriate in the circumstances, and investments included in current assets shall be valued at current cost.

Provisions for reduction in value shall be made in respect of all fixed assets where the reduction is expected to be permanent. Where investments are concerned, a provision for diminution in value may be made even where the reduction in value is not expected to be permanent. Fixed assets with useful economic lives shall be subject to depreciation charges – the cost or alternative valuation less any estimated residual value shall be reduced by depreciation provisions designed to write off that balance by systematic instalments over the asset's useful economic life. Current assets shall be written down to a net realizable value where that value is lower than cost or alternative valuation. Conversely, where a provision for reduction in value is no longer necessary, the provision shall be written back (via the profit and loss account) to the extent that it is no longer necessary.

Current cost accounting
The requirement to prepare and publish current cost accounting (CCA) statements is laid down by SSAP 16; all listed companies and all other business entities above a certain size (and subject to the requirement that

their financial statements should give a true and fair view) are required to produce CCA accounts. There are a number of exemptions, both on grounds of size and on grounds of nature or activity. Companies that can satisfy two out of three of the following criteria are not required to produce CCA statements:

- turnover less than £5.0 million;
- total assets less than £2.5 million;
- average number of United Kingdom employees less than 250;

and CCA statements are not required from companies that are:

- wholly-owned subsidiaries of United Kingdom companies;
- insurance companies;
- property owning, investment and dealing companies;
- investment and unit trusts;
- non-profit-making organizations (such as charities, building societies, friendly societies, trade unions, pension funds, and the like).

Schedule 1 to the 1981 act permits the use of the CCA bases for the valuation of assets and thereby facilitates the preparation of CCA financial statements in fulfilment of the act's requirements.

Current cost financial statements

Companies falling within the ambit of SSAP 16 must include in their annual financial statements a current cost profit and loss account and balance sheet, supported by explanatory notes containing certain specified minimum information. These CCA data may be supplementary to the historical cost financial data or take the place of those historical cost statements; in that latter event, supplementary historical cost statements must be presented or sufficient historical cost data given to satisfy legislative requirements.

The following discussion concerns itself only with the provision of supplementary CCA information; where CCA information is presented in the form of the main statutory financial statements, the disclosures discussed here will need to be made in addition to those discussed elsewhere in connection with the requirements of the Companies Acts.

SSAP 16 requires certain adjustments to be made to the historical cost profit and loss account, to disclose a current cost operating profit and a current cost profit attributable to shareholders. The mechanics of calculating the actual adjustments are not described here in detail; readers are referred either to SSAP 16 and the Guidance Notes thereto or to one of the financial accounting textbooks listed in the Further Reading at the end of this book.

Current cost operating profit is arrived at as a result of adjusting historical cost operating profit before interest. There are four adjustments to be made:

- a depreciation adjustment,
- a cost of sales adjustment,
- a monetary working capital adjustment,
- a gearing adjustment.

Other adjustments will need to be made for the profits or losses of related companies, for gains or losses on foreign currency translations, for sales of fixed assets, and for exceptional items.

The depreciation adjustment represents the difference between the proportion of the value to the business of fixed assets consumed in a period and the depreciation calculated on the historical cost basis; value to the business will generally be determined by reference to some assessment of current replacement cost.

The cost of sales adjustment represents the difference between the value to the business and the historical cost of stock consumed in a period.

The monetary working capital adjustment represents the extent to which changes in input factor prices have affected monetary working capital. For the purposes of SSAP 16, monetary working capital is defined as the aggregate of trade debtors and prepayments, trade bills receivable, and any stocks not subject to a cost of sales adjustment, less trade creditors and accruals, trade bills payable, and any element of interest payable in respect of cash or bank borrowings included in monetary working capital.

Current cost profit attributable to shareholders must be disclosed. It is arrived at by deducting from the current cost operating profit the following items: taxation, extraordinary items, balance of interest payable or receivable, and minority interests. In addition, SSAP 16 requires a gearing adjustment to be made.

The gearing adjustment is based on the entity's gearing ratio – the relationship between average net borrowings and average net current cost operating assets. It seeks to determine the proportion of the operating profit adjustments (described above) that are borne by the providers of loan capital to the entity.

Adjustments have to be made also to the historical cost balance sheet. The current cost balance sheet may be presented in a summarized form, on condition that a full historical cost balance sheet is provided. All fixed assets, stocks subject to a cost of sales adjustment, and investments not included in current assets are to be reported at a figure representing their appropriate value to the business. Current assets (other than stocks subject to a cost of sales adjustment) and liabilities are reported at their unchanged historical cost values. Reserves should include revaluation reserves (whether surpluses or deficits) and the cumulative current cost adjustments.

The explanatory notes to SSAP 16 contain a number of suggestions of ways in which companies might disclose additional CCA-related information. Broadly, these are concerned with reporting the effects of changes in the general purchasing power of money, reporting restated comparative figures for preceding periods, and reporting current cost funds' flows.

There are several considerable difficulties associated with the reporting of current cost results, including the cost of preparation and the application of SSAP 16 to smaller companies. SSAP 16 is recognized to be, at best, an interim solution to a continuing problem, and the Accounting Standards Committee has reviewed the operation of the standard and has issued an exposure draft with a view to bringing in a revised accounting standard with effect from 1 January 1985. That revised standard will require cost accounting data to be disclosed in notes to the financial statements; it is likely that current cost calculations will be made on the same basis as in SSAP 16. As examples of comprehensive CCA financial statements, the BOC report includes CCA profit and loss and balance sheet accounts (pages 176–7); the various adjustments are described at relevant points in the notes.

Revaluation of Assets

Assets may be valued on alternative accounting bases other than the historical cost basis – current cost, market value, or directors' valuation, as may be appropriate. The process of revaluation will 'create' profits or losses that are to be dealt with in a separate reserve. That revaluation reserve may, from time to time, be reduced by any amounts no longer required for the purposes of the company's accounting policies or, for instance, if an expected diminution in value is not realized. Such reductions may usually be taken into the profit and loss account, provided the amount had previously been charged to the profit and loss account or if the amount represents a realized profit. Unrealized profits, such as revaluation surpluses on property and the like, may not be included in the profit and loss account. A simple example may serve to make the points clearer.

A fixed asset costing £300,000 (or previously revalued at that figure) and having accumulated depreciation based on cost (or revalued amount) of £60,000 is revalued at £325,000; the surplus to be credited to the revaluation reserve would be £85,000: £325,000 less (£300,000 – £60,000). The surplus may not be calculated by reference to the gross cost or gross previous valuation of £300,000, with the accumulated depreciation credited back to the profit and loss account.

Losses on revaluation should be debited to the revaluation reserve only up to the amount of any surplus already included in the reserve in respect of a revaluation of the asset in question. Any excess of loss over that amount should be charged to the profit and loss account as a provision for diminution in the value of the asset.

The profit or loss on a sale of a revalued asset is the difference between the net proceeds of the sale and the net book value at the date of sale; the net book value will represent the revalued amount less any provision for diminution or depreciation. When such a profit or loss has been realized, any surplus remaining in the revaluation reserve in respect of the asset in question may be transferred to the profit and loss account.

Treatment of Depreciation

Depreciation is defined in SSAP 12 ('Accounting for depreciation') as the measure of the wearing out, consumption or other loss of value of a fixed asset; those effects may arise from use, through the passage of time, or through obsolescence or technological and market changes. Schedule 1 to the 1981 act is consistent with the provisions of the accounting standard and calls for the allocation to the appropriate accounting period of the proportion of cost less estimated residual value that is 'lost' in that period.

The assessment of depreciation calls for the estimation of at least three factors:

- the cost or valuation of the asset;
- the probable realizable value on disposal at the end of the asset's working life (the residual value);
- the asset's working life (or useful economic life).

It will be appreciated that there are a number of methods for the calculation and imposition of depreciation charges. These may be found enumerated in any financial or managerial accounting textbook. Examples of depreciation rates and policies adopted by The BOC Group plc are given in the statement of accounting policies presented in Appendix A (pages 183 and 184).

Contents

The prescribed contents of post-1981 balance sheets under the alternative formats are summarized below in the order outlined earlier.

Fixed assets

Intangible assets
These must be included on the face of the balance sheet under a main heading, with the following sub-headings included either on the face of the balance sheet or in the notes to the financial statements:

- development costs;
- concessions, patents, licences, trade marks and similar rights and assets;
- goodwill;
- payments on account.

Schedule 1 lays down that an amount may be included in the balance sheet in respect of 'development costs' only in special circumstances, although it does not define those special circumstances. In general, research and development costs may not be capitalized; where they are, a reason must be stated. In most respects, the provisions of the schedule are closely similar to those presented in SSAP 13 ('Accounting for research and development'). SSAP 13 provides certain criteria for the capitalization of research and development costs, and those criteria may be considered analogous to the act's 'special circumstances'. They include the clear identification of a project and the clear identification of specific related expenditure.

'Goodwill' represents the difference between the value of a business as a whole and the value of its net assets (i.e. fixed and current assets less liabilities). Schedule 1 rules that goodwill may appear in a balance sheet only where it has been obtained for a valuable consideration (generally, either cash or shares). There are often two kinds of goodwill present in financial statements: goodwill in a company's own financial statements, and goodwill arising on consolidation in group financial statements. Schedule 1 lays down rules for the accounting for goodwill in a company's own financial statements, but makes no rules about goodwill on consolidation. An accounting standard on the subject of accounting for goodwill will be issued during the course of 1984; an exposure draft, ED30, permitted two alternative approaches:

- writing off goodwill directly to reserves;
- showing goodwill as an asset that is written off systematically over its useful economic life by way of charges against profit and loss account.

The maximum useful economic life is set at twenty years. The exposure draft also discusses the problems of 'negative' goodwill – when the fair value of the separable net assets exceeds the fair value of the consideration given for them. Under those circumstances, companies would either recognize an unrealized profit (to be released as the assets are depreciated or sold) or an amount set aside for losses that are likely to occur (to be released to profit and loss account over the period that the losses are expected to be incurred). Available evidence indicates that most companies write off goodwill immediately on acquisition. Schedule 1 calls for the systematic writing-off of goodwill over a period not exceeding the useful economic life of the goodwill. In the case of goodwill arising on consolidation, there are no statutory provisions, but companies would be expected to adopt one of the generally accepted approaches outlined above.

Tangible assets

The amounts of the following fixed assets must be shown either on the face of the balance sheet or in the notes thereto:

- land and buildings,
- plant and machinery,
- fixtures, fittings, tools and equipment,
- payments on account and assets in course of construction.

The category 'land and buildings' must be further analysed into freeholds, long leaseholds (more than fifty years' unexpired life remaining), and short leaseholds.

It is appropriate here to consider the question of the capitalization of the cost of fixed assets, and to mention items of cost that should be capitalized. In the case of land, capitalized cost should include the purchase price, agents' commissions, legal and surveying fees, draining, clearing, landscaping and demolition costs. Development land tax should be added to the cost of the land where appropriate. If a building is purchased, the capitalized cost should include the purchase price and all repair, alteration and improvement costs. If a building is constructed, the balance sheet cost should include the cost of all work sub-contracted, the cost of materials, labour and other direct production overheads, and all other incidental costs (excavation, obtaining permits and licences, temporary buildings used as construction offices, and professional fees).

The cost in the balance sheet of other fixed assets should include the purchase price plus any freightage, duty and installation charges. Own-built plant and machinery costs will also include the costs of materials, labour and production overheads. In all other cases, the balance sheet total should represent the total cost of relatively permanent items of furniture or fixtures and fittings.

Interest charges on capital borrowed to finance the production of an asset may be capitalized, although there are particular difficulties in identifying the amount of capital borrowed to finance the production of any asset. Where interest is included in the cost of an asset, that interest must be disclosed in a note to the financial statements.

Investments

Under the two alternative formats, investments fall to be reported either in the category of fixed assets or in that of current assets. Under the heading 'fixed assets', the following must be shown either on the balance sheet or in the notes to the financial statements:

- shares in group companies,
- loans to group companies,
- shares in related companies,
- loans to related companies,
- other investments other than loans,
- other loans,
- own shares.

Under the heading 'current assets', the following must be disclosed on the balance sheet or in the notes:

- shares in group companies,
- own shares,
- other investments.

In general terms, the distinction between the two headings relates to the basis on which investments are held. Those held on a relatively short-term basis would be included under 'current assets'.

As mentioned earlier in this chapter, there are alternative valuation bases for these assets – cost, market value or determined value. Listed investments must be distinguished, sub-divided between those listed on a recognized stock exchange (the federated British stock exchanges commonly known as the Stock Exchange and the Irish stock exchanges) and those listed elsewhere.

Where an investment in shares exceeds 10.0 per cent of the allotted share capital of the subject company or of the nominal value of any class of equity share capital, or where the value of the investment exceeds 10.0 per cent of the assets of the investing company, the notes must give additional information:

- the name of the subject company,
- its country of incorporation and/or registration,
- the identity and proportion of the nominal value of each class of shares held.

Companies listed on the Stock Exchange must give additional information, including the principal country of operation of the subject company and the percentage of each class of loan capital attributable to the investing company's interest (direct or indirect).

In its financial statements, The BOC Group presents detailed information about investments in related companies (see note 13 on pages 202-3), revealing that the balance sheet value of investments in related companies at 30 September 1982 was set at £41.9 million, against which £8.9 million had been charged for provisions.

The net value of related companies and other investments is reported at

£64.4 million (net of provisions) in note 13(b) on page 203 and that net value is analysed as between listed and unlisted investments as follows:

	(£ million)
Listed: London	0.9
elsewhere	12.3
Unlisted: directors' valuation	51.2
	64.4

The listed investments had a market value at the balance sheet date of some £21.7 million, as against a cost of £13.2 million.

Other investments

This category will comprise all investments other than those mentioned above in group and related companies, as appropriate, including such items as:

- partnerships and joint ventures,
- building society deposits,
- time deposits with banks,
- insurance policies (generally, life assurance).

Loans

Loans should be included under 'fixed assets' only where they are of a fixed amount and are not repayable in the short term. Generally, this category should include only loans to group and related companies.

Own shares

Only in rare (and for the moment unforeseeable) circumstances would this category appear. British legislation requires own shares purchased or redeemed to be cancelled; it seems unlikely that any investment would appear under 'own shares'.

Current assets

Stocks

Stocks are required to be disclosed as a main heading in the balance sheet. The word 'stocks' must be used; alternatives are not permitted. The category will require the following sub-headings:

- raw materials and consumables,
- work in progress,
- finished goods and goods for resale,
- payments on account.

Directors may adapt the arrangement and the headings where the special nature of a company's business makes such an adaptation appropriate. SSAP 9 ('Stocks and work in progress') had laid down rules concerning the classification of stocks and work in progress into categories appropriate to a company's business activities; those requirements are outweighed by the 1981 act's provisions. The accounting policies adopted in regard to stocks and work in progress must be disclosed. The value to be included in respect of stocks is their purchase price or production cost unless their net realizable value is lower, in which case that lower amount is used. It is permissible to include in the cost of stocks any interest paid or payable on capital borrowed to finance the stocks' production but only to the extent that the interest accrues during the production period; such a course of action depends on the close identification of any capital amounts borrowed to finance stock production. Generally, borrowings are for the activities of a business as a whole and such a close identification would not be possible.

Under both Schedule 1 and appropriate accounting standards, any generally acceptable method of costing stock can be used – for example, 'first-in, first-out' (FIFO), or 'last-in, first-out' (LIFO), or weighted average cost. The 1981 act permits the use of LIFO, but the provisions of SSAP 9 do not. Other methods may include the latest invoice price (again not recommended by SSAP 9), and the retail method or selling price less profit margin method (under which stocks are valued at selling price and then reduced by the deduction of the profit margin).

Detailed consideration of the valuation of work in progress and long-term contracts is not appropriate here, and readers are referred to SSAP 9 and relevant accounting textbook treatments.

In the BOC accounts (see page 177), a value for stocks is shown on the face of the balance sheet – £302.1 million – and an analysis of that total is provided in note 15 to the financial statements (see page 204):

	(£ million)
Raw materials	74.3
Work in progress	110.4
Gases and other finished goods for resale	139.3
Payments on account	(21.9)
	302.1

The note on page 204 provides similarly detailed information about the other categories of current assets and current liabilities referred to below.

Debtors
Debtors must be disclosed as a main heading on the balance sheet and the following items must be disclosed either on the face of the balance sheet or in the notes thereto:

- trade debtors,
- amounts owed by group companies,
- amounts owed by related companies,
- other debtors,
- called-up share capital not paid,
- prepayments and accrued income.

While shown under separate main headings on the alternative formats, the two final items above ('called-up share capital not paid' and 'prepayments and accrued income') may be included under 'debtors' when the amounts are not material.

'Trade debtors' will include amounts owed by customers, suppliers' debit balances, contract retentions, etc., less any provision for bad and doubtful debts, credits for returns, allowances, cash discounts and rebates.

'Other debtors' will include amounts in respect of debts arising from non-trading or lending activities – amounts due from the sale of fixed assets, insurance claims, refundable deposits, and the like. Additionally, the Companies Acts require disclosure under this heading of the following:

- loans to finance share purchases, where such loans are lawful,
- loans to directors,
- loans to officers other than directors.

The final two categories above are dealt with in the course of Chapter 6, although their size, nature and characteristics are required to be disclosed in relation to the balance sheet and its notes.

Cash at bank and in hand
Cash at bank and in hand should not include deposits with building societies or time deposits with banks and the like, which should be shown as current asset investments. All other cash and near-cash items should be shown in this category however: legal tender, cheques, postal orders, credit card vouchers, demand deposits, and the like.

Creditors
Format 1 requires that creditors must be separated into those falling due within one year and those falling due after more than one year. Format 2 provides only one heading for creditors, but the amounts must be shown separately – within one year and after more than one year – and in aggregate. The act lays down that 'creditors' must be shown under the following sub-headings either on the face of the balance sheet or in the notes to the balance sheet:

- debenture loans,
- bank loans and overdrafts,

- payments received on account,
- trade creditors,
- bills of exchange payable,
- amounts owed to group companies,
- amounts owed to related companies,
- other creditors including taxation and social security,
- accruals and deferred income.

The latter heading is shown separately on the alternative formats, but may be included under creditors where not material.

In general terms, the above categories are straightforward and the calculation of the amounts to be reported is fairly easy. There are, however, general disclosure requirements in respect of amounts falling due after more than one year that can usefully be mentioned here.

For each item that is payable wholly or in part after five years from the balance sheet date, there must be disclosed:

- the aggregate amount wholly repayable,
- the aggregate amount repayable by instalments, and the aggregate amount of instalments that fall due after more than five years,
- the terms of payment and the applicable interest rates.

Where large numbers of debts are involved, the disclosure of the latter item may be given in general terms.

Companies listed on the Stock Exchange are required to give more detailed information in regard to the aggregate amounts repayable in one year or less (or on demand), in between one and two years, in between two and five years, and in five years or more.

Provisions for liabilities and charges
This item must be shown on the face of the balance sheet as a main heading; the following sub-headings must be disclosed either on the face of the balance sheet or in the notes thereto:

- pensions and similar obligations,
- taxation, including deferred taxation,
- other provisions.

In general terms, 'provisions' are defined as any amounts retained for the purpose of providing for any liability or loss that is either likely to be incurred or certain to be incurred but where there is uncertainty as to the amount or as to the date on which it will arise.

Capital and reserves

Share capital and share premium
The 1981 act and its schedule require the disclosure of the following items:

- the amount of the authorized share capital,
- the amount of the allotted share capital,
- the amount of the called-up share capital that has been paid,
- the number and aggregate value of each class of allotted shares,
- the earliest and latest redemption dates of any redeemable shares and associated details,
- the reasons for and details of any allotment of shares during the period in question,
- the number, description and amount of any share options,
- the amount and period of any arrears in respect of fixed cumulative dividends,
- details of any holdings of the company's securities by subsidiaries or their nominees.

The legal provisions in respect of the issue of share capital are contained in the Companies Act 1980 and readers are referred thereto for further details.

Where companies issue shares for a consideration in excess of their par or face value, the excess is to be placed in a share premium account. Generally, any balance on that account may be used only for purposes laid down in the Companies Act 1948: the issue of fully paid bonus shares; the writing-off of any preliminary or formation expenses; the writing-off of any expenses, commissions or discounts in connection with the issue of shares or debentures; the provision of any premium payable on the redemption of debentures.

Revaluation reserve
The Schedule 1 formats permit this reserve to be labelled by an alternative name; it is the only 'Roman numeral' heading with that facility. The purpose and nature of the revaluation reserve has already been described in the section on 'Revaluation of assets'. That description also covered the circumstances under which movements to and from revaluation reserve would have impacts on the profit and loss account.

Other reserves and profit and loss account
'Other reserves' will generally be capital redemption reserves or own share redemption reserves. Additionally, a company's articles of association may stipulate the creation of other reserves for specific purposes.

The 1981 act formats require that the retained balance on profit and loss account should be shown on the face of the balance sheet and movements on profit and loss account must be disclosed.

Minority interests

While no format requires a heading for minority interests, it is considered appropriate to show the item as a separate heading in consolidated balance sheets, unless the amount is immaterial. The purpose of the consolidated balance sheet is to reveal the position of the group so far as it relates to members of the group; minority interests should not, therefore, be shown as part of shareholders' funds. Dividends due to minority stakeholders should be shown as liabilities under the heading 'other creditors including taxation and social security'. Similarly, the minority shareholders' share of profits and losses after taxation should be shown separately on the consolidated profit and loss account.

Contingencies and Commitments

Contingencies

It is appropriate here to mention the matter of contingent liabilities and assets. While not directly covered by the 1981 act, the statement in Schedule 1 referring to the principle of prudence in financial statements lends strength to the practice of disclosing contingencies; in terms of best practice, SSAP 18 ('Accounting for contingencies') deals with these matters. The 1981 act does, however, tighten the disclosure provisions laid down in the 1967 act. The earlier act made a general requirement to state the general nature and amount (if practicable to determine clearly) of contingent liabilities; the 1981 act makes that requirement more precise: the amount or estimated amount is to be stated, its legal nature disclosed, and particulars of any security given.

Contingencies are conditions that exist at a balance sheet date but of which the future outcome is uncertain and only confirmed on the occurrence or non-occurrence of one or more uncertain future events – law suits, guarantees, taxation penalties, and the like. Where a contingent loss is probable, it should be accrued in the normal way; where possible, details should be given in the notes to the financial statements; where the likelihood of occurrence is remote, no disclosure is required. Much the same requirements apply to contingent gains.

Commitments

The 1981 act requires disclosure of the following financial commitments:

- capital commitments (expenditure contracted for or authorized at the balance sheet date),
- pension commitments (those that are provided for in the balance sheet and those that are not provided for),
- other financial commitments (purchase commitments in excess of

normal requirements, exposed foreign currency positions, lending or guarantee commitments).

In broad terms, these details are given in respect of any financial commitments that have not been provided for and are relevant to an assessment of the company's affairs.

Post Balance Sheet Events

There is now a requirement to report post balance sheet events, generally defined as events that only become apparent between the balance sheet date and the date of the signing of the balance sheet on behalf of the board of directors. Both Schedule 1 of the 1981 act and SSAP 17 ('Accounting for post balance sheet events') introduced requirements in this respect. SSAP 17 makes a distinction between events that require adjustment of the financial statements ('adjusting events') and those that require disclosure but do not require adjustment to the financial statements ('non-adjusting events'). Examples of adjusting events would include the bankruptcy of a debtor after the year-end, a fall in the selling price of a product causing net realizable value of stocks to fall below cost, changes in the rate of taxation on profits taken up in the financial statements, or the discovery of errors or fraud showing the financial statements to be incorrect. Non-adjusting events might include a fall in the value of property or investments, a change in foreign exchange rates, the issue of shares, or the acquisition or disposal of a business.

The 1981 act requires disclosure in the directors' report (see Chapter 6) of particulars of important events affecting the company and its subsidiaries that have occurred after the year-end.

It is useful in this context to mention the requirements in respect of the signing of the balance sheet. Under the Companies Acts provisions, every balance sheet of a company shall be signed by two directors on behalf of the board of directors. Additionally, SSAP 17 requires that each set of accounts should indicate the date on which the financial statements were approved by the board of directors. That date is important, in that it establishes the date up to which the directors are responsible for disclosing material post balance sheet events. The date will either be shown on the face of the balance sheet, above the signatures of the directors, or as the first item in the notes to the financial statements. Failing that, the date should be stated in the course of the auditor's report. These latter suggestions are not mandatory, but are considered representative of best practice. An example will be found in the accounts of The BOC Group plc (on page 209) of events occurring after the balance sheet date. Between 30 September 1982 and 23 December 1982 (the date on which the financial statements were approved

– see the note on page 177), the group entered into three contracts for the acquisition of businesses. The note reports the considerations payable for those acquisitions and the ways in which those considerations were met – mostly by the issue of ordinary shares as part or full payment.

4 The Funds Flow Statement

This statement, which is often called the sources and applications of funds statement, has become a necessary component of the published financial reports of British companies. It provides helpful supplementary information for the user of financial statements. Broadly, it reports where the company obtained resources and the uses to which they were put. There is no statutory requirement to provide such a funds flow statement, but best accounting practice, as laid down in SSAP 10 ('Statements of source and application of funds'), requires the provision of a statement in the audited financial statements of all companies other than those whose annual turnover or income is less than £25,000.

Format

SSAP 10 and surveys of reporting practice suggest that two alternative forms of funds statement are the more popular. Exhibits 4.1 and 4.2 present two companies' examples of these two alternative forms. One, illustrated in Exhibit 4.1, may be described as the 'change in net liquid funds' type, while the other, illustrated in Exhibit 4.2, may be described as the 'changes in working capital' type. Both are in common use in Britain, although the first variant appears to be the most popular. The consolidated statement form used by The BOC Group plc (reproduced on page 178) represents another type, and incorporates both a current cost profit figure and its modified historic cost equivalent.

The 1981 act says nothing about funds statements, and their provision and format are governed by the requirements of SSAP 10. As with other accounting standards, SSAP 10 permits a variety of approaches, and there are, therefore, no correct or wrong formats. Some are more useful than others, however, and the alternative formats discussed in this chapter are considered to have greater merit than other variants.

Contents

The statement is required to show the profit or loss for the period, with adjustments for the items not involving the movement of funds – such as depreciation charges, deferred taxation provisions – and for profits retained by related or associated companies.

Exhibit 4.1 *Fleet Holdings plc – Consolidated statement of source and application of funds (period from 24 September 1981 to 30 June 1982)*

	(£ thousand)
SOURCE OF FUNDS	
Profits from ordinary activities before taxation	2,932
Adjustments for items not involving the movement of funds:	
Depreciation	2,030
Profit retained in related companies	(10)
Extraordinary item	(306)
Total generated from operations	4,646
Increase in creditors	1,472
Proceeds of issue of share capital	50
Net proceeds of transactions in connection with demerger	9,486
Disposals of tangible fixed assets	402
Decrease in loan to related company	15
Dividend received from related company	7
	16,078

APPLICATION OF FUNDS		
Acquisition of subsidiary	(4,510)	
Satisfied by issue of loan stock	4,510	
		—
Repayment of loan stock		(3,921)
Purchase of tangible fixed assets		(4,668)
Increase in stocks		(678)
Increase in debtors		(2,901)
Tax paid		(162)
Repayment of loans		(173)
Payments from provision for ex gratia pensions		(263)
		(12,766)
INCREASE IN NET LIQUID FUNDS (net liquid funds comprise cash and bank balances less bank loans and overdrafts)		3,312

In addition, the standard requires the reporting of the following items:

- taxation paid,
- dividends paid,
- fixed assets purchased and sold,
- funds raised by increasing equity or loan capital of a medium- or long-term nature,
- funds used in redeeming or repaying loans of a medium- or long-term nature,
- increases in current assets (other than liquid funds),

- decreases in current assets (other than liquid funds),
- increases in current liabilities (other than liquid funds),
- decreases in current liabilities (other than liquid funds),
- changes in working capital,
- movements in net liquid funds.

The final two items may be shown at alternative positions in the statement and are usually divided into their components. Losses should be shown as applications of funds, unless there is a net source of funds after adjustment for non-cash items such as depreciation, etc.

Important items – fixed assets, for example – should be dealt with separately from both a source and an application viewpoint; there should be no 'netting' by the adding together of purchases and sales. Small, relatively unimportant items can be combined. As with other financial statements, comparative figures for the preceding period, calculated on the same bases, should be given.

Funds

Problems have been caused by a too narrow definition of 'funds'. Some preparers have tended to regard 'funds' as either just working capital or just cash. By doing so, statements prepared in that way ignore important financing and investing activities that do not directly affect working capital or cash.

Such financing and investing (or their opposites, disfinancing and disinvesting) activities are important to a proper appreciation of the ways in which the directors obtained and used resources; they should be included in the funds statement. The issue of shares to finance the purchase of a new factory is an important consideration; additionally, the trans-actions represent both a source of funds and an application of those funds. Movements to and from reserves do not affect the financial resources of a company and should not appear in a funds statement.

Taxation

Taxation payments and taxation provisions are not the subjects of precise or even clear rules in SSAP 10. In general, companies treat taxation on a 'tax paid' basis and ignore deferred taxation, unpaid tax and taxation provisions. In that event, the sources computation commences with the calculation of trading profit (or profit on ordinary activities) before taxation. This method has the merit of being simple, and it avoids some of the complications occasioned by such matters as advance corporation tax and changes in the short- or long-term nature of taxation liabilities. An alternative approach takes into account movements on all taxation balances, following the strict accruals concept. In this event, the statement begins with ordinary activities' profit after taxation; adjustments are made for the deferred taxation element that does not require the movement of funds, and increases or decreases in taxation liabilities are shown as sources or applications of funds.

Exhibit 4.2   *Rank Organisation plc – source and application of funds (for the year ended 31 October 1982)*

		(£ million)
SOURCE OF FUNDS		
Within the Group		
Trading profit		33.2
Interest		(34.9)
Dividends received from associated companies		16.9
Extraordinary items before tax		(27.3)
Items included above not requiring funds:		
Depreciation		15.9
Other items		7.5
		11.3
Net proceeds from the sale of		
Investment properties		54.0
Other fixed assets		5.7
Net assets and goodwill of subsidiaries		1.9
Investments		2.0
		74.9
Outside the Group		
Borrowings other than bank overdrafts	52.8	
Issue of preference shares by a		
subsidiary	16.8	69.6
		144.5
APPLICATION OF FUNDS		
Acquisition of net assets of subsidiaries		16.5
Investments in associated companies		13.2
Additions to fixed assets		29.8
Repayment of borrowings other than bank overdrafts		38.3
Repayment of preference shares by a subsidiary		37.6
Dividends paid		26.4
Taxation paid		4.4
		166.2
DECREASE IN WORKING CAPITAL		(21.7)
Comprising		
Decrease in creditors and accrued expenses	0.6	
Decrease in cash and short-term deposits		
less acceptance credits & overdrafts	(13.4)	
Decrease in stock and work in progress	(0.3)	
Decrease in debtors	(8.6)	
	(21.7)	

Dividends
A similar approach is adopted in respect of dividends. Dividends paid are treated as an application of funds, and proposed dividends are ignored – on the grounds that such future dividends do not affect the flow of funds until after they have been approved by the shareholders. The alternative approach treats dividends paid and proposed as applications of funds, and changes in dividends proposed balances are treated as part of the overall changes in creditors.

Extraordinary items
Again SSAP 10 does not deal specifically with extraordinary items. If they involve the movement of funds, they should be disclosed separately in the funds statement. Typically, funds statements will include the net effect of the purchase of a subsidiary as an application of funds; Other examples include the payment of compensation for loss of office, the payment of ex gratia pensions, the net proceeds of demerger or subsidiary sale transactions, and so on.

Related companies
Here again, there are two generally accepted methods of dealing with the results of related companies in the funds statement. The more popular method brings in as a source of funds only those parts of the related company's earnings that are received or receivable by the reporting company. To achieve this, the portion of earnings retained by the related company is shown as an adjustment to the profit figure reported in the funds statement. The alternative method regards all the earnings of a related company as a source and treats the unremitted or retained portion as an application of funds. This method's champions argue that the non-remittance of earnings should be seen as a further investment in the related company by the reporting company. The first method appears to be better supported by commercial good sense.

Constructing a Funds Statement

In essence, the construction of a funds statement is easy: the balance sheet at the end of a period is compared with the balance sheet at the start of that period and the change in each balance sheet item is listed. The notes to the financial statements are used to determine such items as depreciation, fixed asset purchases and disposals, changes in share capital and reserves, and so on. The resulting numbers are then arranged in a funds statement – increases in assets are applications, decreases in assets are sources, increases in liabilities are sources, and decreases in liabilities are applications.

Exhibit 4.3 presents the summarized balance sheets of Addo plc, a general trading company, for the periods ending 31 December 1982 and 1983. From those balance sheets and the summarized profit and loss account presented in Exhibit 4.4, it is possible to construct a funds statement; it will be useful here to look at the principal constituents of Addo's funds flow statement for the year to 31 December 1983.

Exhibit 4.3 *Addo plc – summarized balance sheets (as at 31 December 1982 and 31 December 1983)*

	1983 (£ thousand)	1982 (£ thousand)
FIXED ASSETS		
Tangible assets: Freehold properties	2,280	1,600
Plant and machinery	2,800	2,200
	5,080	3,800
CURRENT ASSETS		
Stock	3,360	2,200
Debtors	1,960	1,280
Cash at bank and in hand	—	400
	5,320	3,880
CREDITORS: AMOUNTS FALLING DUE WITHIN ONE YEAR		
Bank overdraft	170	—
Trade creditors	1,830	1,300
Taxation	570	550
Proposed dividend	280	210
	2,850	2,060
NET CURRENT ASSETS	2,470	1,820
TOTAL ASSETS LESS CURRENT LIABILITIES	7,550	5,620
CREDITORS: AMOUNTS FALLING DUE AFTER MORE THAN ONE YEAR	(2,000)	(1,200)
PROVISIONS FOR LIABILITIES AND CHARGES		
Deferred taxation	(944)	(760)
	4,606	3,660
CAPITAL AND RESERVES		
Called-up share capital	2,200	2,000
Share premium account	600	400
Profit and loss account	1,806	1,260
	4,606	3,660

Exhibit 4.4   *Addo plc – summarized profit and loss account (for year to 31 December 1983) (extracts)*

	(£ thousand)
Turnover	12,500
Profit on ordinary activities before taxation	1,460
(after depreciation £940,000)	
Dividends paid £140,000	
Dividends proposed £280,000	

Notes:
(a) 200,000 ordinary £1 shares were issued during the year at a price of £2 each.
(b) During the year, additions and disposals of fixed assets were as follows:

	Freehold properties	*Plant & machinery*
Additions	£880,000	£1,440,000
Disposals	£120,000	—

The freehold property had a book value of £100,000 (cost of £120,000 less accumulated depreciation of £20,000) and was sold for £180,000 – an extraordinary profit of £80,000.
(c) Corporation tax of £220,000 in respect of 1982 profits was paid on 1 January 1983. Advance corporation tax is payable (at the rate of three-fifths of actual dividend distributions) on dividends; £90,000 was paid in respect of the final dividend for 1982 and £60,000 in respect of the interim dividend for 1983. In all, £370,000 was paid in respect of tax during 1983.
(d) Dividends actually paid in 1983 were as follows: £210,000 as a final dividend for 1982, and £140,000 as an interim dividend for 1983.

The first source item, profit before taxation, is derived from the profit and loss account in Exhibit 4.4, which shows a balance of £1,460,000 profit before taxation. The only adjustment for items not involving the movement of funds is in respect of depreciation, which is reported in the profit and loss account at a total of £940,000 for the year. The total sources from operations, therefore, are £2,400,000. Other sources derive from examining the change in certain items on the balance sheets: issued share capital has increased by £200,000 (from £2,000,000 to £2,200,000); the share premium account has increased by £200,000 (from £400,000 to £600,000); long-term loans have increased from £1,200,000 to £2,000,000 – an increase of £800,000. In addition, proceeds have been received from the sale of freehold buildings: a building valued at £120,000, on which accumulated depreciation totalled £20,000, had been sold for £180,000 (as revealed by the extraordinary profit item in the profit and loss account of £80,000). Total funds from other sources were, therefore, £1,380,000. The total sources identified are £3,780,000.

Turning to the application of funds, the following movements can be identified. Freehold property costing £880,000 has been purchased and plant and machinery costing £1,440,000 has been acquired. Taxation totalling £370,000 has been paid, as have dividends totalling £350,000. The total applications identified so far are £3,040,000.

The increase in working capital, therefore, is calculated at £740,000, which can be divided as follows: stocks have risen by £1,160,000 and debtors have risen by £680,000; on the other hand, creditors have risen by £530,000 and net liquid funds have fallen by £570,000 – cash having fallen by £400,000 and the bank overdraft having risen by £170,000.

These sources and applications and changes in working capital can be brought together in a funds flow statement – as shown in Exhibit 4.5.

Exhibit 4.5   *Addo plc – source and application of funds (for the year ended 31 December 1983)*

	(£ thousand)
SOURCE OF FUNDS	
Profit before taxation	1,460
Adjustment for items not involving the movement of funds:	
Depreciation	940
	2,400
Proceeds of share issue	400
Proceeds of sale of fixed asset	180
Loans raised	800
	3,780
APPLICATION OF FUNDS	
Purchase of fixed assets	2,320
Payment of taxation	370
Payment of dividends	350
	3,040
INCREASE IN WORKING CAPITAL	740
Comprising	
Increase in stock	1,160
Increase in debtors	680
Decrease in creditors	(530)
Decrease in net liquid funds	(570)
	740

The cash flow variant
It is possible, and often valuable, to construct a variant of the funds flow statement – the cash flow statement. Such a statement would seek to explain why the cash balance has fallen from a surplus of £400,000 to an overdraft of £170,000. In essence, that movement can be explained as follows:

	(£ thousand)		
Turnover per profit and loss account			12,500
less Increase in debtors			(680)
Cash received from debtors			11,820
less Payments for goods &			
expenses	10,100		
plus Increase in stocks	1,160		
	11,260		
less Increase in creditors	(530)		
		(10,730)	
Funds from operations:		1,090	
Sale proceeds	180		
Share issue proceeds	400		
Loans raised	800		
		1,380	
		2,470	

So the total cash available to the firm during the year was £2,470,000 plus the opening balance of £400,000. The uses of that cash can be explained as follows:

	(£ thousand)
Purchase of fixed assets	2,320
Payment of tax	370
Payment of dividends	350
	3,040

With a total application of £3,040,000, as against a total source of £2,470,000, there has been a net reduction in cash of £570,000 – the £400,000 opening balance and the £170,000 overdraft.

Usefulness of Funds Flow Statements

In general terms, there is a willing acceptance of the actual or potential usefulness of profit and loss accounts and balance sheets. It is appropriate, therefore, to seek to determine the usefulness of the funds flow statement. Users of accounts are concerned about the viability and future performance of a company, and considerable help can be obtained from considering the income and position statements. The funds flow statement also assists in this task. Information is collected together in a way that helps to answer the questions: What resources did the company have available to it last year, and how did the company use those resources?

It is valuable to appreciate the extent to which funds have been generated from operations and the extent to which they have been raised by other means – including the incurrence of loans and obligations or the disposal of fixed assets. One of the pertinent questions to be asked concerns the payment of tax and dividends. Did the funds generated from ordinary trading operations cover those payments? Or were the funds to pay taxation and dividend obligations raised by long-term borrowings or asset disposals? The acquisition and disposal of fixed assets are prime examples of funding transactions that are not readily apparent from the 'conventional' accounts and yet that are vital to a proper understanding of the company's activities. As such, the information contained in a funds flow statement provides valuable guidance to the reader and user of financial statements.

5 The Value Added Statement

This statement is one of the several additional statements proposed originally in the Accounting Standard Committee's discussion paper, *The Corporate Report* (1975). The essential difference in this statement is that it recognizes that a company or other business entity is operated by, and for the benefit of, a number of different interests – employees, owners, lenders and government. For a thorough analysis and discussion, readers are referred to Cox (1979, 1983). Currently, there are neither statutory nor professional requirements for the presence or format of such an additional statement, but it has come to form part of the customary package of financial statements produced by British companies.

Format

Given the lack of binding requirements, a variety of formats has developed (see Cox, 1979, 1983; or Morley, 1978, for examples). The model format presented in *The Corporate Report* is reproduced in Exhibit 5.1 as a suitable framework for such a statement. The BOC Group plc statement of value added is reproduced on page 179 in the accounts in Appendix A to this book, and that statement demonstrates an effective way of augmenting the value added information – by a regional analysis, and by a calculation of value added per employee.

Exhibit 5.1   *Statement of value added – model format*

Turnover
less Bought-in materials and services
Value added

To pay employees: wages, pensions and fringe benefits
To pay providers of capital: interests on loans; dividends
    to shareholders
To pay government: taxation
To provide for maintenance and expansion of assets:
    depreciation; retained profits
Value added

In broad terms, the value added statement is a simple rearrangement of information given in a profit and loss account and elsewhere in the financial statements. It can be considerably enhanced by the presentation of percentages alongside the various categories of application. As examples of actual formats employed, in addition to the BOC example, Exhibits 5.2 and 5.3 present the value added statements of two companies. It has to be noted that many companies – including several of considerable size and influence – do not provide value added statements.

Exhibit 5.2 *Marley plc – statement of value added (for the 14-month period ended 31 December 1982)*

		(£ million)
VALUE ADDED		
Sales to customers		460.7
Deduct: Bought in materials and services		(310.0)
		150.7
APPLIED AS FOLLOWS		
To employees:		
Wages, salaries, pensions and other employment costs		108.5
To government:		
Corporate taxes		6.8
To providers of capital:		
Interest	16.5	
Minority interests	0.5	
Dividends to shareholders	5.2	
		22.2
Retained in the business:		
Depreciation	15.6	
Deficit for the period	(2.4)	
		13.2
		150.7

Contents

The first item in a value added statement will generally be the turnover figure that appears in the profit and loss account. In most cases, this will be exclusive of value added tax (VAT). From that turnover figure will be deducted the cost of bought-in services, which will typically include the following:

- raw materials,
- heating and lighting,
- professional and specialist services,
- printing,
- audit fees,

and so on. The result will be a figure of value added by the efforts of the enterprise's employees.

The second part of the statement will seek to show that value added has been distributed between the various parties involved. First, the employees' share is reported. This item will comprise all amounts payable to all employees:

- gross pay,
- employers' national insurance contributions,
- employers' pension contributions,
- employers' costs of fringe benefits and facilities.

Exhibit 5.3   *Macarthys Pharmaceuticals plc – value added (year to 30 April 1982)*

		(£ thousand)
SOURCE OF VALUE ADDED		
Sales to external customers		215,114
less goods and materials purchased and services provided		(196,078)
		19,036
DISTRIBUTION OF VALUE ADDED		
Employees:		
Pay	11,696	
National insurance	1,277	
Pensions	702	
Group profit share	526	
		14,201
Government:		
Corporation tax		1,142
Providers of capital:		
Dividends	948	
Interest	744	
		1,692
Retained in the business		2,001
		19,036

Many variations exist at this level of the statement, with some reporters taking the national insurance and PAYE contributions to a separate category to demonstrate the company's relationship with central government more clearly. In that event, the salary and wages figure reported would be the net amount actually paid over to employees.

Next, it is necessary to report the portion of value added that has been paid to the providers of long-term capital. Generally, these will be:

- interest paid and payable on loans,
- dividends paid and payable to shareholders,

and those items will be easy to calculate.

The third category concerns payments to government, and this is the item that demonstrates the greatest diversity in practice. Strictly speaking, the only entry under this general heading should be the amount of corporation tax payable in respect of the period – both mainstream corporation tax and advance corporation tax. Many reporters, however, show all taxes collected on behalf of and paid over to the government – corporation tax, PAYE, national insurance contributions, VAT, local rates, customs and excise duties, and so on.

The final heading is concerned with the extent to which portions of value added are being retained for the future development of the business and the maintenance of the fixed asset base. It is arguable that depreciation should not be included in this category, and should be treated as a deduction from gross value added at the head of the statement.

There are, naturally enough in an accounting statement, a number of less clear-cut matters. For example, many companies enjoy sizeable non-trading incomes (from investments, for example, or from extraordinary activities such as the sale of assets) and these should be shown as additions to the value added by trading. If the company receives a share of the profit or loss of an associated or related company, that too should be shown at the head of the statement as an addition to the value added generated from trading.

Usefulness of Value Added Statements

In terms of the development of value added statements, the statement is still in its infancy. Roughly one in five major companies produce such a statement, and it has been argued that this is because of political or cosmetic needs – the statement offers a useful way of highlighting the very large portion of value added that is paid over to employees and the government.

The statement offers a useful device for formulating additional assessments of a company's performance, and as such is a helpful supplementary statement. There is no standardized format and companies are free to adopt whichever format appeals to them most or, indeed, to create their own. In many cases, the value added statement does not form part of the group of statements reported upon by the auditor.

Nonetheless, despite its comparative infancy and its restricted popularity, the statement is seen to have merit and to offer a useful additional base for analysis. It is likely that current cost-based value added statements will be prepared by many reporters, and the BOC statement shows that segmental value added statements are produced in some instances.

6 The Directors' Report

As a result of the 1981 act, the format and contents of the directors' report have varied considerably, in that a number of items formerly given voluntarily or in accordance with accounting standards in the directors' report have now been compulsorily included in the notes to the financial statements and there have been specific extensions to the items to be included in the post-1981 directors' report. Additionally, the Listing Agreement of the Stock Exchange occasionally calls for wider disclosure than that enjoined by statute or accounting standard; those extra items can conveniently be disclosed in the directors' report or an annex thereto.

There are no formats specified for the report, but the report of the directors of The BOC Group plc (as reproduced on pages 165-174 in Appendix A) offers an excellent example of best practice in this respect. The directors can augment the basic mandatory information as they wish, but the following descriptions are concerned mostly with the requirements of the Companies Acts, accounting standards and the Listing Agreement.

Contents

Broadly, the directors' report is required to give details of and information on the company's activities, its directors, substantial holdings of its shares, its employees, and its charitable and political donations in the year under review. The quantity and quality of those details and information vary considerably from company to company. However, all companies are required by law to present a directors' report, and the same broad pattern is followed by most companies.

Activities and trading results

The directors are required to give details of the principal activities of the company and its subsidiaries during the year, and of any significant changes in those activities during the period. Definitions or examples of principal activities are available, and the following appears to offer a useful guide.

Principal activities are usually taken to mean important categories of diversification, generally in terms of distinct classes of industrial or commercial activity – engineering, leisure, retailing, etc. Vertical classification is not required.

In terms of changes to the company's activities, it is generally suggested that a positive statement be made if there has been no change, or that sufficient details be given of any major changes, such as withdrawal from an industrial sector or a significant class of business.

Companies quoted on the Stock Exchange are required to give an analysis of turnover and profit contribution by geographical regions. Under the provisions of Schedule 1 to the 1981 act, that information must be given by all companies in the notes to their financial statements in respect of turnover. It is suggested also that, as a matter of best practice, some analysis of asset distribution by geographical region would be useful.

The extent to which companies provide such segmental information varies considerably and many give no more than the bare essentials to conform with statutory and regulatory criteria. The disclosure of capital employed and employees by region is voluntary and most companies fail to provide information of that kind.

Developments during the period

Additionally, the directors are required to give a fair review of the development of the company and its business during the period and the position of the company and its subsidiaries at the end of the period. They must give details of any important occurrences affecting the company during the year, and present an assessment of likely future developments.

While there is no real indication of the extent of that 'fair review', there is a general feeling that future directors' reports should be more comprehensive than those that have appeared in the past. As a minimum, the report should include the following:

- a discussion highlighting the turnover and profits from ordinary activities;
- details of exceptional and extraordinary items;
- indications of comparative results for the preceding period;
- a discussion of the main factors that have contributed to any significant change;
- details of acquisitions and disposals of subsidiaries or divisions;
- details of acquisitions and disposals (where significant) of fixed assets;
- (where reported) details of and a discussion concerning the current cost adjusted results.

The requirement to review the position of the company and its subsidiaries at the end of the period might be best met by discussing at least the following:

- changes in, and adequacy of, working capital and its principal components (stock, debtors, creditors, liquid funds);
- borrowings and proposals for financing capital expenditure during the coming period;

- important or significant performance and liquidity ratios (return on assets, solvency, gearing, earnings per share, and so on).

As mentioned in Chapter 3, any post balance sheet events of a 'non-adjusting' kind must be reported; they are to be reported in the notes to the financial statements (according to SSAP 17), and it would be appropriate for the directors' report either to mention those events briefly or to refer to the relevant note to the financial statements.

In terms of meeting the requirement to report on and discuss likely future developments, the directors' report should concern itself with at least the following:

- forecast of earnings during the coming year, expressed in general or trend terms rather than in quantified target terms;
- details of significant plans for new products, acquisitions and disposals, capital investment, expansion and contraction, rationalization, and so on;
- forecasts of probable socioeconomic factors impinging on the company.

These forecasts and predictions are replete with dangers and directors exercise considerable care in framing such 'hostages to fortune'.

The area of research and development must be covered in the report, and directors would be expected to give an indication of progress and likely future directions for research and development, particularly where such innovation is likely to lead to new products or new markets being developed. Directors are naturally reluctant to give sensitive information that would be of value to competitors and imitators.

The report's review of the period must contain details of the dividends paid and to be proposed, and report on actual and planned movements in reserves, where significant.

Directors

The 1981 act and its predecessors, and other regulatory pronouncements, are quite clearly concerned to bring about the disclosure of all significant information about the directors of a company and their relationships with it. The basic requirements are as follows:

- the names of all directors at any time during the period in question;
- the interest of directors in shares and debentures of the company and/or its subsidiaries at the beginning of the period and at the end.

Listed companies must distinguish between beneficial and non-beneficial holdings, and the usual practice is to include the interest of directors' close families in such analyses.

In certain circumstances, details must be given of a director's service contract with the company – usually when he is eligible for re-election. Full details of all transactions and arrangements with directors – particularly loans, quasi-loans and credit facilities – must be presented in the financial statements. Considerable interest has recently been evinced in such matters as the provision of mortgages or favourable-rent houses for directors, and such matters are required to be reported. As mentioned earlier, the emoluments of all directors must be reported in summary form, classified by band in terms of the aggregate amounts of salaries and so on.

Substantial holdings

A person who acquires 5.0 per cent or more of the nominal value of the voting capital of a public company must notify the company within five days of so acquiring that stake or of becoming aware that he has acquired that stake. In this connection, an interest includes that of a spouse or a child or ward. Under the terms of the Listing Agreement of the Stock Exchange, a company's directors must give in their report particulars of any and all substantial holdings (i.e. greater than 5.0 per cent) of any class of voting capital.

Fixed assets transactions

The directors' report must describe and comment upon the following:

- significant changes in fixed assets – both physical actual changes and changes in value;
- substantial differences between market value and balance sheet value of any fixed asset or class of fixed asset.

Such comments will generally extend the information given in the notes to the financial statements, describing and discussing the particular assets in question.

Employees

Under a variety of legislative instruments, including the Health and Safety at Work Act 1974, companies will be obliged to give substantially more information about employees and employment conditions than has hitherto been the case.

In the notes to the financial statements, the total average number of employees must be disclosed and a classified breakdown (as discussed earlier) must be provided. Further, staff costs must be disclosed either on the face of the profit and loss account or in the notes thereto.

Although not yet statutorily enforced, companies are voluntarily providing information on health and safety at work. Since 1980, the directors' report must contain a statement describing the company's policy in respect of the employment of disabled persons. That requirement only applies to companies with an average total number of employed persons during the year of 250 per week or more.

Donations

The directors are required to report political and charitable donations by the company or group of companies where those donations are in excess of £200. In addition, where donations are for a political purpose, the name of the recipient and the individual amount paid must be disclosed. There are considerable areas of confusion about the proper definition of a 'political purpose', but in general terms such payments are readily identified and should be reported. Given the degree of interest in the political-giving activities of British companies, many reports make a point of stating categorically that no payments are made or donations given for political purposes.

Accounting, auditing and taxation matters

Significant departures from accounting standards should (and, in the case of listed companies, must) be disclosed and an explanation given for any departure. Listed companies are expected to conform fully with all extant accounting standards.

The appointment of a company's auditor is a matter for the shareholders in general meeting, but it is customary for the directors' report to refer to the auditor's willingness to be reappointed or, if appropriate, to mention and explain any proposed change to current auditing arrangements. More importantly, however, the 1981 act brought the directors' report more firmly into the auditor's sphere of activity and he is required to determine whether or not the directors' report and its contents are consistent with the audited financial statements. In general terms, the 1981 act gives statutory backing to a practice that had been followed by auditors for several years.

Where a company is held to be subject to the close company taxation liability of any company, that fact should be included in the directors' report; listed companies must report whether or not they are subject to close company provisions.

7 The Chairman's Statement

Many of the matters that used to be contained in the statement to members by a company chairman have now been incorporated in the directors' report and the notes to the financial statements. Nevertheless, the statement remains an influential part of the annual report, and is read widely by shareholders.

In essence, the statement offers an opportunity for a chairman (who is frequently also chief executive) to report in unquantified and unaudited terms on the performance of a company during the past financial period and on the likely future developments. He will usually take the opportunity to comment on directors and other employees, and on the efforts of the management team and the workforce. Quite often, the chairman's statement will be used to make political or social comments about government, taxation, accounting standards or whatever else exercises the chairman at the time of writing.

There is no format, other than the general one that the statement is usually addressed to the shareholders and is conventionally signed and dated by the chairman, and there are no standard or even recommended contents.

Chairmen's statements range in length from half a printed page to more than seven or eight pages. In the latter case, the contents will include a reasonably thorough description of each of the main areas of activity. Based on the usual type of chairman's statement, even though no such abstraction exists in any sensible way, the following contents are proposed:

- descriptions of, and comments on, major corporate developments – such as acquisitions, disposals, demergers, share issues, rights issues, etc.;
- comments on the trading results for the period, and significant influences thereon;
- descriptions of, and comments on, major subsidiaries and their activities and results;
- comments on corporate growth and asset bases;
- details of, and comments on, executive share option schemes, employee participation schemes, and the like;
- forecasts of prospects in the immediate future;
- comments on the recruitment or separation of directors and senior employees;
- comments on the efforts and productivity of employees.

Not all chairmen's statements follow these or any common line, of course, and practice varies considerably from company to company and from chairman to chairman.

Importance and Usefulness

The statement is not audited and, as such, may be considered to be of little real value in assessing a company and its prospects. That is not the view of the users of annual reports; as reported by Lee and Tweedie (1981), professional institutional investment specialists consider the chairman's statement to be an important part of the annual report. The most important were the profit and loss account and the balance sheet, and the chairman's statement was next in terms of relative importance. It is salutary to add here that the auditor's report was considered the least important part of the annual report. Of the 214 readers of annual reports surveyed by Lee and Tweedie, all except one read the chairman's statement briefly or thoroughly; of those readers, the greater majority did not read the auditor's report at all.

In these circumstances, it is perhaps necessary to have a general format for such an important part of the annual report. Additionally, it is necessary to seek a better appreciation of the use made, and the accuracy and verifiability, of information contained in the chairman's statements; some research work is proceeding along those lines.

There is no doubt that, divorced from the strict requirements of the law and the regulatory bodies, the tone and approach of a chairman's statement are valuable indicators of a company's 'state of mind' and useful determinants of the likely future development plans of a company. As such, the statement is clearly helpful to readers.

The BOC Group plc

In order that the above comments may be set in context, and so that chairmen's comments may be compared with, for example, the directors' report, it is useful to consider extracts from the chairman's statement presented in the annual report of The BOC Group plc – the full chairman's statement is not reproduced in Appendix A.

The chairman of BOC, Sir Leslie Smith, began his 1982 statement with a comment that may be familiar to readers of this book:

> I have every sympathy with the shareholder who ploughs his way through our Report and Accounts and tries to decide for himself whether the Company is doing well, badly, or indifferently; how the Company would fare in changed economic circumstances; and how our

performance compares with other British companies or with our international competitors. All of us who have the responsibility for compiling this Report of our stewardship do our best to present a straightforward and true picture of our affairs. Unfortunately the growing complexity of the rules and regulations with which we have to comply and the sheer volume of information which we are required to publish make our task almost impossible.

He went on to say that even the figures themselves are now open to misinterpretation – the impact of inflation on asset values being a particularly strong one.

In discussing the results for the year, he drew attention to the impacts of the worldwide recession, pointing out that most of BOC's businesses serve manufacturing industry and are therefore specially vulnerable to the effects of recession. He mentioned the group's strategy for cutting costs,

> by planned attacks on overmanning and on outdated work patterns, supplemented and supported by cost saving investment. The benefits are particularly noticeable in the UK where the scope for cost reduction was greatest and where the impact of recession came earlier than elsewhere.

He said that management in the group had to be congratulated on their achievements, and that there was much to be optimistic about – profitability had been maintained, productive capacity had been preserved intact, and many of the businesses were doing well.

In discussing the level of international and domestic risk to which the group was exposed, the chairman drew attention to particular strengths of The BOC Group – keeping abreast of technological developments, fostering research, and so on. He argued persuasively against the creation of further barriers to trade:

> As the recent GATT meeting showed all too clearly, every community is devoted to the principles of free trade so long as they are applied to everybody except themselves . . . [I]t is my hope that Government will maintain its policy of the very minimum of protectionism.

He was moved by the particular problem of unemployment, and recognized the difficulties faced by those whom the group had made redundant:

> The truth that 'our strength lies in our people' has become a cliché which has an even emptier ring at a time when we employ thousands less than a year ago. I believe the economic necessity of our actions within the Group companies is understood and accepted by those no longer employed by us.

He concluded by proclaiming the group's continued objective of making an increasing contribution to the wealth not just of the UK, but of all the communities in which BOC operates.

Of its nature, the chairman's statement in the BOC annual report is a model of its kind: wide-ranging, far-sighted, and addressed to matters vital to the continued progress and stability of BOC and its fellows in the international business community. In the case of BOC, the chairman's statement was succeeded by a report from the group chief executive. That latter report went into the detailed descriptions and analyses that, in other companies' reports, would have been found in the directors' report or the chairman's statement. Turnover and profit trends and results were detailed, particular businesses' results were discussed, and forecasts for 1983 were made. The group chief executive used his report to comment on working capital changes, and he finished by commending the group's employees for their work and skills and the group's business partners for their support and continued loyalty.

8 Other Reports and Statements

Following the initiative of the Accounting Standards Committee in seeking to identify desirable components of a rounded and useful corporate report, many additional reports and statements have developed. These are generally of a qualitative nature, supported by quantified information, and broadly they seek to add – in a helpful and promotional way – to the financial data presented in the conventional reports and accounts and their notes. These additional reports and statements can be considered in two categories:

- the provision of new, different additional information – on employment practices, social responsibility, community involvement, and so on;
- the provision of explanatory additional information – a break-down of staff costs by sex or age, information on a company's pension scheme, long-run historical and comparative data, and so on.

The variety of practice in these areas is considerable, and there are no suggested or generally acceptable formats or lists of contents. In terms of the willingness to provide such additional information, certain companies are front-runners; The BOC Group plc is one and Appendix A contains several examples of additional voluntary disclosure. Two other companies have been chosen to represent best practice in these areas – Marks & Spencer plc, and Scottish & Newcastle Breweries plc – and examples of their practices appear in the chapter. There are other companies presenting additional information of these kinds, of course, although the proportion of all companies doing this is still fairly low.

Without devoting a disproportionate amount of effort and space to these additional disclosures, it is useful to consider two general areas in which company practice is developing helpfully – employment-related information, and social or environmental information. There are several academic and practical studies of the theories behind these additional reports and of the practices of British and American companies in their provision; see, for example, studies by Dobbins and Fanning (1981), Fanning (1979), Lee (1981) and Seidler and Seidler (1975).

Employment-Related Information

The 1981 act and other legislation enjoin the provision of certain basic information about employees and employment conditions, as has been described earlier. The practice has developed, however, following one of the recommendations in *The Corporate Report* (Accounting Standards Committee, 1975), of providing wider-ranging information on the employment practices of companies.

The Corporate Report proposed certain contents of an employment statement:

- numbers employed, average for the year and actual for first and last days;
- broad reasons for changes in numbers employed;
- age distribution and sex of employees;
- functions of employees;
- geographical locations of major employment centres;
- major plant and site closures, disposals and acquisitions;
- hours scheduled and worked;
- employment costs, including fringe benefits;
- costs and benefits associated with pension schemes and the ability of such schemes to meet future commitments;
- cost and time spent on training;
- names of unions recognized for collective bargaining, and membership figures;
- information concerning health and safety at work, including frequency and severity of accidents and occupational diseases;
- selected ratios relating to employment.

Since the publication of the Accounting Standards Committee's suggestions, very little has been done by way of researching the need for and purposes of such a report. It had been proposed that legislation should be introduced to make such a report compulsory, but professional opinions held against legislation in this area. Fanning (1979) and others have examined the topic in more depth, but the provision of employment reports remains a relatively rare occurrence. Amongst leading companies, Scottish & Newcastle Breweries plc regularly presents an employment report as part of its annual report and accounts; Exhibit 8.1 reproduces the text of one of the company's recent employment reports. Another leading company, Marks & Spencer plc, presents different information in its employment report and Exhibit 8.2 reproduces extracts from a recent version.

There has been a marked increase in the provision of employment-related data, both as a result of legislation and as a result of voluntary decisions to disclose such information, but comparatively few companies feel moved to augment their existing practices in this way.

Exhibit 8.1   *Scottish & Newcastle Breweries plc – employment report*

1   Numbers employed

The numbers employed in the United
  Kingdom at May 3, 1981 were:

	1981	1980
Production, distribution and wholesaling of beer	6,770	7,115
Wines and spirits, including off-licences and distilleries	1,455	1,515
Group central functions, including finance, management services and personnel	515	535
	8,740	9,165
Hotels, restaurants and public houses		
full-time	6,205	6,955
part-time	10,350	11,425
	25,295	27,545
Former EMI Hotels and Restaurants		
full-time	1,365	—
part-time	260	—
	26,920	27,545

Under Section 18 of the Companies Act 1967, the average numbers of employees working wholly or mainly in the United Kingdom during the financial year to May 3, 1981 were 27,169 (1980 27,830).

2   Remuneration

The aggregate remuneration for the 53 weeks of the financial year was £103,960,000 compared with £85,464,000 for the previous year; in addition the Group's share of national insurance contributions was £10,935,000.

The table which follows shows the number of employees including Directors in the Group whose emoluments exceeded £7,500 during the financial year:

£	1981	1980
over 20,000 (see page 21)	27	16
15,001–20,000	50	33
10,001–15,000	400	202
7,501–10,000	1,598	526
	2,075	777

3   Industrial relations

Time lost through stoppages increased from 1,662 man days to 7,828 man days. 7,003 of these occurred as a result of a single dispute in north-east England.

4   Training

During the year 28,131 man days were spent on off the job training compared to 29,322 in 1980.

5   Health and safety

Accident statistics for our brewery operatives within the UK in the form approved by the Brewers' Society are:

Calendar year	Number of employees	Number of accidents	Number of lost days	Days lost per man
1978	5,217	341	6,270	1.20
1979	4,997	341	6,901	1.40
1980	4,646	241	6,312	1.35

The accident rate per thousand employees compared with the brewing industry:

Calendar year	Breweries with more than 1,000 employees	All breweries	Our breweries
1978	99.82	102.24	64.79
1979	92.96	102.89	68.24
1980	66.13	73.27	51.87

6   Labour turnover

There were wide variances amongst different categories of employees but the statistics excluding employees in hotels and public houses are:

	Total	Own accord	Discharged	End of contract	Retirement and other reasons
1980	17.3%	8.9%	2.1%	1.5%	4.8%
1981	13.8%	4.2%	1.6%	3.3%	4.7%

7   Absenteeism

The consolidated absence rates again mask the wide differences between various sections of the Group but the statistics excluding employees in hotels and public houses are:

	Total	Accidents and sickness	Authorized absence	Unauthorized absence
1980	6.0%	4.6%	0.7%	0.7%
1981	4.9%	3.5%	0.9%	0.5%

8   Trade Unions

The numbers of employees represented by each trade union which is recognized for collective bargaining purposes are:

Employee Group	Representative union	Numbers represented as at May 3, 1981	Known membership percentage 1981	1980	Numbers represented as percentage of total employees
Engineers	AUEW				
Plumbers					
Electricians					
Instrument mechanics	EET & PTU				

Vehicle mechanics	T&GWU (automotive section) AUEW	617	100 100	2
Joiners				
Painters				
Builders	UCATT			
Other craftsmen	ASB, NUSMW, CFGB	5	100 100	—
Production, ware-housing and distribution	T&GWU	3,742	99 99	14
Hotels – staff	G&MWU	4,480	25 25	17
Licensed houses – staff	T&GWU	11,203	12 11	42
managers	NALHM	1,325	68 68	5
Clerical and administrative	ACTSS	1,674	79 72	6
Technical and supervisory	ACTSS	902	82 78	3
Total of negotiating groups		23,948	41 41	89
Management, sales staff and other employees		2,972	11 11	11
All employees		26,920	37 37	100

ACTSS	Association of Clerical, Technical and Supervisory Staff
ASB	Amalgamated Society of Boilermakers, Shipwrights, Blacksmiths and Structural Workers
AUEW	Amalgamated Union of Engineering Workers
CFGB	Coopers' Federation of Great Britain
EET & PTU	Electrical Electronic Telecommunication and Plumbing Trade Union
G&MWU	General and Municipal Workers' Union
NALHM	National Association of Licensed House Managers
NUSMW	National Union of Sheet Metal Workers, Coppersmiths and Heating and Domestic Engineers
T&GWU	Transport and General Workers' Union
UCATT	Union of Construction, Allied Trades and Technicians

Social Responsibility Information

The movements towards corporate social reporting have generally found little adherence outside the ranks of a small number of companies and a loyal number of academics and commentators. Nonetheless, many companies present social and environmental information at different places in their annual financial statements and accompanying reports, even though that information is not collected together in one so-called social report.

The contents of such a social report would include the following disclosures:

- environmental factors (pollution control activities, preventive or remedial environmental measures, and so on);
- energy factors (energy conservation activities, efficient use of energy);
- fair business practice factors (minorities, disabled persons, overseas employment practices, responsibility to lenders and suppliers);
- human resource factors (health and safety, training, welfare and leisure facilities, employee participation, pensions);
- community involvement factors (educational and charitable support, executive secondment, and so on);
- product factors (product safety and reliability, impacts of use);
- general social factors.

Apart from the relatively few provisions of the Companies Acts, mentioned in earlier chapters, there are no regulations calling for the provision of such a social report in its entirety or in part. Companies with interests in South Africa are required, under a European Community code of practice, to submit regular annual reports to the Secretary of State for

Exhibit 8.2   *Marks & Spencer plc – employment report (extracts)*

Benefits
We paid £148.6 million in salaries. Our salary policy gives extra reward for individual merit. We allocated £3.2 million for the acquisition of shares under the Employees' Profit Sharing Schemes. 19,566 now participate in the Schemes. We spent £13 million on welfare and social amenities, mainly on catering subsidies and a wide range of health services concentrating on preventive medicine.

Long Service
We value long service. Nearly 20,000 United Kingdom staff have completed more than 5 years' service and over 10,350 have completed more than ten years.

Equal Opportunities
We recruit and promote men and women on equal terms, regardless of colour, race and religion. All our staff receive training relevant to their jobs and are encouraged to contribute to their fullest ability.

Staff Involvement
Our staff are informed of Company progress and developments. They are encouraged to offer views in those areas where they are directly involved. Communication Groups and Working Parties in which our staff participate have proved to be valuable and constructive.

Trade, detailing employment numbers, practices and policies for South African employees. Multinational companies are encouraged, by various agencies, to provide social and environmental information on a geographical or regional basis.

Companies engaged in the extractive industries in particular feel obliged to make disclosures on environmental matters. Equally, companies active in politically sensitive areas – banking or pharmaceuticals, for example – often take the opportunity in their annual reports of describing and extolling their community involvement.

Individual examples of occasional disclosure of items of social interest abound, but a few may be reported here as representative. Rowntree Mackintosh plc reported as follows:

> The group made charitable donations totalling £233,000 during 1982 (1981 £115,000) of which payments made by UK companies were £204,000 (1981 £83,000). These were given to a wide range of causes but many were linked to projects within the communities in which the group operates. Two sizeable donations arose from promotional activities on confectionery brands: £64,000 to the UK children's charity 'Break' which works to provide holiday and residential care for handicapped children and £50,000 to the Jimmy Savile Appeal Fund for Stoke Mandeville Hospital. The company contributed £1,500 to Britain in Europe.

In addition, the directors reported that the group had supported three local initiatives aimed at helping the formation and development of small businesses. Plans had been completed to provide a number of unemployed young people with training opportunities at the group's factories. Other organizational help was given to young people seeking employment:

> For example, a senior manager was seconded as a full-time coordinator for Project Trident which helps young people have practical experience of working in industry.

The most comprehensive description of the community involvement of Rowntree Mackintosh was given, not in the annual report to shareholders, but in the annual report to employees.

In common with their North American counterparts, who have been closely involved with social and community responsibility activities for many years, the British clearing banks have developed a number of social programmes. The annual report of National Westminster Bank plc recorded that, in 1982, the bank

> gave support to a wide range of community projects; projects which have proved to be of real social benefit and which stimulate community

participation. Major items were grants to develop local voluntary organizations and to initiatives to combat unemployment in inner cities. In the Arts, recognition of our support was marked with an award by the Association for Business Sponsorship of the Arts with particular comment on the varied and imaginative sponsorship programme undertaken by the Bank.

The other clearing banks report similar experiences and degrees of involvement.

By and large, very little of the available social information is quantified, but there appears to be an underlying trend towards greater disclosure of social and environmental matters.

Other Statements

In addition to the statements discussed above and elsewhere in the book, *The Corporate Report* proposed a number of other statements:

- money exchanges with the government;
- transactions in foreign currency;
- future prospects;
- corporate objectives.

It is useful to examine the degree to which these kinds of statement have been produced by United Kingdom companies and, where possible, to present examples from published annual reports.

The statement of money exchanges with the government is intended to report the flow of money between enterprises and government, thereby demonstrating the degree of interdependence between the enterprise and the state. It is suggested that the contents of such a statement should include:

- PAYE collected from employees and paid over to the Inland Revenue;
- VAT collected from customers and paid over to HM Customs & Excise;
- corporation tax and similar taxes paid over;
- rates and similar levies paid over to local authorities;
- other sums collected and paid over to government departments and agencies – social security contributions, training levies, duties;
- money receipts from government, including grants and subsidies.

Very few companies actually produce a regular statement of money exchanges with government; one that does is Marks & Spencer plc, and Exhibit 8.3 presents one of that company's recent statements.

Exhibit 8.3   *Marks & Spencer plc – statement of financial relationship with United Kingdom central and local government*

	(£ million)
Corporation tax on the year's profits amounted to	76.8
In addition to the above the following central and local government charges have also been borne in the United Kingdom:	
Rates	17.4
Import duty	1.7
Contribution for national insurance	14.0
Total cost of United Kingdom central and local government charges	109.9
The Company is also obliged to collect the following taxes for which they are accountable to the United Kingdom government:	
Value added on sales	163.1
Income tax deducted from employees' salaries	25.0
Income tax deducted from interest on debentures	1.0
Employee contributions for national insurance	5.4
Making a total for the year for which the Company is accountable to United Kingdom central and local government of	304.4

The statement of transactions in foreign currency is intended to reveal the extent to which business entities have contributed to balance of payments results and to provide evidence on which to assess the exposure to risk and vulnerability of business enterprises. It is suggested that the contents should include:

- details of UK cash receipts for direct exports;
- details of UK cash payments to overseas concerns for direct imports, distinguishing between capital and revenue items;
- details of overseas borrowings remitted to or repaid from the UK;
- details of overseas investments and loans made from or repaid to the UK;
- details of overseas dividends, interest or similar payments received in the UK or UK dividends, interest or similar payments remitted overseas.

As with the money transactions statement, hardly any companies produce a statement of international monetary transactions.

The Corporate Report proposes that a statement of future prospects be published as part of the annual report and accounts, covering such matters as:

- future profit levels;
- future employment levels and prospects;
- future investment levels;
- details of the assumptions underlying the forecasts.

Such matters are routinely covered in either the chairman's statement, the managing director's report or the directors' report, and no companies produce such an additional quantified statement in line with the Accounting Standards Committee's proposals.

The statement of corporate objectives is seen as a device whereby investors can measure the degree of effectiveness of managements in achieving target objectives and assess the extent of congruence between their individual objectives and the company's corporate objectives. It is intended to be a broad statement of general philosophy or policy and to contain quantified targets in respect of sales, value added, profitability, investment, dividends, employment, social and environmental issues, and so on.

As with the other additional statements proposed by the Accounting Standards Committee, very few companies produce a statement of corporate objectives and even fewer prepare – or at least publish – quantified statements in line with the Committee's proposals.

Conclusion

In a foreword to one of the regular series of annual surveys of published reports, published by the Institute of Chartered Accountants in England and Wales, Sir Douglas Morpeth echoed the comments of many company chairmen when he said that criticism was arising

> that the increasing demands for more information and the restrictions and burden of accounting standards are going too far. All those concerned with increasing demands for information and the development of improved understanding of company accounts should remember that a balance must be struck between the interests of the user and the interests of those whose responsibility is primarily to manage a business and make a profit. It is a responsibility of the accounting standard setters to try to keep such a balance so that the interests of society both in efficient and profitable business and accountability are best served.

It is easy to argue, as so many do, that if more information were available better decisions could be made. There is obviously a tolerance level up to which that argument is valid; beyond that level, however, there are considerable dangers of information overload and even greater dangers that those required to produce additional reports and analyses will refuse to comply with accounting standards, best practice and external suggestions. Part two of this book will reveal the very large extent to which existing levels of information disclosure are sufficient to facilitate the formation of sound and efficient judgements about a company and its position and prospects.

9 The Auditor's Report

In essence, the auditor's report is the *sine qua non* of corporate reporting. As popularly understood, it is the guarantee to the reader and user that the financial statements have been prepared properly and in accordance with legislative and regulatory requirements, that they present the information truthfully and fairly, and that they conform to best accounting practice in their treatment of various measurements and valuations. At the same time, paradoxically, the auditor's report is certainly the least read part of the annual report and probably the least understood as well.

It is a statutory requirement that every company's financial statements must be reported upon by duly appointed auditors, and that this report must accompany every balance sheet and profit and loss account laid before the members of a company. The auditor's duty is to the shareholders of a company, although there have been several instances of that duty being interpreted more widely. They are outside the scope of this present discussion, but readers are referred to any auditing textbook (de Paula and Attwood, 1982, or Woolf, 1979, for example) for accounts of certain pertinent legal actions concerning the duties and responsibilities of auditors to third parties and to those who rely on audited financial statements (see, for example, reports of the Jeb Fasteners Ltd vs. Marks Bloom & Co action in 1981, and subsequent appeals therein, concerning the legal duty of care owed by auditors to strangers of whom nothing was known at the time of an audit).

There are clearly defined formats for auditors' reports under different circumstances and there are clearly delineated contents. This chapter describes the alternative forms of auditor's report and its usual contents and omissions.

It is considered best practice for an auditor's or accountant's report to accompany every set of financial statements issued, for whatever purpose, to third parties or destined to come into the hands of third parties. This chapter (and indeed the whole book) is concerned only with financial statements issued by companies in accordance with statutory obligations and professional recommendations to report the results of a trading period and the position at the end of that period.

Format and Contents

In general terms, the format is straightforward. Most auditors' reports follow a standard pattern, with modifications and extensions incorporated as appropriate. The auditors' report to the members of The BOC Group plc is shown on page 175 of the Financial Review reproduced in Appendix A. Further examples are the following reports made to the members of Fleet Holdings plc and Marley plc. The report to the members of Fleet Holdings plc by the company's auditors, Touche Ross & Co, read as follows:

> We have audited the financial statements on pages 14 to 29 in accordance with approved Auditing Standards. In our opinion the financial statements on pages 14 to 26 give, under the historical cost convention as described in note 2(a), a true and fair view of the state of affairs of the Company and the group at 30 June 1982 and of the profit and source and application of funds of the group for the period then ended and comply with the Companies Acts 1948 to 1981. In our opinion the abridged supplementary current cost financial statements on pages 27 to 29 have been properly prepared, in accordance with the policies and methods described in notes 1 and 2, to give the information required by Statement of Standard Accounting Practice No. 16.

The financial statements directly referred to in the report represented the profit and loss account, company and group balance sheets, notes to the financial statements and the current cost financial statements. In addition, although not reported upon, the auditors will have been required to verify the information contained in the directors' report.

The auditors' report to the members of Marley plc read as follows:

> We have audited the accounts on pages 34 to 46 in accordance with approved Auditing Standards. The accounts have been prepared under the historical cost convention as modified by the valuation of fixed assets. As indicated on page 38 it is not the company's policy to provide for depreciation on freehold and long leasehold buildings which are included at £76 million in the accounts. This is not in accordance with Statement of Standard Accounting Practice No 12 which requires that provision should be made for depreciation of fixed assets having a finite useful life. Except for the effects of not providing for depreciation on freehold and long leasehold buildings, in our opinion the accounts give, under the convention stated above, a true and fair view of the state of affairs of the company and the group at 31st December 1982 and of the profit and source and application of funds of the group for the 14 months period then ended and comply with the Companies Acts 1948 to 1981. In our opinion the supplementary current cost accounts together with the notes thereon on pages 48 to 52 have been properly prepared in accordance with the methods described in the notes, to give the information required by Statement of Standard Accounting Practice No 16.

The report, made by Price Waterhouse, represents an example of a 'qualified' audit report (reporting non-compliance with SSAP 12) and it is appropriate here to examine further the matter of qualified audit reports.

Auditing standards have been formulated by the Auditing Practices Committee of the Consultative Committee of Accountancy Bodies. Under these standards and associated guidelines, an auditor is required to report on the following:

- whether the financial statements have been audited in accordance with approved auditing standards;
- whether the financial statements give a true and fair view of the state of affairs and profit or loss of the company and its subsidiaries;
- whether the financial statements comply with statutory requirements (in British circumstances, the Companies Acts 1948 to 1981, as modified or extended by statutory instrument).

As part of his investigation, the auditor is required to satisfy himself that

- proper accounting records have been kept,
- the financial statements are in agreement with the accounting records,
- the information given in the directors' report is consistent with the financial statements.

An unqualified report is one in which an auditor can report affirmatively on all the specified matters.

Qualified reports are those in which the auditor expresses a reservation, of whatever weight, because of significant departures from legislative or regulatory requirements or of non-compliance with relevant accounting standards. A qualified audit report is issued only after discussion with the board of directors. There are no standard phrases to form a qualified report, since each report will be specific to the particular circumstances of the qualification, but the Auditing Practices Committee has produced a diagram of the types of opinions that are appropriate in different circumstances, as follows:

Nature of circumstances	Material but not fundamental	Fundamental
Uncertainty	'SUBJECT TO' opinion	DISCLAIMER of opinion
Disagreement	'EXCEPT FOR' opinion	ADVERSE opinion

In general terms, qualified reports must not be made unless the matters occasioning the qualification are significant and/or material. Non-compliance with the requirements of the Companies Acts might not be material or, indeed, significant, but such an instance would require mention in the audit report.

A 'subject to' opinion is issued where the auditor is not able to form an opinion on one or more matters that together are not considered fundamental. For example, it may be accounting standard practice to make certain adjustments to a stock or debtors total in certain circumstances; if those adjustments are not made, the auditor would issue an opinion that, subject to the effect of any adjustment that might have been made, a true and fair view has been presented. His opinion would outline the omitted procedures.

A disclaimer of opinion will be made in those very exceptional circumstances where any uncertainty is considered fundamental and where the auditor cannot form an opinion as to the truth and fairness of the financial statements and their compliance with statutory or professional requirements. The auditor would say that he was unable to form an opinion for the reasons stated in his report.

An 'except for' opinion is appropriate in those circumstances in which an auditor disagrees with the treatment or disclosure in the financial statements of items that are not considered fundamental. A report in these circumstances will indicate the nature of the disagreement (as in the auditors' report in respect of Marley plc, quoted earlier) and state that, except for the amount involved in the item causing disagreement, the financial statements are true and fair and comply with all relevant requirements.

An adverse opinion will be issued in circumstances where an auditor disagrees on matters that are considered fundamental to the business. In these circumstances, the auditor would issue an audit report stating that in his opinion the financial statements do not give a true and fair view and do not comply with the relevant statutory and regulatory requirements.

Nevertheless, the issue of an adverse opinion or the disclaiming of any opinion are measures of last resort and should be used only in extreme circumstances. Amongst those circumstances may be found the following:

- the probability of the company being unable to continue in business;
- serious deficiencies in the accounting records;
- serious defects in the quality of the audit evidence;
- doubts or serious misgivings about the integrity of management and the reliability of its representations.

Omissions that do not affect the balance sheet or the profit and loss account – as, for example, the omission of a statement of the source and application of funds – should simply be commented upon in the auditor's report; they would not give rise to a varied or qualified opinion.

Modified audit reports

Certain sizes of company are exempt from the full statutory requirements in respect of accounts delivered to the Registrar of Companies (as discussed earlier), and such companies' filed accounts must be accompanied by a special auditor's report. That report would certify that, in the auditor's opinion, the requirements for exemption had been satisfied and should contain a copy of the full text of the audit report made to members of an exempt company.

Certain modifications to 'standard' auditors' reports are made in respect of certain categories of company – banking, shipping and insurance companies, for example, or dormant and non-trading companies. Additionally, there are suggestions that certain small companies should receive audit reports that express reliance upon the acceptance of management assurances. Such reports fall into the 'subject to' category, basing an opinion on the assurances of a chief executive or the directors that all a company's transactions have been accurately recorded in the accounting records.

Usefulness of Auditors' Reports

It is essential to understand clearly what an auditor's report is, and what it is not. An audit does not guarantee the absolute truth and fairness of a company's financial statements. It certifies that proper accounting records have been kept, that the financial statements are in accordance with those records, and that the Companies Acts have been complied with; additionally, it attests (unless specifically stating otherwise) that generally acceptable accounting principles have been applied properly and consistently. To that extent, it provides a measure of reasonable assurance that the financial statements may be relied upon.

It is no part of the auditor's duty and responsibilities to search for or to prevent the incidence of fraud or misappropriation, or any other managerial or staff misbehaviour; that is the duty of the owners' agents – the directors – as part of their contract with their principals. However, the auditor generally plans his work so that he has a reasonable chance of detecting such incidences; to that extent the audit process acts as a safeguard against fraud.

The form of words used in an auditor's report is crucial; particular attention must be paid to the phrases and conditional statements used. An independent audit lends credibility to a company's financial statements and, to some extent, helps to protect the interests of all those who deal with or have a stake in that company. It is, however, restricted to the matters discussed in this chapter; investors, purchasers and suppliers are not entitled to rely on an auditor's report in all circumstances and a full and thorough independent investigation or clarification is essential.

Nonetheless, the auditor's report is a regulatory requirement in most countries, and a voluntary safeguard in others. As such, it offers an independent objective opinion on the accounts prepared by a company's management.

Part Two:

Interpretation and Assessment

10 Financial Statement Analysis and Comparison

Objectives

Having described and examined the principal components of published financial statements, it is now time to focus attention on the means by which those statements may be analysed to extract information that will be useful in making financial decisions or judgements about a company. The principal tools of financial statement analysis have been developed over a long period and consist in general, of first identifying the important items of both financial and non-financial data and then relating these to one another and also to factors external to the company. This process is usually referred to as ratio analysis. The ratios that are calculated can then be used to evaluate the current performance of a company by comparing them with the ratios of previous years or with those for other companies in the same industry.

Ratio analysis

The decisions that different users may be faced with may be quite varied: for example, lenders will be interested in creditworthiness, employees in information for wage-bargaining purposes, shareholders in profits and dividends prospects, and so on. Nevertheless, it is true to say that just about all users will be interested in evaluating the current performance and financial position of the company and in making predictions about its future. It is necessary, therefore, to consider the role that financial statement analysis has to play in this process.

The figures contained in the financial statements – such as turnover, profit, current assets, total assets, etc. – are absolute amounts that may not by themselves be very meaningful indicators of a good or bad performance or of a satisfactory or unsatisfactory position. For example, the balance sheet of a company may reveal that the current assets figure is £150,000 and the current liabilities figure £75,000. Individually these items may not tell us very much. However, if they are related to one another in the form of a ratio, i.e. £150,000 to £75,000, the resultant ratio of 2 : 1 (or simply 2) may indicate whether there is a sufficient cushion of short-term funds in the business. Similarly, it is possible to take two profit and loss account items, such as net profit of £40,000 and sales of £800,000, and examine their relationships. Any informational value that these two items may have when considered in isolation will be greatly enhanced by calculating the profit to sales ratio of £40,000 to £800,000, or 0.05 : 1. This ratio is usually expressed as a percentage, in this case 5 per cent, which indicates the net profit percentage being earned on each £ of sales value. Further ratios can be obtained by relating items from both the profit and loss account and the balance sheet. For example, the net profit figure used above was £40,000 and an examination of the balance sheet may reveal a figure of £400,000 for total assets employed. By themselves, these figures are difficult to interpret, but if they are related to each other in the form of a ratio, i.e. £40,000 to £400,000, a ratio of 0.1 : 1 or 10 per cent is obtained. This may indicate the adequacy of the profit figure when considered against the total value of the assets available for earning such a profit.

Reducing the large number of financial statement items to a relatively small number of key ratios in this way can help to begin answering the following questions about the economic aspects of a company:

- Is the profit that is being earned satisfactory?
- Is the management of working capital (cash, debtors, stock, creditors) adequate?
- Is the long-term capital structure suitable?
- Is efficient use being made of assets and other resources?

The ratios that have been developed in connection with these questions are described in detail and examined in Chapters 11–14.

Comparision of Financial Ratios

The calculation of ratios is only the first step in financial statement analysis. Although ratios provide a useful means of relating individual items in the financial statements to other items, some standard is needed against which those ratios can be assessed. Unfortunately, there is no such thing as an 'ideal' or absolute standard measure for this purpose. For example, it is not possible to state categorically that the ratio of net profit to total assets for all companies should be 10 per cent and therefore that anything less than 10 per cent is 'bad' and anything greater is 'good'.

The lack of absolute ratio criteria has been overcome in practice in two ways, The first, and the one most frequently adopted, is to calculate the average ratios for all the companies in a particular industrial sector. This gives an 'industry' standard against which the ratios of a particular company can be evaluated. The second method involves the calculation of the relevant ratios for the company under analysis for each of a number of preceding years and using those ratios as a basis for assessing the ratios for the current period. Figures for immediately preceding years are available in the current year's financial statements. In addition, the more important items are shown in summarized form for at least the past five years by all listed public companies.

These 'standards', however, do have certain limitations. There is still no clear guide as to the optimal size of a particular ratio. For example, assume that the industry average for the ratio of current assets to current liabilities is 1.5. If a particular company in that industry has a ratio of 0.5, it is well below the 'standard' and can perhaps be thought of as 'bad'. However, another company in the same industry with a ratio well in excess of the industry average, say 2.5, cannot categorically be thought of as 'good'. Such a high ratio might be the result of cash being allowed to lie idle or of stock levels being higher than necessary. Both of these practices could be instances of bad management of current assets. The answer might seem, therefore, to be to evaluate a company in terms of its deviation below or above the average for the industry. Unfortunately, it is not so simple. Even within the same industry, companies have to face different situations that may justify a substantial deviation from the industry average. Thus, if a particular ratio is out of line with the average for the industry, such a deviation merely indicates an area for further examination. Moreover, it could be argued that the industry average is not the most appropriate standard. After all, the average incorporates the ratios of the best and the worst companies in the industry. Perhaps it might be better to have industry standards based on the ratios of the most successful companies in the industry.

A similar problem is encountered if the 'standard' is based on the ratios of a company in earlier years. Conditions are unlikely to be stable over time and the ratios obtained in previous years may be wholly inappropriate to the current environment in which the company has to operate. Thus, a deviation from previous years' ratios does not permit instant 'good' or 'bad' classifications but might, depending on the size of the deviation, suggest that further examination is necessary.

By themselves, ratios are of limited value. It seems clear that if absolute ratio criteria did exist then ratio analysis would be a mechanical procedure requiring very little expertise. It is because there are no absolute criteria and because of the imperfections in the surrogate 'standards' that a great deal of skill and judgement are required in the evaluation and inter-pretation of ratios. In Chapter 15, the use and limitations of both inter-firm and intra-firm ratio comparisons are considered further.

Ratio Calculation

When calculating ratios, a logical connection between the items being related to each other is essential. For example, the ratio of net profit to total assets is economically meaningful, and the resultant statistic can be used in the evaluation of those profits against the asset base available. A ratio relating the income tax charge in the profit and loss account to the total assets employed, on the other hand, is of doubtful significance. Thus, although it is possible to construct a large number of ratios, from the many items contained in published financial reports, not all of these ratios will have any economic relationship. The implications of this for financial statement analysis are that a few key ratios are in reality all that is needed. Additional support for the view that only a limited number of ratios are required stems from the high degree of correlation among the various ratios. This is mainly because many ratios are made up of items that also appear in other ratios, and so correlation might be expected.

A further requirement that is often proposed for ratio calculation is that the components of the ratios should be determined in a consistent manner. For example, a frequently calculated ratio is that of sales to debtors, i.e. the debtor turnover ratio. However, the debtors figure occurs as a result of credit sales, while the reported sales figure usually includes both credit sales and cash sales, so the same valuation basis is not being used. Such an inconsistency in the method of calculating the components of a ratio does not necessarily invalidate it, but merely suggests care in its interpretation.

Finally, it is often argued that the components of the ratios should have relationships that vary with each other; in other words, the components should be functionally related. For example, when calculating the ratio of net profit to sales, the profit figure is arrived at by deducting from the sales figure all the manufacturing and operating expenses of the company. Some of those expenses will vary more or less directly with the level of sales but others will be fixed whatever the level of sales. Thus, the resultant profit figure is not functionally related to the sales figure.

Ratios, do not, of course, have to be restricted to financial items. In recent years, much more use has been made of non-financial data. Employee-related data are an obvious example of this, and ratios of sales per employee, or profit per employee, or value added per employee are now quite common. Other ratios of a similar nature will depend on the types of activity carried on by a company. For a road haulage company, for example, a useful ratio for comparative purposes might be profit per road mile travelled or per ton carried; for an airline, profit per passenger mile or costs per passenger mile might be useful statistics.

Problems in Ratio Analysis

Some of the problems surrounding ratio calculation and finding suitable bases for comparison have been mentioned earlier. In this section, attention is focused on some of the other frequently cited problems in ratio analysis.

Lack of uniformity in accounts preparation
It was seen in Part One that accountants preparing financial statements are free, within broad limits, to choose from a wide range of generally accepted

accounting principles. Thus, two firms that are identical in every respect may show quite different figures for profit and balance sheet valuations, owing to the use of different accounting policies. The efforts of the Accounting Standards Committee since its inception in 1970 have done much to reduce the range of permitted accounting policies, but choices still exist for the valuation of stocks and work in progress, depreciation methods, deferred tax treatment, the treatment of intangibles and goodwill, accounting for leases, and many other areas. The consequences for ratio analysis are readily apparent. Comparisons are a very important feature of ratio analysis, yet without uniformity in the preparation of financial statements it is impossible to determine whether variations in ratios are due merely to accounting policy differences or to real economic differences.

Even if uniformity of accounting policies existed (for example, a mandatory requirement for straight-line depreciation in all circumstances), differences in estimates of asset lives would still result in variations in depreciation charges. Thus, only total uniformity, with both depreciation method and asset lives being prescribed, would produce truly comparable bases for ratio preparation. Such requirements would, of course, be anathema to the British business community. Different companies do use identical assets in different ways and therefore, in reality, there will be differences in asset lives. Accounting for economic reality, and not simply accounting in accordance with the rules, is a cornerstone of accounting philosophy in the United Kingdom.

The use of historic cost accounting has also had the effect during times of rapidly changing prices of making ratio comparison an exercise of doubtful validity. Using, once again, the ratio of net profit to total assets as an example, it is evident that the denominator of the ratio (total assets) will be different for a firm with equivalent assets purchased more recently.

Diversified companies
Although the growth in acquisitions and mergers of companies has slowed down in recent years, the merger boom of the 1960s and early 1970s resulted in a large number of highly diversified companies. Because, by definition, diversified companies operate in different industries with different degrees of risk and different expected profitabilities, the calculation of ratios based on the aggregated figures is going to be of limited use in financial statement analysis. The problems of aggregating the results of diversified companies have been recognized for a long time. The obvious solution is to report separately the results of the segments of a company that operates in different industries. That will facilitate comparisons by permitting the calculation of ratios not only for the diversified group as a whole but for each of the industrial sectors in which the company operates.

Unfortunately, segment reporting is still high on the list of unresolved problem areas in financial reporting. One of the difficulties as far as ratio analysis is concerned is the allocation to individual segments of costs that are common to the whole company. Head office administrative costs, interest charges on loans, and so on, are examples of common costs that are incurred by the company and have to be allocated on an arbitrary basis to each segment. Such a requirement can distort significantly the results of a particular segment.

Lack of conceptual foundation
It was claimed earlier that the purpose of financial statement analysis is to extract information useful for decision-making purposes. It was also stated that ratio analysis is the principal tool of financial statement analysis. It might therefore be reasonable to assume that ratio analysis would figure largely in microeconomic theories about asset valuation and in theories about securities analysis. However, an examination of the literature in those areas reveals that this is not the case. This is because of the lack of any conceptual foundation surrounding ratio analysis and decision-making. It has been assumed that ratios will be useful without ever establishing that usefulness. Moreover, the strong support for the efficiency of capital markets, which argues that share prices at any time always reflect fully all publicly available information, implies that securities analysis is of little use in assessing share prices.

Even so, ratio analysis is still used in practice. In spite of its apparent limitations, a great deal of time and effort is still spent on calculating and comparing ratios. In fact, as will be described in Chapter 15, decision models consisting of a combination of ratios have proved very effective in making predictions about companies. However, before considering these, it is necessary to examine in detail the mechanics of ratio analysis; this is done in the next four chapters.

11 Profitability and Performance

In Chapter 2 it was shown how information concerning the profit of a company is presented in the annual financial report. Although such information is useful in establishing the absolute level of profit earned during a period, it fails to indicate the performance of a company because it does not take account of the resources available for the generation of the profit. A measure of profitability is therefore required that relates profit earned to other relevant factors. There are several widely used indicators of profitability; this chapter introduces some of the more important of these.

Return on Capital Employed

This ratio, which is usually expressed as a percentage, is calculated as:

$$\frac{\text{profit}}{\text{capital employed}} \times 100$$

Such a ratio is intended to provide information on the performance of a company by concentrating on the efficiency with which capital employed has been utilized. Thus, if two companies are being compared and the reported profit of Company A is £10,000 and that of Company B is £15,000, then Company B has clearly earned the greater profit. However, if it is then observed that the capital employed of Company A was £50,000 and that of Company B was £150,000, the return on capital employed for each company is as follows:

$$\text{Company A} \quad \frac{10,000}{50,000} \times 100 = 20\%$$

$$\text{Company B} \quad \frac{15,000}{150,000} \times 100 = 10\%$$

It is now apparent that, when the profits earned by the two companies are related to their respective investment bases, Company A achieved the better return on capital employed and might therefore be regarded as the more successful. It is at this point, however, that the problem is first encountered of establishing precisely what is meant by the components of financial ratios, and also the methods by which these components might be calculated. Both 'capital employed' and 'profit' can quite sensibly have different meanings attached to them, and before comparisons between the ratios of different companies can be made it is obviously essential to ensure that like is being compared with like.

Capital employed is usually taken to be either the total assets of the company, i.e. fixed assets plus current assets, or the net total assets, i.e. fixed assets plus current assets minus current liabilities. If the amount of total assets is used, the resultant profitability measure is intended to focus attention on the efficiency with which all of the resources available to the managers of the company have been utilized. The argument for the use of net total assets is that the level of current assets is inextricably linked with the level of current liabilities and is very much dependent on the working capital policy of the company. In other words, it is only the net total assets that can be thought of as a resource that is completely at the disposal of management. Any distortions that are caused by variations in working capital policy will be minimized by netting off current liabilities against current assets so that a more comparable asset base is obtained.

In the examples that follow, ratios of return on capital employed have been calculated for The BOC Group plc based on each of the alternative definitions discussed above. It should be noted however that BOC itself has adopted a slightly unusual variation on the net total assets approach when calculating return on capital employed. From the five-year record on pages 212 and 213 it can be seen that the capital employed figure is calculated as net total assets after excluding short-term cash items. Presumably the rationale for using this approach is to provide an investment base that avoids the distortions caused by fluctuations in the short-term cash position.

A further point concerning capital employed relates to the date at which this should be calculated. Because the numerator of the ratio represents a flow of profit earned over the entire accounting period, the denominator ought to reflect the average amount of capital employed during the period. It is usually sufficient for this purpose to take an average of the amounts of capital employed at the beginning and end of the accounting period.

It is also evident that the basis on which the assets have been valued will have important implications for profitability analysis. At times of rising prices, the historical cost of the assets will usually be lower than their current values. This can make comparisons between firms with different asset age structures extremely difficult. Fortunately many companies now include in their annual reports financial statements that have been prepared according to the principles of current cost accounting, or alternatively have adopted the practice of frequently revaluing their fixed assets to reflect current values. The detailed Financial Review of The BOC Group plc for the year ended 30 September 1982 is reproduced in Appendix A (pages 163–216). From this it can be seen that profit and loss accounts (page

176) and balance sheets (page 177) have been prepared on the basis of two separate accounting conventions: the current cost convention and the modified historical cost convention. As these statements will be referred to extensively during this and the succeeding chapters it will be convenient to reproduce them again at this stage. Exhibits 11.1 and 11.2 show the current cost profit and loss account and current cost balance sheet respectively. The profit and loss account and balance sheet prepared under the modified historical cost accounting convention are shown in Exhibits 11.3 and 11.4. The information on accounting policies (page 181) reveals that under this latter convention the fixed assets are stated at the lower of their replacement cost or economic value; this results in identical fixed asset valuations to those obtained from the use of the full current cost accounting convention. The Financial Review also includes a profit and loss account (page 214) and a balance sheet (page 215) based on the traditional historical cost convention, whereby assets are stated by reference to their original cost. In order to bring out the differences that each of these alternative accounting conventions might produce, the return on capital employed calculations for BOC have been prepared by using a capital employed figure based on current cost values, modified historical cost, and, where possible, traditional historical cost.

As far as the profit component of the ratio is concerned, comparability will be improved by using a profit figure that reflects the ordinary activities of the company and excludes the effects of any extraordinary items. Comparability is similarly improved by using a profit figure before deductions for interest and taxation. The amount of taxation paid by a company depends on a variety of circumstances, not all of which are under the control of the company. Distortions caused by differences in liabilities to taxation can therefore be avoided by concentrating on the before tax position. The rationale for excluding interest charges is that the resultant profit figure is then consistent with the calculation of capital employed. If capital employed is taken to represent the total assets of the company, then it is evident that these have been partially financed by the creditors, therefore the profit figure should be the amount before any interest payments to creditors have been deducted. If capital employed is taken to represent the net total assets, then strictly speaking it would be correct to exclude only the long-term interest payments. The interest paid on current liabilities, or received on current assets, should be included in the calculation of profit. Note 3 to the financial statements of BOC (page 188) gives some information on the distinction between interest payments to long-term and short-term creditors, but does not permit an exact calculation to be made. As the amounts involved are relatively small, this distinction has been ignored and the trading profit before interest, taxation and extraordinary items has been taken as the appropriate profit figure to be used in the following return on capital employed ratios for 1982.

Exhibit 11.1   *The BOC Group plc: consolidated profit and loss account for the year ended 30 September, current cost basis*

1981 (£ million)		Notes	1982 (£ million)
1521.7	TURNOVER	1	1534.2
(882.6)	Cost of sales		(920.4)
639.1	Gross profit		613.8
(164.1)	Distribution costs		(164.3)
(325.3)	Administrative expenses		(292.3)
(19.2)	Research and development		(24.9)
(7.9)	Monetary working capital adjustment		(5.6)
7.6	Share of profits of related companies		9.7
1.0	Income from other fixed asset investments		1.2
131.2	OPERATING PROFIT	1	137.6
—	Realised stock holding gains		—
131.2	TRADING PROFIT		137.6
27.4	Gearing adjustment		26.1
(65.7)	Interest payable (net)	3	(65.3)
3.5	Interest capitalised		7.1
	PROFIT ON ORDINARY ACTIVITIES		
96.4	BEFORE TAX		105.5
(37.6)	Tax on profit on ordinary activities	4	(27.6)
58.8	Profit on ordinary activities after tax		77.9
(11.5)	Minority interests		(10.9)
47.3	Earnings		67.0
0.6	Extraordinary items	5	6.0
47.9	PROFIT FOR THE FINANCIAL YEAR		73.0
(16.9)	Dividends	6	(19.5)
31.0	TRANSFER TO RESERVES	18	53.5
	Earnings per Ordinary share (undiluted)	7	
16.49p	nil distribution basis		22.64p
14.34p	net basis (after ACT written off)		20.24p
	Earnings per Ordinary share (fully diluted)		
15.92p	nil distribution basis		20.27p
13.76p	net basis (after ACT written off)		17.86p

Exhibit 11.2 *The BOC Group plc: consolidated balance sheet at 30 September, current cost basis*

1981 (£ million)		Notes	1982 (£ million)
	FIXED ASSETS		
1152.6	Tangible assets	11	1277.6
	Investments (related companies and		
43.9	other investments)	13	71.4
1196.5			1349.0
	CURRENT ASSETS		
278.5	Stocks		305.6
310.3	Debtors		288.2
14.3	Deposits at short call		31.4
12.2	Cash at bank and in hand		6.4
615.3			631.6
	CREDITORS: Amounts falling due within one year		
(58.5)	Borrowings and finance leases		(109.7)
(306.7)	Other		(290.0)
250.1	**NET CURRENT ASSETS**	15	231.9
1446.6	**TOTAL ASSETS LESS CURRENT LIABILITIES**		1580.9
	CREDITORS: Amounts falling due after more than one year	16	
(484.2)	Borrowings and finance leases		(517.4)
(15.2)	Other		(15.8)
(55.5)	**PROVISIONS FOR LIABILITIES AND CHARGES**	17	(58.2)
(554.9)			(591.4)
891.7			989.5
	CAPITAL AND RESERVES	18	
84.8	Called up share capital		85.4
44.3	Share premium account		45.6
376.4	Revaluation reserve		326.9
53.0	Other reserves		135.1
217.3	Profit and loss account		274.7
14.7	Related companies' reserves		18.6
790.5			886.3
101.2	**MINORITY SHAREHOLDERS' INTERESTS**		103.2
891.7			989.5

Exhibit 11.3   *The BOC Group plc: consolidated profit and loss account for the year ended 30 September, modified historical cost basis*

1981 (£ million)		Notes	1982 (£ million)
1521.7	TURNOVER	1	1534.2
(882.6)	Cost of sales		(920.4)
639.1	Gross profit		613.8
(164.1)	Distribution costs		(164.3)
(325.3)	Administrative expenses		(292.3)
(19.2)	Research and development		(24.9)
—	Monetary working capital adjustment		—
7.6	Share of profits of related companies		9.7
1.0	Income from other fixed asset investments		1.2
139.1	OPERATING PROFIT	1	143.2
18.2	Realised stock holding gains		17.6
157.3	TRADING PROFIT		160.8
—	Gearing adjustment		—
(65.7)	Interest payable (net)	3	(65.3)
3.5	Interest capitalised		7.1
95.1	PROFIT ON ORDINARY ACTIVITIES BEFORE TAX		102.6
(37.6)	Tax on profit on ordinary activities	4	(27.6)
57.6	Profit on ordinary activities after tax		75.0
(11.2)	Minority interests		(10.5)
46.3	Earnings		64.5
0.6	Extraordinary items	5	6.1
46.9	PROFIT FOR THE FINANCIAL YEAR		70.6
16.9	Dividends	6	(19.5)
30.0	TRANSFER TO RESERVES	18	51.1
	Earnings per Ordinary share (undiluted)	7	
16.17p	nil distribution basis		21.91p
14.02p	net basis (after ACT written off)		19.50p
	Earnings per Ordinary share (fully diluted)		
15.78p	nil distribution basis		20.19p
13.62p	net basis (after ACT written off)		17.78p

Exhibit 11.4 *The BOC Group plc: consolidated balance sheet at 30 September, modified historical cost basis*

1981 (£ million)		Notes	1982 (£ million)
	FIXED ASSETS		
1152.6	Tangible assets	11	1277.6
	Investments (related companies and		
43.9	other investments)	13	71.4
1196.5			1349.0
	CURRENT ASSETS		
274.8	Stocks		302.1
310.3	Debtors		288.2
14.3	Deposits at short call		31.4
12.2	Cash at bank and in hand		6.4
611.6			628.1
	CREDITORS: Amounts falling due within one year		
(58.5)	Borrowings and finance leases		(109.7)
(306.7)	Other		(290.0)
246.4	NET CURRENT ASSETS	15	228.4
	TOTAL ASSETS LESS CURRENT		
1442.9	LIABILITIES		1577.4
	CREDITORS: Amounts falling due after more than one year	16	
(484.2)	Borrowings and finance leases		(517.4)
(15.2)	Other		(15.8)
	PROVISIONS FOR LIABILITIES		
(55.5)	AND CHARGES	17	(58.2)
(554.9)			(591.4)
888.0			986.0
	CAPITAL AND RESERVES	18	
84.8	Called up share capital		85.4
44.3	Share premium account		45.6
372.9	Revaluation reserve		323.6
10.6	Other reserves		11.6
259.7	Profit and loss account		398.2
14.7	Related companies' reserves		18.6
787.0			883.0
101.0	MINORITY SHAREHOLDERS' INTERESTS		103.0
888.0			986.0

Return on total assets
The formula for this ratio is:

$$\frac{\text{Trading profit before interest,}}{\underset{\text{Average total assets for the period}}{\text{taxation and extraordinary items}}} \times 100$$

Depending on the accounting conventions used, the ratios for The BOC Group plc can be calculated as follows:

Current cost accounting
The average *total* assets for the period can be determined from Exhibit 11.2. The total assets figure at the end of the period (30 September 1982) is the sum of the fixed assets of £1,349.0 million and the current assets of £631.6 million, i.e. a total of £1,980.6 million. Similarly the total assets figure at the beginning of the period (30 September 1981) is made up of fixed assets of £1,196.5 million and current assets of £615.3 million, i.e. a total of £1,811.8 million.

The trading profit before interest, taxation and extraordinary items can be obtained by referring to Exhibit 11.1; it consists of the amount shown as 'trading profit' of £137.6 million plus the 'gearing adjustment' of £26.1 million, a total of £163.7 million. (For an explanation of the gearing adjustment see Chapter 14.)

The return on capital employed can now be calculated as:

$$\text{ROCE} = \frac{163.7}{\frac{1}{2}(1980.6 + 1811.8)} \times 100 = 8.6\%$$

Modified historical cost accounting
Exhibit 11.4 reveals that the total assets at the end of the period consisted of fixed assets of £1,349.0 million and current assets of £628.1 million, a total of £1,977.1 million. The equivalent figure for the beginning of the period is the sum of £1,196.5 million and £611.6 million, a total of £1,808.1 million. Exhibit 11.3 shows that the trading profit before interest, taxation and extraordinary items amounted to £160.8 million. The return on capital employed can now be calculated as:

$$\text{ROCE} = \frac{160.8}{\frac{1}{2}(1977.1 + 1808.1)} \times 100 = 8.5\%$$

Return on net total assets
The formula for this ratio is:

$$\frac{\text{Trading profit before interest,}}{\text{Average net total assets for the period}} \times 100$$

Again, depending on the accounting conventions used, different ratios can be calculated for BOC for 1982 as follows:

Current cost accounting
The net total assets are referred to in Exhibit 11.2 as 'total assets less current liabilities'. At the end of the period these amounted to £1,580.9 million and at the beginning of the period to £1,446.6 million.

$$ROCE = \frac{163.7}{\frac{1}{2}(1580.9 + 1446.6)} \times 100 = 10.8\%$$

Modified historical cost accounting
Exhibit 11.4 reveals that 'total assets less current liabilities' at the end of the period were £1,577.4 million and at the beginning of the period were £1,442.9 million.

$$ROCE = \frac{160.8}{\frac{1}{2}(1577.4 + 1442.9)} \times 100 = 10.6\%$$

Traditional historical cost accounting
To obtain the figures needed for calculating the return on capital employed under this accounting convention it is necessary to refer to the accounting statements shown on pages 214 and 215. The historical cost balance sheet on page 215 shows that fixed assets at the end of the period totalled £1,009.1 million and net current assets (i.e. current assets minus current liabilities) amounted to £214.8 million. The net total assets were therefore £1,223.9 million. Similarly the net total assets at the beginning of the period were £853.1 million plus £234.3 million, a total of £1,087.4 million. The historical cost trading profit before interest, taxation and extraordinary items amounted to £202.8 million, as shown on page 214.

$$ROCE = \frac{202.8}{\frac{1}{2}(1223.9 + 1087.4)} \times 100 = 17.5\%$$

It is not possible to calculate the ROCE using total assets as the denominator under the traditional historical cost accounting convention because the balance sheet on page 215 does not reveal the amount of current assets. However, if the returns on net total assets are examined it is clear that the use of the traditional historical cost accounting convention tends to bias this ratio upwards at times of rising prices and is therefore a less useful measure of performance. Both modified historical cost accounting, as defined by BOC, and current cost accounting produce very similar ratios and, by avoiding many of the distortions in profit measurement and asset valuation that arise from the use of traditional historical cost accounting, might be thought of as better indicators of the underlying economic performance of the company.

Where inter-firm comparisons are being made, it is not possible to state categorically which of the alternatives of return on total assets or return on net total assets is the 'correct' one to use. It all depends on the particular aspects of the company on which the analyst wishes to concentrate. Providing that the components of the ratios are defined in the same way for the companies being compared, then the comparisons should be meaningful. It is also usual to compare the performance of a particular company over time and, ideally, one or more of the above ratios calculated for BOC for 1982 should be calculated for previous years to establish the trend in return on capital employed. However, as was pointed out earlier, BOC has its own method of calculating net total assets and as the only information available for years prior to 1981 is that given in the five-year record on pages 212 and 213 it will be convenient to use the BOC definition for the purpose of time series comparisons. The BOC definition differs from the method described above by excluding short-term cash items. Thus in the five-year record, which has been prepared under the modified historical cost accounting convention, it can be seen that for 1982 net capital employed amounted to £1,649.3 million. This figure can be explained by referring to Exhibit 11.4, which shows that net capital employed has been calculated as total assets less current liabilities of £1,577.4 million, plus short-term borrowings etc. of £109.7 million, minus short-term cash assets of £37.8 million. Using this basis for determining the denominator of the ratio, the returns on capital employed for 1982 and 1981, as shown in the five-year record, have been calculated as follows:

$$\text{ROCE (modified historic cost) } 1982 = \frac{160.8}{\frac{1}{2}(1649.3 + 1474.9)} \times 100 = 10.3\%$$

$$\text{ROCE (modified historic cost) } 1981 = \frac{157.3}{\frac{1}{2}(1474.9 + 1173.2)} \times 100 = 11.9\%$$

If the analysis is extended to years prior to 1981 it can be seen from the five-year record that the return on capital employed for 1982 is the lowest achieved in the past five years and appears to be showing signs of decline.

This brings out the advantage of examining the trend in profitability of a company rather than simply its profit. Over the same five-year period, the trading profit displays an increasing trend, rising from £115.8 million in 1978 to £160.8 million in 1982. The use of trend (time series) analysis is discussed in more detail in Chapter 15.

Return on Equity

The purpose of this ratio is to show the profitability of the company in terms of the capital provided by the owners of the company, i.e. the ordinary shareholders. Return on equity is usually calculated as follows:

$$\frac{\text{Profit after interest and preference dividends but before tax and extraordinary items}}{\text{Average ordinary share capital, reserves and retained profit for the period}} \times 100$$

This ratio therefore focuses attention on the efficiency of the company in earning profits on behalf of its ordinary shareholders, by relating the profits to the total amount of shareholders' funds employed in the company. As with the return on capital employed ratio, it is usually more appropriate to take the figure of profit before tax to avoid distortions caused by differences in the taxation liability of different companies.

In the following ratios that have been calculated for BOC for 1982, the numerator is the amount described in each of the consolidated profit and loss accounts as 'profit on ordinary activities before tax', minus the preference dividend of £0.1 million (see note 6 to the financial statements). The denominator is the average of the opening and closing amounts described in each of the consolidated balance sheets as 'capital and reserves', minus the issued preference share capital of £2.5 million (see note 18 to the financial statements). As it is the intention to concentrate on the returns attributable to the shareholders in BOC, the minority interests (i.e. the interest of outside shareholders in consolidated subsidiary companies) have been excluded from the calculation.

Current cost accounting

$$\text{Return on equity} = \frac{105.5 - 0.1}{\frac{1}{2}(886.3 - 2.5 + 790.5 - 2.5)} \times 100$$

$$= \frac{105.4}{835.9} \times 100 = 12.6\%$$

Modified historical cost accounting

$$\text{Return on equity} = \frac{102.6 - 0.1}{\frac{1}{2}(883.0 - 2.5 + 787.0 - 2.5)} \times 100$$

$$= \frac{102.5}{832.5} \times 100 = 12.3\%$$

Traditional historical cost accounting

$$\text{Return on equity} = \frac{144.6 - 0.1}{\frac{1}{2}(559.4 - 2.5 + 455.6 - 2.5)} \times 100$$

$$= \frac{144.5}{505.0} \times 100 = 28.6\%$$

Earnings per Share

Earnings per share is a widely used variation of the return on equity indicator of profitability. The numerator of this represents the total amount of earnings available to ordinary shareholders after all deductions have been made, i.e. the profit after interest, taxation and preference dividends but before extraordinary items. The denominator represents the number of ordinary shares issued by the company, either at the year end or, if substantial changes have taken place during the year, the average number of shares outstanding during the year. It is now standard practice for earnings per share information to be given in the published accounts of a company (as required by SSAP 3); it is therefore normally unnecessary for the analyst to have to calculate this ratio. However, it might be useful to consider briefly the steps that are involved in this calculation. In the consolidated profit and loss account statements as shown in Exhibits 11.1 and 11.3, four different earnings per share figures are given. To understand these distinctions, it is first of all necessary to consider the taxation position of BOC. Note 4 to the financial statements reveals that after double taxation relief (i.e. relief on taxes paid on overseas profit) there is no liability to mainstream UK corporation tax. When a company pays a dividend to shareholders, an amount of taxation on the dividend has to be paid immediately to the Inland Revenue. This is called Advance Corporation Tax (ACT) and it can usually be set off against the total liability to corporation tax on profits (termed mainstream corporation tax). Because BOC has no liability for mainstream corporation tax, there is no amount against which the advance corporation tax can be offset. Thus every time BOC pays a dividend it incurs a tax liability on the dividend, thereby reducing the after-tax profit position. If no dividend were paid, then no tax liability would be incurred and so the after-tax profit would be higher. The earnings per share figure described as 'net distribution basis' reflects the earnings that would have been available if no dividend had been paid. The earnings per share figure described as 'net basis' reflects the earnings available after deducting the advanced corporation tax on the dividends paid. Note 7 to the financial statements shows the basis on which earnings per share has been calculated.

Using this information, the undiluted earnings per share ratios (i.e. based on the number of ordinary shares outstanding during the current year) can be calculated for 1982 as follows:

Net of ACT

Current cost accounting

Earnings minus preference dividend	£66.9 million
Number of ordinary shares	330.5 million

$$\text{EPS} = \frac{66.9}{330.5} = 20.24 \text{ pence per share}$$

Modified historical cost accounting

Earnings minus preference dividend	£64.4 million
Number of ordinary shares	330.5 million

$$\text{EPS} = \frac{64.4}{330.5} = 19.48 \text{ pence per share}$$

Nil distribution

Current cost accounting

Earnings minus preference dividend	£66.9 million
Add ACT on dividends (see note 4 on page 192)	£8.2 million
	£75.1 million
Number of ordinary shares	330.5 million

$$\text{EPS} = \frac{75.1}{330.5} = 22.72 \text{ pence per share}$$

Modified historical cost accounting

Earnings minus preference dividend	£64.4 million
Add ACT on dividends	£8.2 million
	£72.6 million
Number of ordinary shares	330.5 million

$$\text{EPS} = \frac{72.6}{330.5} = 21.96 \text{ pence per share}$$

These figures approximate to those calculated by BOC. The slight differences are presumably due partly to rounding errors and partly to the fact that the ACT of £8.2 million includes the ACT on the preference dividend of £0.1 million, which has not been adjusted for in the calculations shown above.

It can be seen that information is also given in the BOC consolidated profit and loss accounts (Exhibits 11.1 and 11.3) of the 'fully diluted' earnings per share. The calculation for these particular ratios is similar to that described above except that the denominator now reflects the number of shares that would be in issue if all of the options to take up shares were to be exercised. For example, it is revealed in note 18 to the financial statements that if the holders of the Convertible Unsecured Loan Stock converted this stock into ordinary shares, a further issue of 60,682,370 ordinary shares would be required. Similarly, the various share option schemes described in note 18 would, if the options were exercised, require more ordinary shares to be issued.

As a result of these additional issues, the existing equity base would be diluted, but of course the earnings would benefit to the extent that interest would no longer be payable on the convertible loan stock. The effect of all of these adjustments is captured by the fully diluted earnings per share ratios.

In spite of its widespread use, the earnings per share ratio does have several limitations. For example, if the ratio is used to compare the profitability of different companies, it may be misleading because it is based on the number of shares in issue. Two companies that are identical in every respect except for the nominal value of their ordinary shares will clearly have a different number of shares outstanding and will therefore have different earnings per share. If the profitability of the same company over time is being compared, the ratio will be affected by any bonus issues that have taken place. This has the effect of increasing the number of shares but does not provide any additional capital for the company. Also, because of the effect of retained earnings on the profit of a company, the earnings per share changes will be difficult to interpret correctly. For example, if a company has equity capital of £50,000 (in £1 ordinary shares) on which it currently earns an after-tax return of 20 per cent, then its earnings available to equity will amount to £10,000 and the EPS figure will be 20 pence per share. Of the earnings of £10,000, £2,000 might be distributed as dividends and the balance retained. The equity will now amount to £58,000 and, if the same return on equity is achieved in the next accounting period, then the earnings will be £11,600 and the earnings per share will increase to £11,600 ÷ 50,000, i.e. 23.2 pence per share. Thus the earnings per share will have increased although there has been no corresponding increase in the underlying performance of the company as measured by return on equity.

Price/Earnings Ratio

This ratio is calculated by dividing the market price of the ordinary shares of a company by the earnings per share figure described above. The ratio is therefore made up of a component that reflects the expectations of the market concerning the future earnings of a company (i.e. the market price of the shares) and a component that reflects the earnings available for each ordinary share based on the results of the most recent past accounting period. For example, supposing the current market price of a BOC ordinary share is £2, using the net of ACT current cost earnings per share for the year ended 30 September 1982 of 20.24 pence, then the price/earnings ratio is:

$$\frac{2.00}{0.2024} = 9.88$$

What this means is that, if £2 is paid for these shares, then 9.88 years of current cost earnings of 20.24 pence per share are being bought. Because it is thought that the current market value of a share reflects the expectations of investors concerning the future profits of a company, the ratio is effectively measuring the market's anticipations of future earnings. If the price/earnings ratios of different companies are compared then, all other things being equal, the company with the higher ratio will be the one that is expected to have the better future prospects. Price/earnings ratios differ from the other measures of profitability so far discussed in that the latter are based on the actual reported profit and financial position for a past period. These might therefore offer a better basis for inter-firm comparisons than the price/earnings ratio, which is very much dependent on the subjective opinion of investors concerning future profitability.

Return on Sales and Asset Turnover

The profitability ratios that have been described so far relate profit earned to a specific investment base. An alternative way of examining the performance of a company is to make use of ratios that bring out the relationship between profit and sales, and the relationship between sales and capital employed. The first of these is the return on sales, or profit margin, ratio and this is calculated as:

$$\frac{\text{Profit}}{\text{Total sales}} \times 100$$

The purpose of this ratio is to indicate the performance of the company in achieving the maximum sales possible, whilst at the same time keeping costs to a minimum. The ratio can be thought of as expressing the profit in pounds generated by each pound of sales; in general, the higher it is the better. However, such a ratio by itself may be misleading because it fails to take account of the assets available to achieve the profit margin. In other words, a high return on sales may have been achieved but only after making a considerable investment in resources, resulting in a low return on capital employed.

This problem can be overcome by introducing the asset turnover ratio, which is calculated as:

$$\frac{\text{Total sales}}{\text{Assets}}$$

This ratio is used to measure the performance of the company in generating sales from the assets at its disposal. It is described as the asset turnover ratio because it is, in effect, expressing the number of times assets have been 'turned over' during a period to achieve the sales revenue.

The profit margin ratio and asset turnover ratio, if considered together, provide a useful means of breaking down the return on investment ratios described previously. The relationship between all three ratios can be seen to be:

$$\frac{\text{Profit}}{\text{Total sales}} \times \frac{\text{Total sales}}{\text{Assets}} = \frac{\text{Profit}}{\text{Assets}}$$

Obviously, for such a relationship to hold, the numerator and denominator of each ratio need to be defined in a consistent manner. For example, if we refer to the return on capital employed ratios described earlier, several ways of defining both profit and capital employed were identified. The latter could be the total assets, or the net total assets or, in the case of BOC, the net total assets after adjusting for short-term cash items. For the purpose of comparing the profit margin and asset turnover ratios of BOC in 1982 with the equivalent ratios for 1981 it will be convenient to use their own definition of capital employed.

From Exhibit 11.3 it can be seen that the modified historical cost trading profit of £160.8 million in 1982 was earned from sales (turnover) of £1,534.2 million. Similarly, the 1981 trading profit of £157.3 million was earned from sales of £1,521.7 million. Armed with this information it is possible to calculate profit margin ratios as follows:

$$\text{Return on sales (profit margin) } 1982 = \frac{160.8}{1534.2} \times 100 = 10.48\%$$

$$\text{Return on sales (profit margin) } 1981 = \frac{157.3}{1521.7} \times 100 = 10.33\%$$

Thus, although the return on capital employed (as calculated on page 116) for these two years has declined from 11.9 per cent to 10.3 per cent, the profit margin has shown a slight increase. This might imply that the efficiency with which the capital employed has been used to generate sales has deteriorated and this is confirmed by an examination of the asset turnover ratio. As explained above, the denominator used for calculating this ratio is the net total assets after adjusting for short-term cash items and it is obtained from the BOC five-year record on pages 212 and 213. The ratios are as follows:

$$\text{Asset turnover ratio } 1982 = \frac{1534.2}{\frac{1}{2}(1649.3 + 1474.9)} = 0.98 \text{ times}$$

$$\text{Asset turnover ratio } 1981 = \frac{1521.7}{\frac{1}{2}(1474.9 + 1173.2)} = 1.15 \text{ times}$$

The relationship between profit margin, asset turnover rate, and return on capital employed can now be expressed as follows:

	Profit margin		*Asset turnover*		*ROCE*
1982	10.48%	×	0.98	=	10.3%
1981	10.33%	×	1.15	=	11.9%

It is evident that the increase in profit margin has been insufficient to compensate for the lower rate of asset turnover and this has resulted in an overall decline in return on capital employed. Analysing the profitability of the company in this way therefore provides a better explanation of the change in return on capital employed. Comparisons can now be made with similar companies in the same industry to determine whether the trends isolated for BOC are repeated elsewhere.

Profit margin ratios and asset turnover ratios can of course be related to other returns on investment ratios, such as return on equity, or earnings per ordinary share. Providing that the numerator and denominator of the ratios are calculated consistently, the break-down of these measures of return can provide a useful analysis of profitability for inter-firm and time series comparisons.

Segmental Analysis

So far the analysis of the profitability of The BOC Group plc has made use of the figures contained in the consolidated financial statements. The process of consolidation involves the aggregation of the results of many subsidiary companies with those of the parent company to produce one single figure for trading profit, for tangible fixed assets, and so on. However, with a diversified company such as BOC, the various companies making up the group are involved in a variety of lines of business or operate in different parts of the world, and an analysis based on simply the aggregate position might fail to reflect the performance of the different industrial or geographical segments of the group. Differences in profitability and risk are likely to attach to different industries and to different geographical locations, and comparability, either with other companies or over time, will be improved by extending the analysis of profitability to the major segments of The BOC Group's activities.

Segmental information concerning BOC is given in note 1 to its financial statements. The information provided is based on the modified historical cost accounting convention and the profit figure used is that described in Exhibit 11.3 as 'operating profit' (i.e. the trading profit used in earlier analyses minus the realised stock holding gains). The capital employed is the net total assets after adjusting for short-term cash items. Using this information, it is possible to isolate the profitability of each line of business or geographical location. For example, for the two principal areas of business activity in terms of contribution to overall profit – industrial gases and cryogenic plant, and health care – the position is as follows:

	Return on capital employed	
	1982	1981
Industrial gases and cryogenic plant	$\frac{103.6}{882.4} \times 100 = 11.74\%$	$\frac{96.5}{797.0} \times 100 = 12.11\%$
Health care	$\frac{39.6}{192.8} \times 100 = 20.54\%$	$\frac{20.8}{162.2} \times 100 = 12.82\%$

Because capital employed information is not given for 1980, the analysis has been based on the year-end figures for 1982 and 1981 rather than the more usual average capital employed in each period.

Such an analysis is useful for highlighting the changes that have taken place in the profitability of each major segment and may help to create a better picture of the performance of the company in past periods and also of the prospects for the future profitability of the group as a whole. Moreover, comparisons can now be made with companies in the same industry, for example with other companies, or segments of other groups, operating in the industrial gases industry.

Segmental analyses need not, of course, be limited to return on capital employed; they could also concentrate on profit margin and asset turnover ratios as described previously. Once again using the information contained in note 1 to the BOC financial statements, the picture that emerges for the two business segments of industrial gases and cryogenic plant and health care is as follows:

Industrial Gases and Cryogenic Plant

	Profit margin (1)	Asset turnover (2)	ROCE (1)×(2)
1982	$\frac{103.6}{695.8} = 14.88\%$	$\frac{695.8}{882.4} = 0.789$ times	11.74%
1981	$\frac{96.5}{660.4} = 14.61\%$	$\frac{660.4}{797.0} = 0.829$ times	12.11%

Health Care

	Profit margin (1)	Asset turnover (2)	ROCE (1)×(2)
1982	$\frac{39.6}{243.6} = 16.26\%$	$\frac{243.6}{192.8} = 1.263$ times	20.54%
1981	$\frac{20.8}{207.4} = 10.03\%$	$\frac{207.4}{162.2} = 1.278$ times	12.82%

The decline in return on capital employed on industrial gases can be seen to be primarily due to a worsening in the utilization of capital employed. For health care, the substantial increase in return on capital employed is due almost entirely to the improvement in profit margins for this line of business.

Obviously, where diversification does exist the ability to be able to undertake this kind of detailed profitability analysis for the principal industrial and geographical segments should provide a useful supplement to the analysis of overall group profitability.

Unfortunately, the current lack of uniformity in segmental reporting means that comparisons with other companies will be affected by differences in the definitions of profit and capital employed, differences in valuation methods, differences in transfer pricing policies, and differences in the treatment of costs common to the whole group. Until a standard approach to segmental reporting is adopted by all companies, the results of any inter-firm comparisons must be interpreted with caution.

12 Efficiency and Effectiveness

The profitability ratios described in the previous chapter were concerned with the overall efficiency of a company in generating profits from a given investment base. In addition it is often useful to calculate ratios that concentrate on the performance of the management of a company in terms of specific resources such as stock, debtors, employees, etc. This chapter considers how such ratios might be calculated and interpreted for The BOC Group plc.

Debtor Turnover and Collection

It is established practice in British industry for sales to customers to be made on credit terms. In other words, the goods or services supplied are paid for not immediately but after an agreed period of time. Such a policy requires part of the capital of a company to be used to finance these unpaid sales; the total amount outstanding at the end of the financial year is recorded as debtors in the balance sheet. The questions that then arise are concerned firstly with whether the amount of resources tied up in debtors is reasonable, and secondly with whether the company has been efficient in converting debtors into cash. Because the level of debtors at the end of the year might be expected to vary with the level of sales during the year, these questions are usually examined by calculating the following ratios:

$$\text{Debtor turnover} = \frac{\text{sales}}{\text{debtors}}$$

$$\text{Average collection period (in days)} = \frac{\text{debtors}}{\text{sales}} \times 365$$

The sales figures used in these ratios should, of course, reflect only the credit sales of the period. Where there is a marked seasonal variation in sales, then it would be more accurate to relate the year-end debtors to the sales of the last few months of the year. However, information on the distinction between cash and credit sales, or on the timing of sales, is not usually given in published annual reports and the following ratios for BOC have been calculated by using the total figure for sales as shown in Exhibit

11.3. Similarly, the debtors figure should ideally be the amount outstanding in respect of credit sales, i.e. the 'trade debtors'. Note 15 to the BOC financial statements (see page 204) gives a break-down of the total debtors figures included in the modified historical cost balance sheet. The trade debtors for 1982 and 1981 were £230.3 million and £238.2 million respectively.

	Debtor turnover	*Average collection period*
1982	$\frac{1534.2}{230.3} = 6.67$ times	$\frac{230.3}{1534.2} \times 365 = 54.8$ days
1981	$\frac{1521.7}{238.2} = 6.38$ times	$\frac{238.2}{1521.7} \times 365 = 57.1$ days

There has therefore been some improvement in debtor turnover and in the average collection period between 1981 and 1982, but in both years the debtor turnover ratios seem rather low (normally the higher the ratio the better). Comparisons with similar companies will give some indication of relative performance.

The average collection period can also be compared with the stated credit terms of BOC. For example, if the credit terms are 'thirty days', then this is usually taken to mean thirty days from the end of the month in which the invoice is issued. This would imply an average collection period of about forty-five days. Any variation between the stated and actual credit duration might be thought of as an indication of inefficiency in the collection of amounts due from debtors. However, as was pointed out in the previous chapter, the trading operations of BOC are undertaken in many different parts of the world and credit terms may differ from country to country, depending on local customs and practice. A more meaningful analysis would therefore be to calculate the average collection period for different geographical locations. Unfortunately this is not possible because a geographical break-down of debtors is not provided.

Creditor Turnover and Payment

The system of supplying goods and services on credit terms also affects the purchases of a company. Any purchases that have not been paid for by the end of the year are shown as creditors in the balance sheet. The above exercise for debtors can therefore be repeated for creditors to show the average time taken to pay for the goods and services purchased. Information on purchases is not usually provided directly, but an approximate amount can be obtained by adjusting the 'bought in materials, services and depreciation' figure in the value added statement (see page 179) as follows:

	(£ million)
Bought in materials, services and depreciation	955.1
Less depreciation	(122.6)
Add closing stock (1982)*	305.6
Deduct opening stock (1981)*	(278.5)
Approximate purchases for 1982	859.6

The purchases figure used in the following ratios should, of course be the credit purchases, but as information is not available on the distinction between cash and credit items the amount as calculated above has been used. Since the purchases figure includes both trade purchases and services purchased, the creditors figure taken is the total of 'trade creditors' and 'other creditors' as shown in note 15. Presumably the latter figure includes the amounts unpaid on services received such as rates, electricity, and so on.

The ratios for BOC for 1982 are as follows:

$$\text{creditor turnover ratio} = \frac{\text{purchases}}{\text{creditors}} = \frac{859.6}{167.6} = 5.13 \text{ times}$$

$$\text{creditor turnover period} = \frac{\text{creditors}}{\text{purchases}} \times 365 = \frac{167.6}{859.6} \times 365 = 71.2 \text{ days}$$

Because of the imprecision in the calculation of the components of this ratio, it can be used only as an approximate indication of the creditor payment policy of BOC. Generally speaking, the longer the credit period achieved the better, because the operations of the company are being financed interest free by suppliers' funds. However, if too long a period is taken to pay creditors, the credit rating of the company may suffer, thereby making it more difficult to obtain supplies in the future.

Stock Turnover

An important aspect of the management of a company concerns the levels of stocks that should be held. Very often a considerable amount of capital is tied up in the financing of raw materials, work in progress and finished goods. It is therefore important to ensure that the level of stocks is kept as

---

* Because the consolidated statement of value added has been prepared in accordance with the principles of current cost accounting, the current cost values for opening and closing stocks have also been used.

low as possible. However, if the level falls too low there is the danger that customers' orders could not be fulfilled in time and sales may be lost to competitors. A sound system of stock management is therefore crucial. One way of assessing this is by calculating the stock turnover ratio as follows:

$$\frac{\text{Cost of sales for the period}}{\text{Stock at the end of the period}}$$

If the closing stock figure is not typical of the amount of stock held during the period, an alternative way of arriving at the denominator of the ratio would be to use the average stock held. Because information is not given on the levels of stock held at different times of the year, a simple average of the opening and closing stock amounts is often used. It is important to use the cost of sales rather than sales as the numerator of the ratio because stock is generally valued at cost. The following stock turnover ratios for BOC have been computed from the modified historical cost information contained in Exhibits 11.3 and 11.4.

	Stock turnover rate	*Stock turnover period*
	$\dfrac{\text{Cost of sales}}{\text{Stock}}$	$\dfrac{\text{Sales}}{\text{Cost of sales}} \times 365$
1982	$\dfrac{920.4}{302.1} = 3.05 \text{ times}$	$\dfrac{302.1}{920.4} \times 365 = 119.8 \text{ days}$
1981	$\dfrac{882.6}{274.8} = 3.21 \text{ times}$	$\dfrac{274.8}{882.6} \times 365 = 113.6 \text{ days}$

The stock turnover period ratios reveal that the average period for which stock was held before being sold in 1981 was 113.6 days and that this has lengthened to 119.8 days in 1982. Generally speaking, the higher the stock turnover ratio, or conversely the lower the stock turnover period, the better, but whether these ratios should be classified as 'good' or 'bad' depends very much on the nature of the business. Manufacturing companies such as BOC might be expected to have longer stock turnover periods than, say, a company primarily involved in food retailing. What is an optimal level depends on balancing such factors as the lead time for manufacturing processes, the need to hold reserve stocks of raw materials to insure against uncertainties in supply, the normal holding period of finished goods, and the requirement to keep the amount of capital tied up in stock to a minimum. However, systematic changes over time or deviations from the ratios of similar companies might suggest that the stock position needs careful scrutiny. The worsening position for BOC between 1981 and 1982 might be due to the existence of obsolete or slow-moving stock items, or perhaps a building up of stocks of finished goods rather than cutting back on production. When comparing the BOC ratios with those of other companies it would be useful to be able to examine the position for each industrial segment, but unfortunately there is insufficient information available in the annual report to enable this to be done.

In addition to the assessment of managerial performance in the use of resources and liabilities such as debtors, creditors and stock, these particular items also have important implications for the liquidity of the company and this will be considered in the following chapter. These resources can also be combined into one ratio, the sales to working capital ratio, which is intended to indicate the adequacy of the total reservoir of liquid funds in supporting the level of sales.

Employee Ratios

The BOC consolidated statement of value added (page 179) reveals that the total employment costs for 1982 amounted to £448.8 million. The significance of this amount in terms of the overall operations of BOC can be appreciated by relating it to the sales figure of £1,534.2 million. The wages to sales ratio is seen to be:

$$\frac{446.8}{1534.2} \times 100 = 29.12\%$$

In other words, for every £1 of sales achieved almost 30 pence is paid in employee costs. Its significance is even more striking if it is related to the amount of value added. The consolidated statement of value added shows that 76 per cent of value added is applied in payments to employees. Because wages costs form such an important part of the total operating costs of a company, the efficiency with which this particular resource is utilized needs to be carefully assessed.

There are a variety of ratios that could be calculated to focus attention on the utilization of labour, such as sales per employee, profit per employee, value added per employee, and so on. In Exhibit 12.1, employee ratios analysed by line of business have been determined for BOC for 1981 and 1982. Information on average number of employees has been extracted from note 10 to the financial statements, and the sales, operating profit, and capital employed figures have been extracted from note 1.

The overall sales figure per employee in 1982 of £38,277 shows some improvement from 1981. The same is true of operating profit, which has increased from £3,545 to £3,798. However, an examination of the ratios of the different business segments reveals a widely fluctuating position. The

Exhibit 12.1 The BOC Group plc: employee ratios by line of business

Business Line	Average number of employees		Sales per employee				Operating profit per employee				Capital employed per employee			
			Sales		Per employee		Operating profit		Per employee		Capital employed		Per employee	
	1982	1981	1982 £m.	1981 £m.	1982 £	1981 £	1982 £m.	1981 £m.	1982 £	1981 £	1982 £m.	1981 £m.	1982 £	1981 £
Industrial gases and cryogenic plant	15,750	15,980	695.8	660.4	44,178	41,327	103.6	96.5	6,578	6,038	882.4	797.0	56,025	49,875
Health care	6,540	6,700	243.6	207.4	37,248	30,955	39.6	20.8	6,055	3,104	192.8	162.2	29,480	24,209
Carbon, graphite and carbide	2,980	3,110	134.5	143.0	45,134	45,980	3.3	13.9	1,107	4,469	280.2	195.3	94,027	62,798
Welding	8,340	9,370	269.9	282.3	32,362	30,128	(7.4)	4.7	(887)	502	202.2	201.9	24,245	21,547
Other businesses	5,750	5,010	162.8	150.6	28,313	30,060	10.4	6.5	1,809	1,297	106.8	96.5	18,574	19,261
Total	39,360	40,170	1,506.6	1,443.7	38,277	35,940	149.5	142.4	3,798	3,545	1,664.4	1,452.9	42,287	36,169

lines of business that give most cause for concern are carbon, graphite and carbide, and welding.

The welding division sustained a loss per employee in 1982 and even though sales per employee have increased slightly there would seem to be a need for further examination of the number of employees. Perhaps more worrying is the performance of the carbon, graphite and carbide division. Profit per employee has fallen significantly in 1982 even though this is the most capital intensive of the divisions as measured by capital employed per employee. Generally speaking, the more capital intensive an industry is the fewer employees are needed and, providing that the asset capacity is being fully utilized, the profit per employee should be high.

The advantages of a segmental analysis of this nature are obvious. Analysts can compare the employee ratios with other directly comparable firms operating in each line of business. Assessments of the future profitability of the whole group will be facilitated by a knowledge of the position in the principal segments, and the variations in performance over time can be more meaningfully evaluated.

A similar type of analysis could be undertaken to isolate variations in the different geographical segments of BOC by combining the information in note 1 to the financial statements with that given in the report of the directors (page 173). An examination of the value added per employee offers a further means of assessing the performance of management in the utilization of labour. The value added statement (page 179) provides the following details of value added per employee:

	1982	1981
	(£)	*(£)*
Europe	13,500	10,400
Africa	8,900	9,600
Americas	18,300	17,100
Asia	2,200	3,000
Pacific	14,400	15,800
Overall	14,300	13,000

Thus, although there has been an overall improvement in value added per employee from 1981 to 1982, the regional analysis indicates that in three of the geographical areas there has been a reduction in this ratio.

As far as inter-firm comparisons are concerned, ratios of value added per employee must be used with caution. There is as yet no standard accounting practice concerning the preparation of value added statements. Not all companies make use of current cost accounting values and many companies adopt the gross approach rather than the net approach used by BOC. In addition, value added on its own may give a misleading indication of performance. It is therefore perhaps best used in conjunction with profit per employee or sales per employee ratios.

Other Ratios

There are several other aspects of operational efficiency that could be highlighted by the use of ratios. These usually consist of attempts to break down some primary measure of profitability (such as return on sales) into its component parts to try to pin-point the reasons for differences in the profit margin from that of previous periods or from that of other companies. For example, in order for BOC to sustain total sales of £1,534.2 million in 1982 it was necessary to incur expenditure on administration, distribution, research and development, and so on. Ratios that relate these expenditure items to sales could be calculated from the modified historical cost profit and loss account (Exhibit 11.3) as follows:

$$\frac{Distribution\ costs}{Sales} \qquad \frac{Administration\ costs}{Sales} \qquad \frac{R\&D\ costs}{Sales}$$

$$1982 \quad \frac{164.3}{1534.2} \times 100 = 10.7\% \quad \frac{292.3}{1534.2} \times 100 = 19.1\% \quad \frac{24.9}{1534.2} \times 100 = 1.6\%$$

$$1981 \quad \frac{164.1}{1521.7} \times 100 = 10.8\% \quad \frac{325.3}{1521.7} \times 100 = 21.4\% \quad \frac{19.2}{1521.7} \times 100 = 1.3\%$$

The asset turnover ratio, as calculated in Chapter 11, could similarly be broken down to bring out the relationship between sales and specific categories of assets, such as plant and machinery, land and buildings, total current assets, and so on.

13 Liquidity and Stability

An analysis of the profitability of a company may reveal a satisfactory position and yet if there are insufficient funds available to pay bills as they fall due the company will be unlikely to survive for very long. A problem that often faces highly profitable and fast-expanding companies is that of 'overtrading'. This arises because most of the profits are needed to finance the additional fixed assets, stocks and debtors required to sustain the expanding level of business, and this results in a shortage of liquid resources for meeting short-term obligations. It is therefore important to assess not only the profitability of a company but also its liquidity and stability. The principal methods adopted to focus attention on short-term liquidity are considered in this chapter.

Working Capital Ratio (Current Ratio)

This ratio relates the current assets of a company to its current liabilities. Current assets consist of cash plus those items that can normally be expected to be converted into cash in the near future (i.e. debtors and stocks); together these are thought of as providing a reservoir of liquid resources for meeting the payments due to short-term creditors. The working capital, or current ratio, is calculated as:

$$\frac{\text{Current assets}}{\text{Current liabilities}}$$

From the modified historical balance sheet shown in Exhibit 11.4, it is possible to calculate ratios for The BOC Group plc as follows:

$$\text{Working capital ratio } 1982 = \frac{628.1}{399.7} = 1.57$$

$$\text{Working capital ratio } 1981 = \frac{611.6}{365.2} = 1.67$$

Thus between 1981 and 1982 there has been a slight worsening of BOC's current ratio. As was pointed out in Chapter 10, it is not possible to state categorically what the ratio should be. Generally speaking, if it is less than 1 this might give cause for concern because it would indicate that the liquid resources are insufficient to cover the short-term payments. Bearing in mind the time lag for converting debtors and stock into cash, it should perhaps be greater than 1. In the previous chapter it was shown that the average collection period for BOC's 1982 debtors was 55 days, and the average stock turnover period was 120 days. This compares with an average payment period of trade and other creditors of 71 days. In addition, an examination of note 15 to the financial statements reveals that a substantial part of the total of creditors of £399.7 million is made up of items other than trade and other creditors. The precise payment times of loans and bank overdraft, taxes, dividends and so on may vary from almost immediately to several months in the future. Because of known and unknown variations in the time lags affecting the components of the working capital ratio, it might be considered safer for the ratio to be nearer to 2 than to 1. However, too high a ratio might be due to cash or stock levels being higher than is strictly necessary and might therefore be indicative of the bad management of working capital requirements. Even a comparison with some 'standard' ratio for the industry might be misleading because of different circumstances facing individual companies. Moreover, differences in accounting practices concerning the valuation of stocks and work in progress, and the susceptibility of the working capital ratio to 'window dressing', can cause problems with inter-firm comparisons. Window dressing involves manipulating the working capital position by accelerating or delaying transactions close to the accounting year end. The following example shows how an inferior ratio could be improved by the use of window dressing so that a healthier picture of the company's liquidity might be presented.

Supposing that towards the end of the accounting period a company forecasts that if it follows its normal pattern of stock purchasing and creditor payment, then the net current assets positions will be as follows:

Stocks	£9,000
Debtors	5,000
Cash	6,000
	20,000
less Creditors	(15,000)
Net current assets	5,000

This will result in a working capital ratio of 20,000 ÷ 15,000, i.e. 1.33.

This ratio could be improved substantially by delaying stock purchases of, say, £4,000 until just after the end of the year. This would reduce the stock figure to £5,000 and creditors to £11,000. The position could be further improved by using, say, £4,000 of the surplus cash to accelerate the payments to creditors, thereby reducing cash to £2,000 and creditors to £7,000. The net current assets would then appear as:

Stocks	£5,000
Debtors	5,000
Cash	2,000
	12,000
less Creditors	(7,000)
Net current assets	5,000

Thus, although the net current assets position remains the same, the working capital ratio of 12,000 ÷ 7,000 i.e. 1.71, would appear much healthier to external analysis.

Nevertheless, in spite of its imperfections, the working capital ratio is of use in providing an approximate indication of a company's liquidity, and is widely used as such.

Quick Ratio (Acid-Test Ratio)

A frequent criticism of the working capital ratio is that the numerator includes items that could not be converted very readily into cash if the need arose to pay creditors at short notice. BOC is not untypical of manufacturing companies in having quite a lengthy stock turnover period and therefore stock is generally thought of as lacking liquidity. The quick ratio overcomes this problem by excluding stock from the numerator. It is calculated as:

$$\frac{\text{Current Assets minus stocks}}{\text{Current liabilities}}$$

An examination of Exhibit 11.4 reveals that the modified historical cost ratios for BOC are as follows:

$$\text{Quick ratio } 1982 = \frac{628.1 - 302.1}{399.7} = 0.81$$

$$\text{Quick ratio } 1981 = \frac{611.6 - 274.8}{365.2} = 0.92$$

This ratio, by concentrating on the more readily realizable of the current assets, is thought to provide a much stricter test of liquidity than the working capital ratio.

The question of what is a 'good' or 'bad' ratio still depends on a variety of circumstances. In general, the quick ratio should not fall too far below 1 because this means that if all of the creditors requested early repayment there would be insufficient liquid, or nearly liquid, resources available to meet the request. In other words, the company will fail the 'acid test' of being able to pay the short-term obligations and would therefore be in danger of becoming insolvent. The ratio for BOC has deteriorated between 1981 and 1982 and, if the long-term trend is downwards, the ratio of 0.81 might begin to give some cause for concern.

The quick ratio does provide a useful indicator of potential liquidity problems and, because it avoids the distortions in stock valuations caused by different accounting practices, it gives a better basis than the working capital ratio for comparisons with other companies. However, the ratio can still be affected by 'window dressing' and it could be accused of over-simplifying the position. In reality the debtors of a company may not be very liquid. Certainly the prepayments and accrued income may be difficult to convert quickly into cash and at times of recession the trade debtors may be seeking longer periods of credit because of their own liquidity problems. Attempts to press for earlier payment might force the debtors into bankruptcy. In fact, if recessionary conditions do exist, the raw materials component of the total balance sheet figure for stock may be more immediately realizable than the debtors. Even though the market for finished goods, and therefore work in progress, might be depressed, it should be relatively easy to sell raw materials, either back to suppliers, or to other manufacturers.

One of the most important factors concerning liquidity appraisal is the extent to which loan and overdraft facilities are available. If a company has unused overdraft facilities that could be drawn on, then, even in the extremely unlikely event of all of the creditors requiring immediate payment, there would be a cushion to compensate for a low quick ratio. On the other hand, if overdraft facilities are currently being utilized up to the limit, a low quick ratio might be very serious. Unfortunately, information on loan and overdraft availability, limits, and repayment times is not normally given in annual financial reports.

Funds Flow Analysis

A disadvantage of both the current and the quick ratios is that they measure liquidity at a single point in time rather than over a period of time. The liquidity position of a company such as BOC will be constantly changing in response to the cash flows into and out of the company, and therefore a ratio that merely reflects the liquidity at the balance sheet date fails to capture the extremely important relationship between cash inflows and outflows.

As was explained in Chapter 4, it is now standard accounting practice for a statement of sources and applications of funds to be included in the annual financial report of a company. This statement is extremely useful in providing the external analyst with an explanation for the changes in liquidity over the year. An examination of the consolidated statement of sources and applications of funds for BOC (page 178) reveals that, although in 1981 borrowings were reduced by £33.5 million, in 1982 they increased by £75.7 million. The cash flows from operations were similar in both years and the payments of interest, tax and dividends and the effects of acquisitions and disposals were not significantly different. The main reasons for the change in borrowings between the two years were the higher level of capital spending on fixed assets in 1982, and the changes in working capital due to increases in stocks and decreases in the amounts owing to creditors. Note 21(b) to the financial statements shows that of the extra amount of £75.7 million borrowed in 1982, £59.3 million was of a short-term nature. This may go a long way to explaining the deterioration in the working capital and quick ratios between 1981 and 1982.

A major purpose of liquidity analysis is to try to assess the potential liquidity problems that a company may face in the near future. If the 1982 situation were to be repeated in future years, with insufficient funds being generated from operations to finance the total capital expenditure requirements, and if the shortfall in sources of funds was met primarily by short-term loans, then the liquidity position of the company might look quite vulnerable. However, in the report of the directors (page 172) there is an indication that capital expenditure is expected to fall after 1983. In the absence of any predicted funds flow information, which is what the analyst would obviously prefer, it is necessary to evaluate information from a variety of sources when attempting to assess the viability of a company.

Defensive Interval

A variation on the dynamic approach to liquidity appraisal is to determine the defensive interval of a company. This is achieved by dividing the quick assets (i.e. current assets minus stock) by the operating cash outflows that will be required to be paid for out of those quick assets. From Exhibit 11.3 the operating cash outflows of BOC can be calculated very approximately as:

	1982 *(£ million)*	1981 *(£ million)*
Cost of sales	920.4	882.6
Less depreciation*	122.6	111.9
	797.8	770.7
Distribution costs	164.3	164.1
Administration	292.3	325.3

Research & development	24.9	19.2
Interest	65.3	65.7
Tax*	25.6	27.5
	1,370.2	1,372.5

* The figures for depreciation and tax have been taken from the statement of sources and applications of funds (see page 178).

The inclusion of dividends or interest depends on whether the defensive interval is calculated from the point of view of all providers of capital, or just the providers of equity capital. Assuming that the analysis should be from the point of view of shareholders, then dividends should be excluded and the cash outflows during 1981 and 1982 would have been approximately as above.

The first stage in calculating the defensive interval is to compute the amount of operating cash outflows per day as follows:

$$1982 \quad \frac{£1370.2}{365} = £3.75 \text{ million per day}$$

$$1981 \quad \frac{£1372.5}{365} = £3.76 \text{ million per day}$$

This reveals the average amount of operating cash outlows that would be required each day during 1982 and 1981 respectively.

The next stage is to relate the average daily requirement for cash to the quick assets available. From Exhibit 11.4 it can be seen that the quick assets were £628.1 million minus £302.1 million, i.e. £326.0 million, at the end of 1982 and £611.6 million minus £274.8 million, i.e. £336.8 million, at the end of 1981. Assuming these amounts were typical of the position throughout each year, then the defensive interval can be calculated as:

$$\frac{\text{Quick assets}}{\text{Average daily operating cash outflows}}$$

$$1982 \quad \frac{£326.0}{£3.75} = 87 \text{ days}$$

$$1981 \quad \frac{£336.8}{£3.76} = 90 \text{ days}$$

These ratios show the number of days that the company could survive at its present level of operating activity if no inflow of cash from sales or other sources took place. Ideally, forecasts of future operating cash outflows should be used, but unfortunately this information is not normally provided. However, an analysis of the trend in the defensive intervals of past periods may offer a very useful dynamic approach to the assessment of the liquidity of a company. The ratio can also be used for comparisons with other companies and, because depreciation charges and stock values are excluded from the components of the ratio, the distortion effects caused by differences in accounting practices will be reduced and comparability will therefore be improved.

14 Capital Structure and Financial Risk

In addition to an assessment of the short-term liquidity position of a company, it is also important to examine the overall means by which a company finances its operations. It is usual for a company to be financed partly by loans from banks and other lenders, and partly by the funds of its ordinary shareholders. These two sources of finance are normally referred to as debt and equity respectively, and the relationship between the two gives a measure of the gearing of the company. Gearing has important implications for the long-term stability of a company because of its effect on financial risk. This is because debt and equity have quite different characteristics. The providers of loan capital require a fixed amount of interest to be paid to them each year, irrespective of the level of profits earned. The providers of equity capital do not enjoy fixed rewards each year but are entitled to the residual profits after all other payments, including interest charges, have been met. This residual amount will vary depending on the fortunes of the company. Because the existence of loan capital imposes a fixed commitment in the form of interest charges, the higher the proportion of debt to equity in the capital structure of a company then the more volatile the residual rewards available to equity will become and the greater will be the financial risk perceived by ordinary shareholders. For example, if an all-equity firm earns operating profits after tax of £200,000, then the amount accruing to ordinary shareholders, either as dividends or retained profits, will be £200,000. If in the next year the profits fall by 25 per cent to £150,000, then the amount accruing to ordinary shareholders will also fall by 25 per cent. However, if the company were geared, i.e. if it were financed partly by loans requiring a fixed interest payment of, say, £75,000 per year, then the profits available to ordinary shareholders in the first year would be £125,000 (£200,000 minus interest of £75,000), but in the second year these would fall to £75,000 (£150,000 minus interest of £75,000), a decline of 40 per cent. Conversely, if profits had risen by 25 per cent to £250,000, the earnings available to the ordinary shareholders in the geared company would have increased to £175,000 (£250,000 minus £75,000), an increase of 40 per cent.

A similar argument applies to the riskiness attached to capital repayments. In the event of the liquidation of a company, the providers of loan capital have priority over the ordinary shareholders as to capital repayment. Therefore, the higher the level of gearing, the greater is the chance of ordinary shareholders not being repaid in full.

It is not only the shareholders who are affected by gearing. Looked at from the point of view of creditors, it is clear that a high proportion of debt to equity will increase the risk of interest payments not being met, or the loan repayments and amounts owing to suppliers not being made in full. Even though lenders have the benefit of priority over shareholders for annual interest payments and on liquidation, the value of this benefit steadily declines as more and more of the operations of the company are financed by the lenders and the 'cushion' that the equity financed part provides becomes less and less.

Nevertheless, gearing does have its advantages. It might be reasonable to expect that the benefits of a fixed amount of interest every year and priority over shareholders on liquidation should make the cost of debt capital cheaper than that of equity. In other words, the average return required by lenders should be lower than the average return expected by shareholders. Furthermore, the interest payable on loan capital is an allowable expense when determining taxable profit, whereas dividends are a distribution out of the after-tax profits. Thus, for a company that pays corporation tax at the rate of say 50 per cent on its taxable profits, the after-tax cost of interest payments will be effectively halved, because every £100 paid in interest will reduce taxable profit by £100 and therefore tax payable by £50. To the extent that debt is a less expensive source of finance than equity, then initially the use of gearing might be beneficial, providing that the advantages of lower-cost debt more than compensate for the disadvantages caused by increased financial risk. However, as gearing increases, the financial-risk effect will begin to outweigh the benefits of low-cost debt. This implies the existence of some optimal level of gearing that a company should try to achieve.

A careful examination of gearing is obviously of crucial importance in an evaluation of the appropriateness of the capital structure of a company and in the following sections of this chapter the gearing position of The BOC Group plc is analysed.

Capital Structure Ratios

There are several ways of examining the gearing position of a company, depending on whether it is the long-term capital structure or the overall financial structure that is being analysed.

Long-term debt to equity ratio
From the point of view of long-term capital structure, the most widely used ratio is that of debt to equity. This is calculated as:

$$\frac{\text{Long-term loans plus preference shares}}{\text{Ordinary shareholders' funds}} \times 100$$

Preference shares are usually included in the numerator because preference shareholders are entitled to a fixed rate of dividend. (It should be noted, however, that preference dividends are only payable if sufficient profits have been earned; therefore, if a dividend has not been declared, it might be more appropriate to exclude preference capital from the ratio.) Ordinary shareholders' funds are usually taken to mean the ordinary share capital plus retained profits and reserves. The treatment of provisions can be somewhat problematical: depending on their nature, they might be thought of as part of ordinary shareholders' funds or as liabilities that should be included with long-term loans. In the ratios that have been calculated for BOC, provisions have been excluded and the components of each ratio are made up as follows:

Long-term loans plus preference shares (see notes 16 and 18 to the financial statements)

	1982 (£ million)	1981 (£ million)
Loans other than from banks	255.1	153.3
Bank loans and overdrafts	250.0	316.7
Obligations under finance leases	12.3	14.2
Preference share capital	2.5	2.5
	519.9	486.7

Obligations under finance leases represent the present value of the future rental payments for assets financed under leasing agreements. Because this method of financing asset acquisitions gives rise to an interest payment that is included in the rental amount, the *capital* element has been included with long-term loans.

Ordinary shareholders' funds (the modified historical cost accounting basis as shown in Exhibit 11.2 has been used)

	1982 (£ million)	1981 (£ million)
Called up ordinary share capital	82.9*	82.3*
Share premium account	45.6	44.3
Revaluation reserve	323.6	372.9
Other reserves	11.6	10.6
Profit and Loss account	398.2	259.7
Related companies' reserves	18.6	14.7
	880.5	784.5

* The preference share capital of £2.5 million has been deducted from the called up share capital amounts shown in the consolidated balance sheet.

The debt to equity ratios for BOC can now be calculated as:

$$\text{Debt to equity ratio } 1982 = \frac{519.9}{880.5} \times 100 = 58.94\%$$

$$\text{Debt to equity ratio } 1981 = \frac{486.7}{784.5} \times 100 = 62.04\%$$

Long-term debt to total long-term finance ratio
An alternative way of considering the debt to equity relationship is to calculate the ratio in such a way that it expresses the amount of debt finance as a proportion of total long-term finance, i.e. by calculating:

$$\frac{\text{Long-term loans plus preference shares}}{\begin{array}{l}\text{Long-term loans plus preference shares plus}\\ \text{ordinary shareholders' funds}\end{array}} \times 100$$

Using this approach, the ratios for BOC are as follows:

$$\text{Debt to total long-term finance ratio } 1982 = \frac{519.9}{519.9 + 880.5} \times 100 = 37.13\%$$

$$\text{Debt to total long-term finance ratio } 1981 = \frac{486.7}{486.7 + 784.5} \times 100 = 38.29\%$$

Whichever method is used, the resultant ratio is meant to bring out the relationship between funds that require a fixed amount of interest and dividend to be paid each year and the funds provided by ordinary shareholders. The higher the ratio, the higher the proportion of debt in the capital structure of a company, and therefore the higher the amount of interest charges that might be expected.

In order to be able to decide whether the slight change in the level of gearing between 1981 and 1982 should be thought of as an improvement or not, a knowledge of the optimal capital structure of the company is required. Although it is not possible to state precisely what this should be, a comparison with some industry 'standard' might give an indication of the appropriateness of the ratio. However, much depends on the individual circumstances facing each company. A company that experiences a low level of business risk, with operating profits tending to be stable from period to period, can withstand a higher level of financial risk, and therefore a higher level of gearing, than a company whose operating profits fluctuate widely. Companies that are highly diversified might be expected to have relatively stable profits, because of the wide spread of activities, and so could operate at higher levels of gearing than non-diversified companies.

Total debt to total assets ratio

The gearing ratios that have been considered so far have concentrated on the long-term financial structure of BOC. An alternative way of examining gearing is to bring short-term debt into the picture to show the proportion of the total assets of the company that are financed by borrowed funds, both short-term and long-term. This is the total debt to total assets ratio and is calculated as:

$$\frac{\text{Long-term loans plus short-term loans}}{\text{Total assets}} \times 100$$

One advantage of including short-term loans in the numerator is that this gives recognition to the fact that short-term bank loans and overdrafts are often almost automatically renewable and are therefore effectively a source of long-term finance.

To calculate the total debt to total assets ratio for BOC it is first of all necessary to determine the components of the ratio as follows:

Total debt

	1982 (£ million)	1981 (£ million)
Long-term loans and obligations under financial leases (see note 16 to the financial statements)	517.4	484.2
Short-term loans and obligations under financial leases (see note 15 to the financial statements)	109.7	58.5
	627.1	542.7

Total assets (obtained from the modified historical cost balance sheet (Exhibit 11.4))

Fixed assets	1,349.0	1,196.5
Current assets	628.1	611.6
	1,977.1	1,808.1

The following ratios can now be calculated:

$$\text{Total debt to total asset ratio } 1982 = \frac{627.1}{1977.1} \times 100 = 31.72\%$$

$$\text{Total debt to total asset ratio } 1981 = \frac{542.7}{1808.1} \times 100 = 30.01\%$$

This ratio shows that of the total value of the assets of BOC at 30 September 1982 (determined by the modified historical cost accounting basis) 31.72 per cent were financed by borrowed funds. This gives some indication of the extent to which interest payments will have to be made. Once again, it is not possible to state categorically whether this is 'good' or 'bad'. However, the report of the directors (page 172) reveals that the directors are of the opinion that the gearing level is acceptable. They do in fact warn that gearing will be higher in 1983, due to the need to finance additional capital expenditure, but after 1983 it is expected to fall.

Current cost accounting gearing adjustment
Finally, it should be noted that a further variation on the above approaches is the gearing adjustment used when determining current cost accounting profit. Statement of Standard Accounting Practice No. 16 (SSAP 16) required gearing to be calculated as the relationship between net monetary liabilities and the total of net monetary liabilities and shareholders' funds. The formula for this ratio is:

$$\frac{\text{Net monetary liabilities}}{\text{Net monetary liabilities plus ordinary shareholders' funds}} \times 100$$

The net monetary liabilities of BOC are the total of long-term and short-term loans minus cash and short-term deposits. The total of long-term and short-term loans has previously been calculated as £627.1 million for 1982 and £542.7 million for 1981. From Exhibit 11.2 it can be seen that cash and short-term deposits for 1982 amounted to £37.8 million, and for 1981 to £26.5 million. Ordinary shareholders' funds totalled £883.8 million in 1982 and £788.0 million in 1981. Armed with this information, the SSAP 16 gearing ratios can be calculated as:

SSAP 16 gearing ratio 1982 =

$$\frac{627.1-37.8}{(627.1-37.8)+883.8} \times 100 = \frac{589.3}{589.3+883.8} \times 100 = 40.00\%$$

SSAP 16 gearing ratio 1981 =

$$\frac{542.7-26.5}{(542.7-26.5)+788.0} \times 100 = \frac{516.2}{516.2+788.0} \times 100 = 39.58\%$$

Current cost accounting requires the traditional historic cost accounting profit to be adjusted to reflect the additional depreciation, cost of sales and monetary working capital that will be needed to maintain the operating capacity of an organization at times of rising prices. These are the basic current cost accounting adjustments. However, if prices are rising then the organization also benefits from the fact that loans and overdrafts represent constant monetary liabilities that will be repaid out of a depreciated currency. The purpose of the SSAP 16 gearing adjustment is to reflect this 'purchasing power' gain by reducing the total of the basic current cost adjustments by the proportion that is effectively being financed by net monetary liabilities. In other words, of the total of the basic current cost accounting adjustments for BOC in 1982, 40 per cent will be credited to the profit and loss account as a gearing adjustment. It can be seen from the consolidated current cost profit and loss account for 1982 (Exhibit 11.1) that this amounted to £26.1 million.

The above treatment is just one example of a gearing adjustment; it is likely that others will be introduced in the revised current cost accounting standard to be issued later in 1984, as mentioned on page 47. There is a considerable amount of support for alternative gearing adjustment methods; in addition to the method outlined in SSAP16, other methods include applying a general index to net borrowing (producing an interest charge in real terms) or adding to the SSAP16 adjustment some estimate of the proportion of unrealised holding gains which have been funded by borrowing.

Interest Cover

An alternative way of analysing gearing is to concentrate on the income position rather than on capital structure. Under this approach, gearing is measured as:

$$\frac{\text{Profit before interest and tax}}{\text{Gross interest payable}}$$

This ratio is meant to focus attention on the relationship between interest payments and the profits available for meeting those payments. It shows the number of times interest is 'covered' by profits and therefore indicates the risk of non-payment of interest. Note 3(a) to the financial statements reveals that the gross interest payable by BOC amounted to £72.5 million in 1982 and £71.1 million in 1981. The amount of modified historical cost accounting profit before interest and tax that was available for meeting these interest payments is the trading profit for each year as shown in Exhibit 11.3. Interest receivable of £7.2 million in 1982 and £5.4 million in 1981 (see note 3(a) to the financial statements) would also be available to meet interest payments and should therefore be included in the numerator.

$$\text{Interest cover ratio } 1982 = \frac{160.8 + 7.2}{72.5} = 2.32$$

$$\text{Interest cover ratio } 1981 = \frac{157.3 + 5.4}{71.1} = 2.29$$

This means that the interest payable was covered 2.32 times in 1982 and 2.29 times in 1981. An alternative way of looking at this is to say that the profits available for paying interest in 1982 are 2.32 times the interest payable in that year. In other words, the profits could fall by a factor of 2.32 and there would still be a sufficient amount available to meet interest charges. From the point of view of providers of loan capital, the ratio indicates the protection they have if profits fall; therefore, the higher the ratio the better. Ordinary shareholders would also like to see a high interest cover ratio because this will indicate that the risk of non-payment of dividends is reduced. As with capital structure ratios, the adequacy of the interest cover is very much dependent on the business risk facing the company. For a company whose profits fluctuate a great deal from period to period, a cover of 2.32 times might be thought of as quite low. For a company that achieves stable profits over time, the cover might be satisfactory.

Because the interest cover ratio is meant to indicate the ability to pay interest charges it might, perhaps, be more appropriate to define the numerator in terms of cash flows rather than profit. When using profit, the numerator is affected by items that do not require a cash flow out of the business. Under the cash flow approach the interest cover ratio is expressed as:

$$\frac{\text{Cash flows from operations before interest and tax}}{\text{Gross interest payable}}$$

A measure of cash flows available for meeting interest payments can be obtained from the statement of sources and applications of funds. This reveals that the gross cash flows from operations amounted to £277.4 million in 1982 and £270.8 million in 1981. To these amounts must be added the interest receivable in each of the years.

$$\text{Interest cover ratio (in terms of cash flows) } 1982 = \frac{277.4 + 7.2}{72.5} = 3.92$$

$$\text{Interest cover ratio (in terms of cash flows) } 1981 = \frac{270.8 + 5.4}{71.1} = 3.88$$

The ability of BOC actually to pay its interest charges, i.e. to generate sufficient cash from operations, shows a much healthier position. The cash flows in 1982 were almost four times the interest payments.

Dividend Cover

A similar ratio to the interest cover ratio involves examining the amount by which profits could fall before leading to a reduction in the current level of dividends. The dividend cover ratio is calculated as:

$$\frac{\text{Profits available for paying ordinary dividends}}{\text{Ordinary dividends}}$$

The numerator of this ratio should be the final amount that is left after all other deductions have been made. As it is the intention to show the amount available from ordinary activities, the extraordinary items are usually excluded. The modified historical cost accounting profits available to the ordinary shareholders of BOC are therefore taken as £64.5 million in 1982 and £46.3 million in 1981. The ordinary dividends are the amounts shown as 'dividends' in Exhibit 11.1 minus the preference dividend of £0.1 million in each year. The dividend cover ratios are calculated as:

$$\text{Dividend cover ratio } 1982 = \frac{64.5}{19.4} = 3.32$$

$$\text{Dividend cover ratio } 1981 = \frac{46.3}{16.8} = 2.76$$

These ratios show that ordinary dividends were covered 2.76 times in 1981 and that this has improved to 3.32 times in 1982. This means that the profits of 1982 could have been 3.32 times less than they actually were before there would have been insufficient current profits to pay the dividend. This margin of safety might be a useful means of predicting the possibility of the current level of dividends being maintained in the future.

15 The Use of Financial Ratios

The preceding four chapters have shown how financial ratios for The BOC Group plc could be derived from the published annual report to focus attention on different economic aspects of the group's activities. The purpose of ratio analysis is to provide a profile of the past performance and financial strength of a company that might be useful for decision-making. The use that is made of ratios will vary, therefore, depending on the decisions that are faced by users and on the amount of detailed information available. Managers, for example, will be interested in comparing their actual performance with some predetermined budget performance, and also with the performance in previous years or with that of other companies. Because managers have access to a great deal of detailed information about the company, the ratios they can calculate will range from those that reveal overall performance down to those that concentrate on specific manufacturing processes. The information available to external users, on the other hand, is usually restricted to what is provided in the annual financial report, supplemented by other published data such as industrial or economic statistics. It is with the use of ratios by external users that this chapter is primarily concerned.

Although there are many groups of external user who might benefit from ratio analysis, the exercise is usually thought of in terms of the needs of the principal providers of financial resources – the ordinary shareholders and the creditors.

The decisions facing ordinary shareholders are, in effect, whether they should buy, sell or retain shares in a company, i.e. share trading decisions. Such a decision requires information on the future returns that might be expected from holding shares in a particular company – in the form either of future dividends or the future disposal value of the shares – and also the riskiness of the returns. As there might be expected to be a close relationship between dividends, future share prices and future profits, this suggests the need for ratios that might be useful in predicting the future profitability and long-term stability of a company.

Creditors comprise long-term and short-term lenders, such as debenture holders and bankers, and also the suppliers of goods and services on credit terms. Like shareholders, creditors will be interested in predicting the future profitability of a company. They will also be particularly concerned with evaluating the creditworthiness of the company and the likelihood of insolvency.

Both shareholders and lenders, therefore, are clearly in need of information that will help them to predict future events. As far as the prediction of insolvency is concerned, there is strong evidence to support the value of ratio analysis in accurately forecasting the failure or survival of a company; this is discussed further later in this chapter. The extent to which an examination of past data through the use of ratio analysis can be useful in predicting future returns is somewhat more equivocal. The annual reported financial results of a company form only part of the information used for share trading decisions. Even so, there is evidence of a significant relationship between share trading activity and profit announcements; it is less clear whether this is simply a reaction to the absolute level of reported profit, or occurs as a result of detailed financial ratio analysis.

Nevertheless, it seems reasonable to assume that a starting point in the predictive process would involve an assessment of the current performance of a company by the use of ratio analysis, together with an analysis of the position in previous years and a comparison with other companies.

Time Series Analysis

Time series analysis involves the calculation of the ratios of a company not just for the current or preceding year but for each of the past five or ten years or more. The objectives of such an analysis are firstly to provide a 'standard' against which the current performance and financial stability might be compared, and secondly to attempt to isolate trends over time that might enable future values of the ratios to be predicted.

When conducting a time series analysis, it is obviously important to ensure that there has been consistency in accounting practices; where changes have occurred, these must be corrected for before the analysis is undertaken. It is also possible that the reasons for changes over time in a particular variable, such as sales or profits, may be due to economy- or industry-wide factors outside the control of a particular company. Simply to compare one period with another without adjusting for those factors would be misleading.

The statistical techniques used in time series analysis involve the isolation of four separate components of trends:

- the secular component (the regular movement in trends caused by factors whose influence tends to be in the same direction over a long period);
- the seasonal component (the short-term movement in trends caused by seasonal variations);
- the cyclical component (the movement in trends caused by medium- and long-term cyclical fluctuations);
- the residual component (the irregular movement in trends caused by random and unpredictable events).

Having identified the components of trends affecting a series of past ratios, it is possible, through the use of the mathematical technique of least squares regression, to determine a trend line for each ratio under consideration. (The mathematical technique necessary is not discussed here; readers are referred to an appropriate managerial mathematics text-book – such as Mepham, 1980.) It is this trend line that determines the yardstick against which the ratios of the current year should be compared and provides the starting point for assessing whether the performance of the current period might be thought 'good' or 'bad'. The trend line also provides a base for predicting future values of the ratios.

This kind of time series analysis is a time-consuming and expensive exercise. In the preceding four chapters, ratios were calculated for The BOC Group plc for just two years. This is clearly too short a period to subject to a rigorous time series analysis as outlined above, but if the ratios are brought together in summary form an examination of the differences might enable some commonsense observations to be made (see Exhibit 15.1).

Exhibit 15.1   *The BOC Group plc – summarized ratios*

	1982	1981
PROFITABILITY		
Return on capital employed (%)	10.30	11.90
Undiluted earnings per share (pence)	19.48	14.02
Profit margin (%)	10.48	10.33
Asset turnover (times)	0.98	1.15
EFFICIENCY		
Debtor turnover (times)	6.67	6.38
Stock turnover (times)	3.05	3.21
Sales per employee (£)	38,277	35,940
Operating profit per employee (£)	3,798	3,545
LIQUIDITY		
Working capital ratio	1.57	1.67
Quick ratio	0.81	0.92
Defensive interval (days)	87	90
CAPITAL STRUCTURE		
Gearing: long-term debt/equity (%)	58.94	62.04
total debt/total assets (%)	31.72	30.01
Interest cover (times)	2.32	2.29
Dividend cover (times)	3.32	2.76

From a comparison between 1981 and 1982, the following points emerge. Profitability, as measured by return on capital employed, has deteriorated, even though the profit margin improved slightly. In part, this is due to a decline in the profitable use of the group's assets, as shown by the asset turnover ratio. Earnings per share have improved, but some of that improvement is due to a reduction in taxation as a result of unused depreciation allowances in the United States being effectively sold for cash (see note 4 to the financial statements in Appendix A). If this cannot be repeated in future years, and if the decline in profitability continues, the earnings per share position will suffer.

Efficiency in the collection of amounts due from debtors has improved, but stock turnover has worsened, due perhaps to stocks being maintained at too high a level. The improvement in sales per employee and operating profit per employee has occurred mainly because of reductions in manpower levels. Since the directors' report reveals that the number of people employed is expected to continue to decline, further improvements might be expected.

Each of the three measures of liquidity shows a worsening position. Even though debtors are paying more quickly, the acid test or quick ratio has deteriorated, largely due to the substantial increase in short-term borrowings. If a company is to continue in business, it is essential that it has the ability to meet its short-term commitments. A worsening liquidity position, combined with a decline in profitability, might begin to cause concern to lenders and suppliers of goods on credit.

From the point of view of long-term stability, the position reveals some improvement. Even so, the interest cover of 2.32 times in 1982 is still somewhat low. Analysts tend to look for a more substantial cushion of income to cover future levels of interest payment.

When time series analysis is used for prediction purposes, the examination of segmental information is crucial. The information for share trading and lending decisions is drawn not only from a company's annual report but also from many other sources – forecasts of growth in particular industries and countries, general economic trends, details of major contracts awarded, details of major customers, the introduction of new manufacturing processes, new products, competitors' activities, changes in legislation, changes in key personnel, and so on. Much of this information is specific to particular lines of business or geographical locations. The overall performance of a diversified group of companies is obviously affected by the individual performances of specific segments, which will in turn be affected by the environment in which they operate. Any prediction of overall performance will therefore require segmental information so that all the factors that might have an effect on the performances of segments may be taken into account.

Cross-Sectional Analysis – Inter-Firm Comparison

Cross-sectional analysis offers a further means of providing a 'standard' against which performance can be measured. A comparison of the ratios of a particular company, either with those of individual companies in the same industry or with some aggregate of companies in the industry, will be useful in assessing relative performance. To the extent that the investment decision facing shareholders and lenders involves choosing in which companies to invest or to which to lend, the use of ratio analysis to compare the performance of different companies is helpful. There are, however, a number of problems associated with such inter-firm comparisons.

The first difficulty is in deciding on the appropriate industrial classification of a particular company. Many of the industrial groupings contain companies that are surprisingly different. Moreover, diversified companies will, by definition, be involved in a range of quite different activities, each of which might belong to a different industrial classification. In the Stock Exchange industrial classification scheme, BOC is included in the 'general chemicals' sector – which places it among companies with which it has very little in common, such as ICI, Allied Colloids, British Tar Products, and so on.

The second difficulty concerns the effects of size. When comparing the results of individual companies, it is not sufficient merely to ensure that the companies operate in the same industry. They should also be more or less comparable as to size. Even though one of the supposed benefits of ratio analysis is its ability to adjust for size differences, there are occasions when this breaks down. For example, many ratios make use of the annual sales figure. If Company A has annual sales of £150 million and these represent the major part of the total industry sales, an increase of 10.0 per cent may require a significant effort. If Company B has annual sales of just £1 million, an increase of 10.0 per cent may be achieved much more easily. A further difference caused by size is the degree of risk associated with the company. Large companies usually have better access to the capital markets than their smaller competitors and find it easier to raise long-term finance; during particularly difficult periods, such large companies might often be supported by governments. Small companies are often restricted to the relatively riskier short-term credit and overdraft sources. Large companies might also be expected to benefit from the use of more sophisticated technology and superior marketing channels.

A further difficulty facing inter-firm comparison is that ratio analysis by itself may fail to reflect the true position of the different companies. For instance, the ratios of Company X may be superior in every way to those of Company Y, or superior to the industry average. However, if nine-tenths of the output of Company X is taken up by just one customer, it may be relatively more risky than its comparators. As with time series analysis, cross-sectional ratio analysis must be supplemented with information drawn from a variety of sources.

Perhaps the most serious obstacle to effective inter-firm comparison is the existence of variations in accounting policies and practices. Even though some firms now make use of current cost accounting, a wide range of accounting treatments are permissible for such items as depreciation, stock valuation, intangibles, and the like. Such differences obviously affect the validity of the comparison exercise. The only way that this particular problem can be overcome is through a standardized comparison scheme. The Centre for Interfirm Comparison operates one such scheme and seeks to ensure that the figures supplied by participant companies are truly comparable by providing detailed instructions – about the definition of terms, valuation principles, and so on. Only by pursuing such an approach is it possible to attribute differences in ratios solely to differences in operational performance and economic position rather than to differences in accounting terminology and treatment. Unfortunately, the information and data produced by the Centre for Interfirm Comparison are available only to participating companies and not to all external users of company reports. Appendix B gives details of a number of sources of comparative statistics and data.

The Prediction of Bankruptcy

An ability to predict the likelihood of the bankruptcy or failure of a company would be of obvious benefit to shareholders, lenders, suppliers and managers alike. Over the past forty years, a substantial amount of research has been undertaken on the extent to which ratio analysis might be useful in making such predictions. Much of the research effort has been based on American data, and the methodology generally adopted has involved the comparison of the ratios of failed companies for several years prior to failure with those of companies that did not fail.

The results of the research have been impressive, showing that significant differences were discernible between the ratios of failed and non-failed companies for up to five years before failure. Earlier research concentrated on the ability of a single ratio to predict failure – the 'univariate' approach – and perhaps the best-known examples of the use of this approach are in the earlier work by Beaver (1966). He selected a sample of seventy-nine companies that had either become bankrupt or had defaulted on the payment of interest or preference dividends. These he classified as failed companies; each failed company was then paired with a company from the same industry and of equivalent size that had not failed. For each of the pairs of companies, Beaver calculated thirty of the more conventional financial ratios for each of the five years prior to the failure of the failed company. He found that the mean ratios of the failed companies were substantially worse than those of the non-failed companies over the five-year period.

However, simply detecting differences in the mean values of ratios does not necessarily indicate predictive ability, and Beaver went on to test for that. He assumed that, for each pair of companies, the one with the poorest ratio would be the one most likely to fail, and made that the basis of his prediction. The prediction was compared with the actual outcome to determine the extent to which mis-classification occurred. Obviously, if this particular basis of prediction had no predictive ability at all, the classification would be correct for 50.0 per cent of the time and incorrect for 50.0 per cent of the time. Beaver found that, from the thirty ratios he used, some were particularly successful in predicting failure – success being measured in terms of the lowest number of incorrect classifications. The most successful of all was the cash flow/total debt ratio, with only 10.0 per cent of the companies incorrectly classified one year prior to failure and 22.0 per cent incorrectly classified five years prior to failure. Somewhat surprisingly, the current ratio, which is often thought of as an important indicator of liquidity, was not a particularly good predictor: 20.0 per cent of the companies were incorrectly classified one year prior to failure and 31.0 per cent five years prior to failure.

An alternative to the univariate approach is the 'multivariate' approach, which considers several different ratios simultaneously. The major initial research work on the use of multivariate models to predict failure or non-failure was carried out by Altman (1968). He used the statistical technique of multiple discriminant analysis, which is designed to classify observations into distinct groupings depending on the characteristics of the observations. In Altman's case, the observations were individual companies and he was seeking to classify them as 'failed' or 'non-failed' depending on the various economic characteristics of each company (size, profitability, liquidity, and so on). The use of multiple discriminant analysis facilitates a linear combination of the economic characteristics that best discriminate between failed and non-failed companies. This linear combination is known as a discriminant function and is of the form

$$Z = b_1 X_1 + b_2 X_2 + b_3 X_3 \ldots + b_n X_n$$

where X_1, X_2, X_3, etc., are the various financial ratios, where b_1, b_2, b_3, etc., are the discriminant coefficients, and where Z is the discriminant score. It is the discriminant score that is used to classify companies as either failed or non-failed.

Altman used the paired sample method and selected thirty-three manufacturing companies that had failed and paired them with manufacturing companies that had not failed. Size and industry were the criteria for pairing. For each company, he computed twenty-two accounting and non-accounting measures and then considered these in various combinations as predictors of failure. The following linear combination was found to be the best discriminator of the bankruptcy of a company, and it contained just five of the variables:

$$Z = 0.012 X_1 + 0.014 X_2 + 0.033 X_3 + 0.006 X_4 + 0.0099 X_5$$

where X_1 = working capital/total assets, X_2 = retained earnings/total assets, X_3 = profit before interest and taxes/total assets, X_4 = market value of equity/book value of total debt, X_5 = sales/total assets.

This model would be applied in solvency evaluation by calculating each of those five ratios for the company under consideration, feeding them into the discriminant function, and calculating the discriminant score (usually known simply as the Z-score). The value of the computed Z-score would be compared with the cut-off point that best discriminated between failed and non-failed companies. Altman established cut-off points as follows: all companies with a Z-score greater than 2.99 could be classified as non-bankrupt, and all companies with a Z-score less than 1.81 were classified as bankrupt. The group of companies with Z-scores falling between 1.81 and 2.99 included both bankrupt and non-bankrupt companies; on balance, Altman suggested that a cut-off point of 2.675 caused least mis-classification.

Altman tested the predictive power of his model by examining the frequency of incorrect classifications. Using data from one year prior to bankruptcy, 95.0 per cent of the total sample was correctly classified; data from two years prior to bankruptcy resulted in the correct classification of 72.0 per cent of the sample.

Although Altman's model offers a useful framework for predicting the likelihood of failure, it should be noted that his results are not capable of general application. The sample he used was far too small and was based on data from the period 1946–1965 for US manufacturing companies. Before the model could be applied to current data for UK companies, it would have to be reformulated and retested to take account of the time that has elapsed since its original development and the economic changes since that date.

In 1977, Altman and colleagues (see Altman, Haldeman and Narayanan, 1977) extended the original Altman model and applied it to newer evidence on corporate bankruptcies. In the new model, they employed seven variables: the return on assets ratio, the stability of earnings, the interest coverage ratio, the retained earnings/total assets ratio, the current ratio, the equity/total capital ratio, and the absolute size of total assets. They found that this revised model was an even better predictor of bankruptcy up to five years in advance.

British research has been conducted using the technique of multiple discriminant analysis – notably by Taffler (1983) who tested balance sheet and profit and loss account ratios, four-year trend measures and ratios constructed from funds flow statements. He found that the final two sources did not provide any significantly better improvement over the more conventional types of ratio and eventually derived the following four-variable model:

$$Z = C_0 + C_1 R_1 + C_2 R_2 + C_3 R_3 + C_4 R_4$$

where C_0 is a constant measuring half the distance between the respective Z-scores of failed and solvent companies, and where C_1, C_2, C_3 and C_4 are weights or coefficients to be applied to the ratios, R_1, R_2, R_3 and R_4. In Taffler's model, the contributing ratios were: R_1 = profit before tax/average current liabilities; R_2 = current assets/total liabilities; R_3 = current liabilities/total assets; and R_4 = a defensive interval measure, defined as defensive assets less actual liabilities/projected daily operating expenditure. The nature of Taffler's commercial interests in employing his model for clients precludes a full examination of its validity, but his published results indicate a high degree of reliable prediction from the model. The failed cut-off point was found to be set at $Z = (1.95)$ and his tests found a high degree of discrimination between failing and solvent companies.

A combination of quantitative and qualitative factors has been developed by Argenti (1976), producing an *A*-score based on both financial statement data and qualitative assessments of management performance. That approach has the merit of not just concentrating on the accounting data but also evaluating the defects and mistakes, or otherwise, of a company's management.

Although any particular predictive model may never be applicable at all times and under all circumstances, the models that have been developed do appear to have had quite definite predictive ability. Because of the potential payoff from being able to develop a proven predictive model, research continues apace. Most of the published research results have involved a retrospective analysis, being based on past data for firms that actually failed, and are subject to statistical shortcomings. Nonetheless, the evidence is impressive and has helped in the identification of those crucial ratios that have a strong measure of predictive ability. Thus, although the role of financial ratio analysis in the prediction of future profits, dividends and share prices may be somewhat unclear, its importance in the prediction of future solvency appears much clearer.

Part Three:

Appendices

Appendix A

Financial Review of The BOC Group plc for the Year Ended 30 September 1982

REPORT OF THE DIRECTORS

The presentation of this year's Financial Review has been changed to follow the form prescribed by The Companies Act 1981. The Act calls for only a marginal increase in the amount of information we normally present to shareholders, but alters considerably the structure of both the Accounts and Directors' Report. The Group is considering a filing with the United States Securities and Exchange Commission (SEC) which would involve further disclosure. The more significant elements of such a filing have been incorporated in this Financial Review.

ACCOUNTING CONVENTIONS

The Group's mainstream accounts are based on the historical cost convention but give equal prominence to results based on the current cost convention (CCA).

In the historical cost accounts the majority of assets have been revalued to net replacement cost and depreciation is charged on those replacement values. This variant of pure historical figures is described as 'modified historical cost' (MHC). The effect of the revaluation has narrowed the gap between the historical cost and current cost conventions. The asset values in the two sets of accounts are the same except for a minor difference in the valuation of stocks. In the Profit and Loss account the difference is limited to the net effect of the cost of sales, monetary working capital and gearing adjustments. The depreciation charge is the same under each convention.

ACCOUNTING POLICIES

The Group has made a number of changes to its accounting policies, details of which are given in Note 2, page 23. The most important of these is the decision to capitalise interest on major fixed asset additions. In the year under review the net effect was to increase the profit before tax by £6.5 million. The changed policy is in line with that previously adopted by the Group's larger overseas subsidiaries and with the mandatory accounting standard for United States companies.

As a result of the changes in policies adjustments have been made to the comparative figures for 1981.

GROUP TRADING RESULTS

Sales at £1 534.2 million were less than 1 per cent up on 1981. The transatlantic welding businesses and the US gas and carbon businesses suffered from falling demand and in some areas lower selling prices. Elsewhere there were modest increases in volume but little upward movement in prices. Exchange rate movements on the translation of overseas sales were not a major factor this year. The strength of the US dollar against sterling was offset by a decline in the value of the Australian dollar and the South African rand. The underlying sales growth of the Group's continuing businesses was only 4 per cent against 17 per cent achieved in the previous year.

The MHC trading profit of £160.8 million was £3.5 million above 1981. The profit is after a £10.7 million increase in depreciation and £9.5 million redundancy costs in continuing businesses.

The CCA operating profit of £137.6 million was £7.7 million above 1981 after taking account of a currency translation adjustment of £1.3 million. The regional breakdown shows that improvements were achieved everywhere except the Americas.

For comparison, the 1981 figures shown below have been restated at exchange rates ruling at 30th September 1982. The difference between the total on restatement and the original figures for 1981 give rise to the exchange adjustment

	1982 £ million	1981 £ million
Europe	51.2	25.1
Africa	20.4	18.9
Americas	28.0	53.7
Asia	2.7	2.3
Pacific	35.3	29.9
	137.6	129.9
Exchange adjustment	—	1.3
CCA Operating profit	137.6	131.2

During the year interest rates in the UK and the US fell from the high levels experienced in 1981 and, despite higher borrowings, the interest burden before capitalisation fell by £0.4 million. During 1982 £6.5 million of interest net of amortisation was capitalised. The corresponding figure for 1981 was £3.3 million. Profit before tax in CCA terms were just over 9 per cent above 1981 (MHC, just under 8 per cent). If the benefit from capitalisation of interest and the effect of currency

REPORT OF THE DIRECTORS
(continued)

movements is excluded then the improvement was 6.1 per cent.

In spite of the improvement in profits before tax, the taxation charge was substantially reduced from 1981. The main reason was the Group's ability to sell surplus US tax allowances under the provisions of the US Economic Recovery Tax Act. The benefit in the year was £8.3 million against £2.2 million in 1981.

Before extraordinary items MHC earnings were 39 per cent up and CCA earnings rose 42 per cent.

After extraordinary items the improvement was even greater with disposable earnings increasing by more than 50 per cent.

REVIEW OF BUSINESS SECTORS

The Group's four main businesses are industrial gases and cryogenic plant; health care; carbon-based products; and welding. Its other businesses include vacuum engineering, educational and food services. A review of these businesses for the year ended 30th September 1982 is given below. Segmental analyses of sales and operating profits are given in Note 1, page 22.

INDUSTRIAL GASES AND CRYOGENIC PLANT

1982 was an extremely difficult year for most of our companies involved in the production and distribution of industrial gases. The creditable operating performance was only achieved by timely management action in response to the varying economic environments. The satisfactory Group results, however, represent a combination of mixed fortunes in our main markets.

In the US, the predicted moderate growth in the economy for 1982 was replaced by one of the sharpest declines in economic activity within memory, and that country remains in its deepest recession since the 1930s. The industries which suffered most are steel, where operating rates have declined to below 40 per cent of capacity; metal fabrication; and the automobile and related industries. As a principal supplier to these industries and in common with our competitors, the results for the Americas inevitably suffered. In the very competitive bulk liquid market, liquid oxygen sales were marginally down, but liquid nitrogen showed a significant increase due to the continued exploitation of new applications.

The benefit of this increased revenue was

offset by substantially higher power charges not fully recovered by price increases.

In spite of the current situation investment in new, more efficient, plants and in applications development continues. Two plants from the new range of BOC standardised designs were ordered for California and South Carolina and a third came on stream at Fostoria, Ohio. The number of engineers and scientists engaged in developing new markets has also been increased significantly.

Despite the difficult trading conditions in the UK, the managements there pursued further cost-effective measures to ensure that the trading position remained profitable whilst securing a firm base for the hoped-for resurgence of activity. Unfortunately the current plight of the British steel industry gives no hope for an up-turn.

The gains in productivity so far achieved have enabled us not only to report an extremely effective performance, but have also allowed us to hold prices at well below the rate of inflation. Thus we are doing our best to stimulate the use of our products and also make British industry in total more cost effective. As part of this process, a new oxygen/nitrogen plant was authorised in the UK to meet any future growth in the market, and also to improve further our cost base.

The success of our applications development activity can be illustrated by the fact that some 25 per cent of our UK liquid business is for applications introduced to new customers over the last three years.

In previous years our companies in South Africa and Australia have operated in more buoyant economies. Inevitably, the current worldwide recession has affected our businesses in these areas. Both companies experienced marked down-turns in activity in the latter half of 1982, as competitive pressures mounted and margins were squeezed. That they have done as well as they have is a tribute to the effectiveness of their reaction to these circumstances.

Contracts in our worldwide tonnage business generally ensured that, in spite of reduced off-take by customers, we were able to maintain overall profit performance. However, reduced tonnage demand does have a significant effect on the availability of argon. We have therefore turned to other sources to obtain this valuable gas, and will be commissioning a plant in the US next year to recover argon from an ammonia process stream.

The smaller but important Special Gases activity made good progress in the US and the UK in enhancing its capabilities and production sources. A new krypton recovery plant was inaugurated in the US and an additional unit will be installed in the UK. Production capacity is also being increased to satisfy the fast growing market for gases in the electronics industry.

The Group enjoys a very substantial position in the US carbon dioxide (CO_2) market. In spite of the economic situation, significant volume gains were made, particularly through the development of applications for modern highly efficient food freezing and chilling technology. Additional capacity for this market was brought on stream at Pekin, Illinois, and capacity at Hopewell, Virginia significantly expanded. The US CO_2 business during the year was under pressure from price erosion and affected by the closing down of a number of ammonia plants, from which much crude CO_2 is obtained.

Our increased involvement in enhanced oil recovery combines the technologies of both applications development and plant development. This embraces our purchase of a CO_2 source and a 66 mile pipeline running from Sterlington, Louisiana to Phillips Oil Fields in Bradley County, Arkansas; our development of large nitrogen generators for on-site installation; and continuing growth of BOC-Nowsco, our related company in Europe and the Far East in oilwell stimulation activities.

Cryogenic plant

The UK cryogenic plant and equipment division had a successful year, with export contracts making a vital contribution to performance. This indicates a continued favourable response by overseas customers to a new standard range of oxygen plants and liquefiers recently developed.

In addition to satisfying the cryogenic plant requirements of the Group, third party sales were secured for a 230 tonnes per day (tpd) oxygen plant and 150 tpd liquefier for New Zealand Steel Development to be erected and operated by our New Zealand subsidiary; large tonnage plants for shipment to steel producers in Yugoslavia and India; and major installations in South Africa and the Philippines.

There was also a considerable increase in the production of on-site gas generators enabling us to provide customers with cost-effective alternatives for supply of product.

HEALTH CARE

The first full year since the establishment of a world health care business saw a number of the strategic advances, initiated last year, come to fruition. The four main divisions moved ahead strongly in sales, with substantial improvements in profitability. Overall, health care profits almost doubled.

Medical equipment and pipelines

Impressive sales gains were achieved, mainly with established products, although recent product range additions – especially in the area of advanced electronics – are showing early promise. The international medical gas pipeline business achieved an outstanding profit improvement, and medical equipment after-sales service continues to present opportunities for profitable growth in many parts of the world.

Considerable effort is being focused on a number of key areas, including product line rationalisation and the strengthening of research and development, manufacturing and marketing resources. One such project is the global rationalisation of two major product groups: vaporizers and patient monitoring systems. This is already resulting in more effective utilisation of both research and manufacturing know-how, and thus providing a more powerful Group presence in the world market.

Ohio Medical Products*

Ohio Medical Products had a good year. Cost containment, combined with concentrated selling effort on total anaesthesia and monitoring systems, secured improved margins, especially in the US domestic market. The recent acquisition of electronic ventilator technology is proving to be a key factor and generating enthusiastic acceptance among Ohio customers.

Other significant developments included greater penetration of key market segments as a result of geographical and product rationalisation, and a reorganisation of Ohio's medical supplies business implemented at year-end.

Medishield Equipment*

The Medishield Equipment division, having moved well towards recovery during 1981, achieved a significant return to profitability in 1982.

REPORT OF THE DIRECTORS
(continued)

A stronger organisational structure, higher productivity and stringent cost controls, together with a 22 per cent increase in sales transformed the preceding year's break-even figure to a healthy operating profit, with a substantial improvement in return on capital employed.

For the first time since 1976 all Medishield Equipment operations were profitable, with complete turn-rounds at BOC Medishield's Harlow factory in the UK and ATM Pesty (France) and a continuing high level of productivity at the Cyprane factory (UK).

Strategic moves initiated at year-end to improve production facilities include the consolidation of Mediada operations at a new location in Gothenburg, Sweden, and a factory expansion at ATM Pesty.

In Australia, the CIG Medishield Ramsay medical equipment business was depressed due to government restrictions on hospital expenditure.

Anaesthetics and pharmaceuticals
Ohio Medical Anesthetics achieved significant growth in sales and profits. North American performance was stimulated by the rapid market acceptance of Forane* (isoflurane) and the continuance of Ēthrane* (enflurane) dominance of the inhalation anaesthetic market.

Manufacturing and research facility expansion programmes were initiated to meet the needs for increased production and new product opportunities for the worldwide anaesthetic pharmaceutical market. The Guayama, Puerto Rico, manufacturing facility doubled its Forane capacity. The division's research facility in Murray Hill, New Jersey, US, is undergoing extensive expansion which will be completed in the coming year.

The applications for Ēthrane and Forane have been expanded with recent clinical advances. The US Food & Drug Administration approved the use of Ēthrane as an analgesic for routine childbirth, while Forane was approved for use with children under two years of age.

Geographic expansion of the division's marketing activities was initiated in co-ordination with the expanded research and new products programme. Alyrane* (enflurane) was marketed for the first time for human and veterinary applications in Europe and the Far East.

Intravenous products
Medishield Intravenous Products' otherwise excellent performance was marred by setbacks associated with efforts to establish a viable position in North America.

Viggo* Europe increased sales by 20 per cent and operating profit by 40 per cent, with a healthy return on capital employed.

The trend towards creating local sales operations in high-potential export territories continued in the Middle East, South Africa, Japan and Denmark.

British Viggo sales were up 44 per cent, and its new Swindon factory came on stream as a source of products for international markets.

Viggo's factory at Helsingborg, Sweden, continues to be the division's main source of products and further investments will be made in order to maintain high productivity and reduce costs.

Increased emphasis has been placed on creating a stronger product development organisation. Encouraging results are already evident, with the launch of ranges of central venous catheters, pressure monitoring products and an improved version of the Vasculon* product in the US.

Medical Gases
Demand for medical gases remained firm worldwide. In the UK, sales of cylinder oxygen for use in the home continued to grow strongly, reflecting increased medical awareness of the benefits of oxygen therapy. This trend is expected to accelerate but the methods of providing oxygen will widen, as it has in the US, to include the use of domestic oxygen concentrators. The Group is currently sponsoring trials in the UK, whilst in US, this market will be developed through interests in Glasrock Medical Services.

Superconductors
This activity is included within the health care section for the first time.

In previous years, the Group's superconductor operations were based mainly on US government nuclear fusion and high energy physics programmes. Deep cuts in Federal funding for these projects led to a major contraction in sales during 1982 and the business operated at a loss.

As a result, the business has been re-organised to lessen dependence on government contract work as a jointly owned venture with the UK-based Oxford Instruments Group – a world leader in the design and production of nuclear magnetic resonance (NMR) imaging magnets (the largest market for superconducting wire).

NMR imaging devices are considered safer and more precise than X-ray technology, and represent a significant advance in the diagnostic field – equivalent to the CAT scanner. They should make substantial inroads in the medical equipment area.

CARBON, GRAPHITE AND CARBIDE PRODUCTS

Carbon and graphite products suffered in 1982 from the worldwide recession. US graphite electrode sales were the most severely affected, and were 27 per cent down on the previous year, in line with the drop in US electric furnace steel production.

Nevertheless, sales of graphite electrodes to the non-US steel industry increased by 30 per cent. Almost a third of Group sales of graphite electrodes are now to non-US customers which represents progress toward the Group's long-range goal of becoming a major producer for the worldwide electric furnace steel industry.

Electrode production in 1982 was reduced 14 per cent and manpower levels by 31 per cent in response to recessionary pressures.

The substantial programme to expand and modernise our graphite electrode manufacturing plants continued during 1982. New modern facilities were completed at St Marys, Pennsylvania, increasing capacity by 11 000 tonnes. Most important was the commencement of construction of our new graphite electrode plant in Ridgeville, South Carolina. At year-end, construction was 20 per cent complete. This plant will incorporate the most modern electrode manufacturing technology. It will include a high degree of automation which should improve labour productivity some $2\frac{1}{2}$ times that of our older plants.

During 1982, construction began on the Seadrift, Texas, plant which will produce premium needle coke, the key raw material for the manufacture of graphite. At the end of the year, construction was 16 per cent complete. Start-up of both plants is expected in the last quarter of 1983. The results of our work on a premium needle coke pilot plant give us confidence that we will develop premium needle cokes to the high standards of consistency and quality required.

The speciality carbon products business continued to make progress during 1982 although many markets were adversely affected by the US recession. Our substantial share in the high-growth market for graphite used in growing silicon crystals for the semiconductor industry, was increased. A new bright-clad gouging rod was successfully introduced and graphite moulds made a good penetration into the carbide tool industry.

Carbide-Acetylene Products

Worldwide, the down-turn in the steel industry had a similar impact on our calcium carbide business. In the US sales of calcium carbide and acetylene were 8 per cent down on the preceding year with the major drop occurring during the second half of 1982. Against this trend was the continued successful market introduction of calcium carbide based steel desulphurisation reagents where tonnage increased 30 per cent despite the recession.

In Norway, the re-instatement of the large 50MW calcium carbide furnace was completed. It is now delivering product to markets in the UK and elsewhere.

WELDING

Welding, with its dependence on the metal fabricating industries, suffered a massive setback in demand. The inevitably disappointing overall performance concealed a series of significant achievements during the year in reducing the underlying cost base of the business.

Against 1981's heavy loss in the UK and small profit in the US, there has been a major change in performance.

In Europe, demand remained depressed throughout the year. With exports substantially reduced, sales overall were further reduced in real terms. However, in the UK some significant market share gains have been achieved following the continued development of distributor trading.

Costs have been reduced by a substantially larger percentage than the reduction in sales as the benefits of the restructuring and other changes of the last two years begin to show through. This has led to an improved performance. With continued, though reduced trading losses, there is still a good way to go before we can be satisfied.

In the Americas, demand for welding collapsed in the year. Sales were more than 20 per cent down despite some market share gain. These

5

REPORT OF THE DIRECTORS

(continued)

difficult market conditions were met with substantial cost reductions. However we were not able to eliminate costs at a rate to match the fall in sales. In addition, there was a prolonged strike at the Canadian filler metals factory.

Significant trading losses were incurred to which must be added further costs incurred in scaling down both facilities and inventories to the new levels of demand.

The Australian and South African markets, having earlier retained much of their sparkle despite the world recession, felt the full impact of economic difficulties in the second half of the year. Our companies there experienced sharp reductions in sales levels at that stage together with some pressure on margins. These factors combined to reduce the profitability of both businesses for the year as a whole.

Despite this deterioration in performance, both the Australian and South African welding businesses continue to be in good shape.

The remainder of the Group's welding businesses – largely within the smaller companies – maintained profitable performance during the year although margins overall were lower as, almost universally, trading conditions became more difficult.

The year, therefore, has primarily been one of continued retrenchment and, particularly in the UK, consolidation of changes initiated earlier. A number of new products have been introduced including improved welding electrodes, a new line of gas welding and cutting equipment particularly suited to the requirements of some of our key export markets, a new range of composite MIG welding sets and the initial models of a planned range of solid state welding equipment. The focus continues to be on standard products for volume markets and all the new items introduced during the year fall in this category.

OTHER BUSINESSES
Vacuum products

In spite of the heavy impact of the recession, both Temescal* (the US-based operation) and Edwards (UK-based) showed good improvement and both are well placed to take advantage of any upturn in world economies.

During the year, Temescal consolidated its technological lead in solar and semi-conductor products. A new glass coating research and development centre went into operation midyear at Concord, California, with a large in-line coater capable of applying four coating layers on 1-metre by 2-metre glass.

Construction was started on an expansion to house a production glass coater to serve the Glass Division of Ford Motors. The unit will initially coat high-curvature privacy glass for Ford 1983 model vans and recreational vehicles. By December 1983, Temescal will be supplying Ford with up to 14 million square feet of coated glass annually from the new plant scheduled to be built at Claremore, Oklahoma, by February 1983.

Negotiations were also completed to supply two architectural glass coating systems for the Guardian Glass Company plants in Corsicana, Texas, and Carleton, Michigan. Sales to the reflective glass industry are expected to improve from the introduction of Superglass* coatings developed specifically for the residential window market. The coatings combine high visible light transmission with low heat emissivity and are reported to be superior to any other available coatings.

In late 1982, a facility to manufacture systems and components used in the fabrication of semi-conductor wafers was opened at Salt Lake City, Utah. It will produce the newly developed Plasma-Sette* production equipment for plasma or dry etching semi-conductor layers, and Cryomax* cryogenic vacuum pumps. Commercial production of the Magnesette* 'cassette to cassette', fully automatic magnetron sputtering equipment introduced during the year, will begin at the plant in January 1983.

The Edwards basic product line is world competitive technically and the manufacturing base now has the capacity to support growth. Major growth is available, particularly in the US.

The issue confronting Edwards is the need for a significant increase in sales volumes, and for a dramatic reduction in costs, especially in the UK. Despite progress in many areas, Edwards still has some distance to go to reach a satisfactory level of performance.

In the UK, the general productivity of Edwards factories has continued to improve, and the installation of modern machine tools and systems has made Shoreham one of the most efficient rotary vacuum pump factories in the world.

Our industrial freeze drying business, based

on manufacture at our plants in Italy and Germany, has continued to prosper.

Development of new products continues and this has won orders from government agencies, major industrial companies and research organisations worldwide.

Educational Services

Sales and profits in our US welding, computer and secretarial training school operations reached all-time highs in 1982 for the third year in a row. These record results were achieved in the face of significant difficulties brought on by the deep economic recession, as well as cutbacks in Federally-funded student financial aid programmes.

There are now 18 welding and business schools in operation and construction is nearly complete on two new computer training schools in Paramus, New Jersey and Houston, Texas. It is also intended to expand the successful Washington School for Secretaries.

Food Services

BOC Transhield, the UK transport company which distributes chilled food and other merchandise exclusively to Marks and Spencer, had a good year based upon steady volume growth and consolidation of many new working practices. These included improved utilisation of our labour and vehicles resources.

The new national six-depot network operated efficiently and handled volumes well in excess of original estimates, reflecting the good co-operation and support we receive from our unions and employees.

ACQUISITIONS AND DIVESTMENTS

The programme to rationalise the Group's business portfolio continued. During the year the Group sold the major part of its interest in its UK-based computer services activity, the cutting machines businesses based in Germany and the UK, and the remaining parts of its UK chemicals activity. After the year-end, the Software Sciences subsidiary in the United States was also sold.

During the year the Group reached agreement with Oxford Instruments to establish a joint venture in the United States for the manufacture of superconducting magnets for NMR scanners. The Group's existing superconductor activity has been merged into this venture.

After the year-end, industrial gases companies operating in Venezuela, Colombia and Aruba were acquired and a 43 per cent interest obtained in Osaka Sanso Kogyo KK, a major Japanese industrial gas company. In the health care area agreement has been reached with Glasrock Medical Services Corp., subject to their shareholders' approval, to acquire that company's interests in the domiciliary oxygen service business and its 26 per cent holding in Mountain Medical Equipment Inc., a US manufacturer of oxygen concentrators. The Group already holds a 26 per cent interest in Mountain Medical.

TAXATION

The tax charge is based on the UK accounting standard (SSAP 15) and no provision is made for deferred tax which is unlikely to become payable in the foreseeable future.

If the Group had provided fully for deferred tax regardless of the probability of its becoming payable, the tax charge of £27.6 million would have been increased to £48.8 million. With a large capital investment programme, the Group benefits from the rapid depreciation allowances given in the UK and US and from investment tax incentives in the US. In the UK the only tax paid is Advance Corporation Tax (ACT) on dividends, which is written off. The majority of the tax charge arises from operations in Australia and South Africa and from the smaller companies trading in developing countries. No Federal tax is payable in the US and therefore the Group has entered into certain leasing transactions under the US Economic Recovery Tax Act whereby it effectively sells some of its surplus US tax credits. Further transactions have been effected since 30th September 1982 but changes in the legislation make tax credit sales in 1983 unlikely.

DIVIDENDS

The disposable earnings for the year after the extraordinary profit and writing off ACT on the proposed dividend were £70.6 million (MHC) and £73.0 million (CCA). An interim ordinary dividend of 2.6p per share amounting to £8.7 million was paid in October 1982. The directors recommend for payment on 5th April 1983 a final ordinary dividend of 3.14p per share amounting to £10.7 million. After deducting the total ordinary and preference dividends of £19.5 million the balance of MHC

REPORT OF THE DIRECTORS
(continued)

profits retained in the Group in respect of the year to 30th September 1982 is £51.1 million.

The total ordinary dividend for the year (including tax credit) has been increased by 12.3 per cent. At this level it is covered 2.9 times by disposable CCA earnings (before writing off ACT of £8.2 million).

On a fully diluted basis, assuming full conversion of the outstanding loan stock and exercise of the options granted under both the employee SAYE scheme, and the Senior Executives' Share Option Scheme, the CCA dividend cover would be reduced to 2.7 times.

CASH FLOW
Net borrowings of the Group including finance leases, increased by £73 million to £589 million. The main reason for the increase in debt was the need to finance the Group's heavy capital investment programme. In the last decade the Group has been increasingly dependent on medium term bank finance at interest rates that varied with short term changes in the market. In September 1982 the opportunity was taken to refinance part of this debt through the issue of £100 million of 12¼ per cent Unsecured Loan Stock. This reduced the Group's dependence on variable rate debt although with heavy capital expenditure during 1983, the adjustment is only temporary. If interest rates throughout the world continue to fall the Group would expect to take further opportunities to issue long term fixed rate debt.

At 30th September 1982 net borrowings represented 36 per cent of total capital employed. This is a slight increase compared with 30th September 1981 but remains at a level that the directors consider acceptable.

In 1983 fixed capital expenditure will increase to over £300 million. Some increase in working capital may be necessary when the world economies expand. As a result, the absolute level of borrowings will increase substantially by 30th September 1983. Existing facilities contractually committed to the Group by banks and other lending institutions are more than sufficient to cover this expected debt level. However, the expected growth in the Group's debt was a factor in the decision to issue further equity as consideration for the Group's acquisitions in South America, Japan and the United States.

Borrowings as a percentage of capital

employed will increase during 1983 but in subsequent years with a lower level of planned capital expenditure the gearing level should fall.

GROUP INVESTMENT
The total fixed capital expenditure in the year was £221.7 million against £155.8 million in 1981.

	1982 £ million	1981 £ million
UK	24.3	26.5
Rest of Europe	8.2	3.7
Africa	17.6	25.1
Americas	131.6	68.1
Asia	0.9	0.2
Pacific	39.1	32.2
	221.7	155.8

In 1982 the increase in expenditure was due largely to the continuing investment in the industrial gases business and the major expansion of the US carbon business. Many of the facilities under construction will be completed in 1983 and thereafter the level of expenditure is expected to fall.

INTERNATIONAL TRADE
The main business of the Group – industrial gases – is not generally involved in international trade; the nature of the products require that they are produced close to the customers.

Certain other businesses of the Group, especially cryogenic equipment, welding products, health care, carbide, and high vacuum depend on exports for much of their success.

The main companies of the Group involved in international trade are BOC Ltd in the UK, Airco in the US, CIG in Australia, Odda Smelteverk in Norway and Medishield companies in Europe.

The value of goods exported by the Group from the UK was as follows:

	1982 £ million	1981 £ million
to Group Companies	22.7	19.5
to others	42.2	37.8
	64.9	57.3

Trade between Group companies is conducted at fair market prices.

In addition to export earnings the UK benefited from dividends and interest received from overseas totalling £50.9 million after withholding taxes.

RESEARCH AND DEVELOPMENT

Total Group expenditure on R & D during 1982 was £24.9 million, a 30 per cent increase over 1981. Major efforts in technical development were in industrial gases and cryogenic equipment, health care products, carbon and graphite products, welding products and high vacuum equipment. Some of the Group's businesses require little or no R & D whereas others (including those mentioned above) require significant technical effort to ensure that, in our products and processes, the Group is the equal of the world's best.

PEOPLE AND EMPLOYMENT

The number of people employed by the Group fell in the year by 3 760 (9 per cent). Regionally the employment pattern at the year-end was:

	1982 number	1981 number
Europe	13 780	16 180
Africa	5 190	5 450
Americas	13 110	14 310
Asia	1 060	910
Pacific	5 230	5 280
	38 370	42 130

The average number employed was:

	1982	1981
UK	12 380	14 970
Overseas	28 040	28 380

The remuneration of employees was:

	£ million	£ million
UK	109.0	114.3
Overseas	272.9	252.4

The sale of a number of businesses accounts for half of the change. The low demand and need to improve productivity in the remaining businesses resulted in reductions beyond that achievable through normal employee turnover and redundancy was unavoidable. The number of people employed is expected to decline further in 1983.

The consolidated statement of value added on page 15 gives some indication of the change in productivity in the year.

EMPLOYMENT POLICIES

The Group operates worldwide. Its employment policies vary to meet local conditions and requirements, but are established on the basis of best practices in any given country. These policies favour and encourage the provision of employment opportunities for disabled people, racial minorities and other disadvantaged groups, and the provision of employment opportunities for women.

Throughout the world there is close consultation between management and other employees on matters of concern. The practice varies between countries depending on the customs and legal structure in each location. Overall the Group endeavours to keep its employees well informed about the progress and position of their company and the Group so that they may participate fully in these matters.

In line with the request of the UK Government, detailed information about wages and conditions of black employees in the African Oxygen group of companies is available on request from the Company Secretary of The BOC Group plc.

PENSIONS

There have been no major structural changes in the Group's pension schemes during the year. Benefits in a number of areas were improved.

The majority of Group companies fund their pension liabilities through self-managed schemes. In most cases the fund assets cover accrued liabilities. The situation of the Airco funds is an exception and is commented on in Note 20, page 44. Periodic actuarial valuations have shown that the financial basis and funding arrangements of the schemes are satisfactory in relation to the actuarial liabilities.

Except for Airco, any other fund deficits are immaterial in a Group context.

. In the UK, a separate Report and Accounts of the Pension Fund is made available to all members.

CORPORATE DISCLOSURE

During the year ended 30th September 1982 Group companies made charitable payments of £651 000, of which £138 000 was by companies in the United Kingdom. No political contributions were made by the Group in the United Kingdom.

REPORT OF THE DIRECTORS
(continued)

DIRECTORS AND AUDITORS

The directors are named on pages 6 and 7 of the first section of the Annual Report.

The directors retiring by rotation, all of whom are willing to be re-appointed, are Mr D J Craig, Mr R C Hesketh-Jones, Mr D W N Pitts and Mr R D Reich.

Mr P J J Rich has agreed to become a director and at the Annual General Meeting it will be proposed that he be elected to the Board.

The auditors, Coopers & Lybrand, retire in accordance with the provisions of Section 14 of the Companies Act 1976 and a resolution for their re-appointment will be proposed at the Annual General Meeting.

The directors' interests in shares and debentures of the Company and its subsidiaries, and in contracts with the Company, are disclosed in Note 9(a), page 31.

The service contracts of the directors offering themselves for re-election are:

Mr D J Craig has a service contract with Airco, Inc., to age 62 (i.e. to 29th September 1987)

Mr R C Hesketh-Jones has no service contract.

Mr D W N Pitts has a service contract with the Company to age 60 (i.e. to 28th August 1990), with provision for earlier termination.

Mr R D Reich has a service contract with Airco, Inc., expiring on 30th September 1983, with provision for earlier termination.

ALLOTMENT OF RELEVANT SECURITIES

At the Extraordinary General Meeting held on 25th February 1981 the directors were authorised generally to allot up to 107 635 557 Ordinary Shares of 25p each at any time or times before 26th February 1986. Of this authorisation 104 374 649 Ordinary Shares are still available to be allotted, although 60 682 370 of those shares have been reserved for the conversion of the 9 per cent Convertible Unsecured Loan Stock 2001/06.

At the Annual General Meeting held on 17th February 1982 when the authorised capital was increased by £25 000 000 to £140 000 000 the directors were given authority to allot relevant securities up to the aggregate nominal amount of £25 000 000, effectively to the conclusion of the forthcoming Annual General Meeting. Since that resolution was passed, £2 075 000 (8 300 000 Ordinary Shares) have been allocated to the Senior Executives' Share Option Scheme (approved by shareholders on 30th July 1982), and a further £6 357 289 (25 429 158 Ordinary Shares) have been allotted in respect of acquisitions. Accordingly, relevant securities with a nominal value of £16 567 711 remain available, and the directors now invite shareholders to renew the authorisation for a period to expire on 30th April 1984. However, 29 000 000 Ordinary Shares (£7 250 000 nominal) have, at the date when this Report was printed, been conditionally allotted subject to the closing of the Glasrock acquisition: if that closing takes place before the date of the Annual General Meeting, this authority will apply only in respect of £9 317 711 of relevant securities (equivalent to 37 270 842 Ordinary Shares).

The directors have no present intention of issuing any of the unissued capital other than in respect of existing commitments and the extended authority and power to allot will be subject to the same undertakings to The Stock Exchange that were referred to in last year's Report of the Directors, namely that in the absence of further prior specific approval by shareholders, relevant securities may not be issued:

(a) for cash, otherwise than proportionately to the holders of existing Ordinary Shares or other equity securities, nor

(b) for any transaction which would effectively alter the voting control of the Company.

A Special Resolution dealing with this matter appears as resolution No. 8 in the notice convening the Annual General Meeting.

By order of the Board
P G Bosonnet
Secretary

London
23rd December 1982

(* Trade Marks of the BOC group of companies)

REPORT OF THE
AUDITORS

To the Members of The BOC Group plc

We have audited the financial statements on pages 12 to 47 in accordance with approved Auditing Standards. As explained in the accounting policies on page 17, the financial statements have been prepared to give information under the historical cost convention (as modified by the inclusion of certain assets at a revaluation) and the current cost convention as described in Statement of Standard Accounting Practice No. 16.

In our opinion the financial statements give, under the respective conventions described above, a true and fair view of the state of affairs of the Company and the Group at 30th September 1982 and of the profit and sources and applications of funds of the Group for the year then ended and comply with the Companies Acts 1948 to 1981.

London   Coopers & Lybrand
23rd December 1982   *Chartered Accountants*

CONSOLIDATED PROFIT AND LOSS ACCOUNT

Years ended 30th September

The amounts shown in the right hand columns are stated on the modified historical cost basis; the amounts shown in the shaded area are stated on the current cost accounting basis. These bases are described on page 17. The 1981 figures have been restated as a result of changes in accounting policies (see Note 2, page 23).

Current Cost 1981 £ million	Current Cost 1982 £ million		Notes	Modified Historical Cost 1982 £ million	Modified Historical Cost 1981 £ million
1 521.7	1 534.2	**TURNOVER**	1	**1 534.2**	1 521.7
(882.6)	(920.4)	Cost of sales		**(920.4)**	(882.6)
639.1	613.8	Gross profit		**613.8**	639.1
(164.1)	(164.3)	Distribution costs		**(164.3)**	(164.1)
(325.3)	(292.3)	Administrative expenses		**(292.3)**	(325.3)
(19.2)	(24.9)	Research and development		**(24.9)**	(19.2)
(7.9)	(5.6)	Monetary working capital adjustment		—	—
7.6	9.7	Share of profits of related companies		**9.7**	7.6
1.0	1.2	Income from other fixed asset investments		**1.2**	1.0
131.2	137.6	**OPERATING PROFIT**	1	**143.2**	139.1
—	—	Realised stock holding gains		**17.6**	18.2
131.2	137.6	**TRADING PROFIT**		**160.8**	157.3
27.4	26.1	Gearing adjustment		—	—
(65.7)	(65.3)	Interest payable (net)	3	**(65.3)**	(65.7)
3.5	7.1	Interest capitalised		**7.1**	3.5
96.4	105.5	**PROFIT ON ORDINARY ACTIVITIES BEFORE TAX**		**102.6**	95.1
(37.6)	(27.6)	Tax on profit on ordinary activities	4	**(27.6)**	(37.6)
58.8	77.9	Profit on ordinary activities after tax		**75.0**	57.5
(11.5)	(10.9)	Minority interests		**(10.5)**	(11.2)
47.3	67.0	Earnings		**64.5**	46.3
0.6	6.0	Extraordinary items	5	**6.1**	0.6
47.9	73.0	**PROFIT FOR THE FINANCIAL YEAR**		**70.6**	46.9
(16.9)	(18.5)	Dividends	6	**(19.5)**	(16.9)
31.0	53.5	**TRANSFER TO RESERVES**	18	**51.1**	30.0
		Earnings per Ordinary share (undiluted)	7		
16.49p	22.64p	nil distribution basis		**21.91p**	16.17p
14.34p	20.24p	net basis (after ACT written off)		**19.50p**	14.02p
		Earnings per Ordinary share (fully diluted)			
15.92p	20.27p	nil distribution basis		**20.19p**	15.78p
13.76p	17.86p	net basis (after ACT written off)		**17.78p**	13.62p

CONSOLIDATED BALANCE SHEET
at 30th September

The amounts shown in the right hand columns are stated on the modified historical cost basis; the amounts shown in the shaded area are stated on the current cost accounting basis. These bases are described on page 17. The 1981 figures have been restated as a result of changes in accounting policies (see Note 2, page 23).

Current Cost 1981 £ million	Current Cost 1982 £ million		Notes	Modified Historical Cost 1982 £ million	1981 £ million
		FIXED ASSETS			
1 152.6	1 277.6	Tangible assets	11	1 277.6	1 152.6
43.9	71.4	Investments (related companies and other investments)	13	71.4	43.9
1 196.5	1 349.0			1 349.0	1 196.5
		CURRENT ASSETS			
278.5	305.6	Stocks		302.1	274.8
310.3	288.2	Debtors		288.2	310.3
14.3	31.4	Deposits at short call		31.4	14.3
12.2	6.4	Cash at bank and in hand		6.4	12.2
615.3	631.6			628.1	611.6
		CREDITORS: Amounts falling due within one year			
(68.5)	(109.7)	Borrowings and finance leases		(109.7)	(58.5)
(306.7)	(290.0)	Other		(290.0)	(306.7)
250.1	231.9	**NET CURRENT ASSETS**	15	228.4	246.4
1 446.6	1 580.9	**TOTAL ASSETS LESS CURRENT LIABILITIES**		1 577.4	1 442.9
		CREDITORS: Amounts falling due after more than one year	16		
(484.2)	(517.4)	Borrowings and finance leases		(517.4)	(484.2)
(15.2)	(15.8)	Other		(15.8)	(15.2)
		PROVISIONS FOR LIABILITIES AND CHARGES	17		
(55.5)	(58.2)			(58.2)	(55.5)
(554.9)	(591.4)			(591.4)	(554.9)
891.7	989.5			986.0	888.0
		CAPITAL AND RESERVES	18		
84.8	85.4	Called up share capital		85.4	84.8
44.3	45.6	Share premium account		45.6	44.3
376.4	326.9	Revaluation reserve		323.6	372.9
53.0	135.1	Other reserves		11.6	10.6
217.3	274.7	Profit and loss account		398.2	259.7
14.7	18.6	Related companies' reserves		18.6	14.7
790.5	886.3			883.0	787.0
101.2	103.2	**MINORITY SHAREHOLDERS' INTERESTS**		103.0	101.0
891.7	989.5			986.0	888.0

The financial statements were approved by the Board of Directors on 23rd December 1982 and are signed on its behalf by:

R C Hesketh-Jones   Director
P G Bosonnet   Director

13

THE BOC GROUP plc

CONSOLIDATED STATEMENT OF SOURCES AND APPLICATIONS OF FUNDS
Years ended 30th September

This statement shows how the Group has obtained and used the funds needed to finance its activities. For both years opening and closing balance sheet items have been translated at year-end exchange rates thereby eliminating the effect of exchange adjustments on these items. The accounting bases indicated in the statement – MHC and CCA – refer to the modified historical cost and current cost conventions respectively and are described on page 17. The 1981 figures have been restated as a result of changes in accounting policies (see Note 2, page 23).

	Notes	1982 £ million	1981 £ million
Inflows/(Outflows)			
Operating profit (CCA basis)		137.6	131.2
Monetary working capital adjustment		5.6	7.9
Operating profit (MHC basis)		143.2	139.1
Realised stock holding gains		17.6	18.2
Adjustments for non-cash items			
Depreciation		122.6	111.9
Profit before tax retained in related companies		(7.2)	(5.3)
Other		1.2	6.9
Gross cash flow from operations		277.4	270.8
Capital expenditure (net of disposals)		(204.5)	(137.5)
Increase in working capital			
Stocks		(32.6)	(13.5)
Debtors		0.2	(4.2)
Creditors		(9.8)	40.9
		30.7	156.5
Interest paid (net)		(65.3)	(65.7)
Tax paid		(25.6)	(27.5)
Sale of US tax benefits		10.7	—
Dividends paid		(22.4)	(20.7)
		(71.9)	42.6
Acquisitions of businesses	21(a)	(31.2)	(14.8)
Disposals of businesses	21(a)	25.5	3.0
		(77.6)	30.8
Applied to/(Funded by):			
Issues of shares		(1.9)	(2.7)
Net change in borrowings	21(b)	(75.7)	33.5
		(77.6)	30.8

CONSOLIDATED STATEMENT OF VALUE ADDED

Years ended 30th September

Value added is a measure of the amount of wealth that the Group creates by its activities throughout the world. This statement shows the value added in 1982 and how it has been shared among those contributing towards its creation. The amounts are stated on the current cost accounting basis. The 1981 figures have been restated as a result of changes in accounting policies (see Note 2, page 23).

	1982 £ million	%	1981 £ million	%
Turnover	1 534.2		1 521.7	
Bought in materials, services and depreciation	(955.1)		(961.4)	
Value added	579.1		560.3	
Investment income	2.8		3.5	
Extraordinary items	6.0		0.6	
	587.9		564.4	
Applied as follows:				
To employees as pay or as contributions to pensions and welfare schemes	446.8	76.0	429.8	76.2
To banks and other lenders as interest	65.3	11.1	65.7	11.6
To governments as taxes on profits	24.0	4.1	35.0	6.2
To partners in companies not wholly owned by the Group	7.6	1.3	6.5	1.2
To shareholders	19.5	3.3	16.9	3.0
	563.2	95.8	553.9	98.2
Amount retained within the Group	24.7	4.2	10.5	1.8
	587.9	100.0	564.4	100.0

Regional analysis:	Value added 1982 Total £ million	Per employee £	Value added 1981 Total £ million	Per employee £
Europe	203.7	13 500	184.3	10 400
Africa	47.2	8 900	52.2	9 600
Americas	251.2	18 300	240.8	17 100
Asia	2.3	2 200	2.7	3 000
Pacific	74.7	14 400	80.3	15 800
	579.1	14 300	560.3	13 000

BALANCE SHEET OF THE BOC GROUP plc
at 30th September

*All amounts are stated on the modified
historical cost basis, as described on
page 17.*

	Notes	1982 £ million	1981 £ million
FIXED ASSETS			
Tangible assets	11	38.1	40.7
Investments (subsidiary and related companies)	12	362.2	278.7
		400.3	319.4
CURRENT ASSETS			
Debtors		2.1	3.6
Deposits at short call		10.6	4.7
		12.7	8.3
CREDITORS: Amounts falling due within one year		(56.6)	(41.0)
NET CURRENT LIABILITIES	15	(43.9)	(32.7)
TOTAL ASSETS LESS CURRENT LIABILITIES		356.4	286.7
CREDITORS: Amounts falling due after more than one year	16	(142.3)	(116.8)
		214.1	169.9
CAPITAL AND RESERVES	18		
Called up share capital		85.4	84.8
Share premium account		45.6	44.3
Revaluation reserve		—	1.4
Other reserves		15.5	15.5
Profit and loss account		67.6	23.9
		214.1	169.9

The financial statements were approved by the Board of Directors
on 23rd December 1982 and are signed on its behalf by:

R C Hesketh-Jones Director
P G Bosonnet Director

ACCOUNTING POLICIES AND DEFINITIONS

There have been certain changes in accounting policies, details of which are given in Note 2, page 23.

1 GENERAL

(a) *Accounting conventions*
This Financial Review presents information based on two accounting conventions:

(i) *Modified Historical Cost ('MHC').* Where information is given on this basis, it has been drawn up under the historical cost convention which permits the revaluation of fixed assets. As described in more detail below (see 8 – tangible fixed assets), the Group's tangible fixed assets are stated on replacement cost (or economic value if lower) and depreciation is charged accordingly. This basis is referred to in these accounts as the 'modified historical cost basis', to distinguish it from the standard historical cost basis under which tangible fixed assets and depreciation would be stated strictly by reference to original cost.

(ii) *Current Cost ('CCA').* Information presented on this basis has been drawn up under the current cost accounting convention, which is based on the principle of providing for the maintenance of the operating capacity of the Group's businesses, having regard to the extent to which that capacity is financed by borrowed funds.

MHC information is given in the consolidated profit and loss account, consolidated balance sheet and the balance sheet of The BOC Group plc.
CCA information is given in the consolidated profit and loss account, consolidated balance sheet and consolidated statement of value added.

The consolidated statement of sources and applications of funds is not affected by the accounting convention used.
The accounting policies apply to both conventions, except where otherwise stated. The notes on financial statements contain supplementary information in support of the statements referred to above; the information thus relates to both conventions, according to context.

(b) *Basis of consolidation*
The Group accounts include the accounts of the parent company and (with minor exceptions) of all subsidiaries for the years ended 30th September. The results of companies acquired or sold during the year are dealt with from the date of their acquisition or to date of sale. A subsidiary is not consolidated in the Group accounts where, in the opinion of the directors, effective control can no longer be exercised, such that the inclusion of its results in the Group accounts would be misleading.

The Group share of profits less losses of related companies is included on the equity accounting basis where significant commercial and financial influence exists and the Group interest is between 20%–50%. Companies so treated are listed in Note 13. Where audited accounts are not co-terminous with those of the Group, the share of profits less losses has been arrived at from the last audited accounts available and unaudited management accounts to 30th September.

Investments in related companies are included in the consolidated balance sheet at the Group's share of the net assets of the related companies.

Accounting policies and definitions continued overleaf

ACCOUNTING POLICIES AND DEFINITIONS
(continued)

(c) *Discontinued businesses*
The trading results, assets and liabilities of businesses which have been discontinued are included in the financial statements up to the date of sale or decision to cease operations. Profits or losses attributable to the sale or closure are dealt with as extraordinary items.

Where information by business segment is shown in the financial statements (Notes 1 and 10), amounts relating to discontinued businesses (including those in course of divestment or closure) are shown separately.

(d) Certain subsidiary and related companies operate in countries subject to political instability and economic risk. Appropriate provision is made against profits earned in cases where the ability to repatriate dividends or capital is regarded as uncertain.

(e) *Overseas companies*
Certain overseas subsidiary and related companies of the Group publish accounts in their respective countries in accordance with local requirements. In some cases, in order to comply with local accounting rules and practice, it is necessary to use different accounting policies from those of the Group, and appropriate adjustments are made to the amounts included in these accounts.

(f) *Investment income*
Income from investments not consolidated as related companies is included in trading profit only if received, or declared and receivable.

(g) *Exchange rates*
All amounts denominated other than in sterling are translated at rates of exchange approximating to those ruling at the financial year-end. Because of the fluctuations in exchange rates, this process gives rise to exchange differences. Where these arise through the translation into sterling of the opening net asset position of the accounts of overseas subsidiaries, they are taken to reserves in order not to distort the profits of the year.

Where exchange differences result from the translation of foreign currency borrowings of UK companies, raised to acquire overseas assets, they are taken to reserve and offset against the differences arising from the translation of those overseas assets. All other exchange differences (including those arising from currency conversions in the normal course of trading) are dealt with through the profit and loss account. The main exchange rates against sterling used in the preparation of these accounts were:

	1982	1981
US $	**1.70**	1.83
Australian $	**1.78**	1.60
South African rand	**1.95**	1.74

(h) *Goodwill*
Differences between the fair value of attributable net tangible assets at the date of acquisition and the cost of shares acquired are transferred to capital reserves.

2 TURNOVER

Turnover is based on the invoiced value of sales, excluding inter-company sales, VAT and similar sales-related taxes.

3 RESEARCH AND DEVELOPMENT EXPENDITURE

Group revenue expenditure on research and development is written off when incurred.

Accounting policies and definitions continued on opposite page

4 MONETARY WORKING CAPITAL ADJUSTMENT

Current cost
In arriving at current cost operating profit an adjustment is made, calculated by reference to the value of trade debtors less trade creditors, which has the effect of making provision for the increase in monetary working capital required because of increases in prices or costs.

5 OPERATING PROFIT

Operating profit reflects the results of the ordinary activities of the various businesses which constituted the Group during the year. In arriving at operating profit, the amount included in cost of sales for stocks consumed during the year is based on replacement cost (or net realisable value if lower) at the time of consumption; operating profit thus excludes stock holding gains.

Items not expected to recur frequently or regularly are included in operating profit if they relate to continuing businesses (for example, rationalisation or relocation costs). Where such items derive from events or transactions outside the ordinary activities of the businesses (for example, profits or losses on the sale of a business), they are not reflected in operating profit, but shown separately as 'extraordinary items'.

6 STOCK HOLDING GAINS

Stock holding gains occur when price increases cause the replacement cost of stock items to be higher than their original cost of purchase or manufacture. Realised holding gains are those relating to stocks consumed during the year; unrealised holding gains relate to stocks held at the balance sheet date.

Modified historical cost
In the MHC statements, realised stock holding gains are included in the profits of the year. The term 'trading profit' represents the sum of operating profit and realised stock holding gains. Unrealised holding gains are not recorded anywhere in the MHC statements, since stocks are valued by reference to historical cost.

Current cost
In the CCA statements, all stock holding gains are credited directly to reserves, and thus excluded from profits. Realised gains are included in current cost reserve; unrealised gains are included in revaluation reserve.

7 GEARING ADJUSTMENT

Current cost
The gearing adjustment in the current cost statements recognises that the burden of price changes falls proportionately on both lenders of money and providers of equity capital. It is calculated by applying an average gearing percentage to the total of:
(i) additional depreciation on fixed asset revaluations
(ii) cost of sales adjustment (equivalent to the amount of realised stock holding gains)
(iii) monetary working capital adjustment.

8 TANGIBLE FIXED ASSETS

(a) The gross book value of most Group fixed assets is recorded at current replacement cost or economic value if lower.

(b) No depreciation is charged on freehold land or construction in progress. Depreciation is charged on all other fixed assets on the straight line basis over the effective lives except for certain tonnage plants (principally those commissioned in the UK

ACCOUNTING POLICIES AND DEFINITIONS
(continued)

since 1st October 1969) where depreciation is calculated on an annuity basis over the life of the contract.

Straight line depreciation rates vary according to the class of asset, but are typically:

Freehold buildings	2% pa
Leasehold land and buildings	2% pa
(or at rates based on the life of the lease, where shorter than 50 years)	
Plant and machinery	7%–10% pa
Cylinders	4%–7% pa
Motor vehicles: general	20% pa
distribution vehicles	7%–10% pa

(c) Interest costs incurred during the construction period on major fixed asset additions are capitalised and form part of the total asset cost. Depreciation is charged on the total cost, including such interest, on the bases set out above. This accounting policy has been adopted for the first time in these accounts: further details are given in Note 2, page 23.

(d) Where assets are financed by leasing agreements that give rights approximating to ownership ('finance leases') the assets are treated as if they had been purchased outright at the present value of the total rental payable during the primary period of the lease and the corresponding leasing commitments are shown as obligations to the lessor.

Depreciation on the relevant assets is charged to profit and loss account.

Leasing payments are treated as consisting of capital and interest elements and the interest is charged to profit and loss account.

All other leases are 'operating leases' and the annual rentals are charged wholly to profit and loss account.

9 STOCKS

Modified historical cost
Stocks, including work in progress, are valued at cost or net realisable value whichever is lower, and cost where appropriate includes a proportion of overhead expenses. Work in progress is stated at cost less progress payments received or receivable. Work in progress on major construction contracts includes attributable profit less provisions for all known and anticipated losses.

Cost is arrived at principally on the average and 'first-in, first-out' (FIFO) bases.

Current cost
Stocks are restated in the current cost balance sheet at the lower of replacement cost and net realisable value.

10 DEFERRED TAX

The Group provides for deferred tax, on the liability method, in respect of the excess of capital allowances given for tax purposes over historical cost depreciation, and other timing differences, but not where, in the opinion of the directors, the potential tax liability is unlikely to become payable in the foreseeable future.

11 REVALUATION RESERVE

In the modified historical cost statements the revaluation reserve represents the uplift on the net book value of tangible fixed assets from historical cost to revaluation amount. In the current cost statements, the revaluation reserve also includes unrealised stock holding gains.

Accounting policies and definitions continued on next page.

12 CURRENT COST RESERVE

The current cost reserve incorporates:
  (i) the additional depreciation charged in the profit and loss account arising from the revaluation of tangible fixed assets
 (ii) realised stock holding gains (cost of sales adjustment), monetary working capital adjustment, and gearing adjustment included in the current cost profit and loss account
(iii) the net revaluation surplus or deficit realised on the disposal of tangible fixed assets.

13 PENSIONS

The Company and its major subsidiaries operate pension schemes whose assets are independent of the Group's finances. The schemes are funded by contributions partly from the employees and partly from the companies at rates determined by independent actuaries. When benefits are increased, the additional actuarial liability (to the extent that it is not covered by an existing actuarial surplus) is generally funded by contributions from the companies spread over future periods. Full actuarial valuations are made at regular intervals, usually every one to three years, and contribution levels set accordingly.

NOTES ON FINANCIAL STATEMENTS

1 SEGMENTAL INFORMATION

(a) Turnover

(i) 1982

TURNOVER BY BUSINESS	Europe £ million	Africa £ million	Turnover by country of origin Americas £ million	Asia £ million	Pacific £ million	Total £ million
Industrial gases and cryogenic plant	245.7	58.2	271.3	5.3	115.3	695.8
Health care	73.8	7.5	133.8	0.7	27.8	243.6
Carbon, graphite and carbide	8.1	—	126.4	—	—	134.5
Welding	42.5	38.4	119.2	2.2	67.6	269.9
Other businesses	75.8	28.6	50.0	—	8.4	162.8
Continuing businesses	445.9	132.7	700.7	8.2	219.1	1 506.6
Discontinued businesses	27.6	—	—	—	—	27.6
	473.5	**132.7**	**700.7**	**8.2**	**219.1**	**1 534.2**
Turnover by destination (customer location)	**449.7**	**140.2**	**688.4**	**28.0**	**227.9**	**1 534.2**

(ii) 1981

TURNOVER BY BUSINESS	Europe £ million	Africa £ million	Turnover by country of origin Americas £ million	Asia £ million	Pacific £ million	Total £ million
Industrial gases and cryogenic plant	235.2	60.2	249.7	4.6	110.7	660.4
Health care	70.3	1.1	109.8	0.5	25.7	207.4
Carbon, graphite and carbide	8.1	—	134.9	—	—	143.0
Welding	43.6	41.1	132.7	2.5	62.4	282.3
Other businesses	66.9	26.9	43.8	—	13.0	150.6
Continuing businesses	424.1	129.3	670.9	7.6	211.8	1 443.7
Discontinued businesses	56.1	21.6	0.3	—	—	78.0
	480.2	150.9	671.2	7.6	211.8	1 521.7

(b) Profit, capital employed and capital expenditure

(i) Regional Analysis	Operating profit 1982 £ million	1981 £ million	Capital Employed 1982 £ million	1981 £ million	Capital Expenditure 1982 £ million	1981 £ million
Europe	52.7	26.5	435.1	376.5	32.5	30.2
Africa	20.6	21.7	143.3	142.6	17.6	25.1
Americas	31.8	55.2	830.4	732.7	131.6	68.1
Asia	2.7	2.4	7.5	8.2	0.9	0.2
Pacific	35.4	33.3	233.0	214.9	39.1	32.2
	143.2	139.1	1 649.3	1 474.9	221.7	155.8

Note 1 continued on opposite page

1(b) continued

(ii) *Business Analysis*	Profit before tax		Capital Employed		Capital Expenditure	
	1982 £ million	1981 £ million	1982 £ million	1981 £ million	1982 £ million	1981 £ million
Industrial gases and cryogenic plant	103.6	96.5	882.4	797.0	118.3	90.6
Health care	39.6	20.8	192.8	162.2	9.6	15.2
Carbon, graphite and carbide	3.3	13.9	280.2	195.3	56.8	23.2
Welding	(7.4)	4.7	202.2	201.9	16.8	9.0
Other businesses	10.4	6.5	106.8	96.5	15.5	14.0
Corporate	(5.9)	(5.0)	(16.3)	(1.4)	4.0	0.3
Continuing businesses	143.6	137.4	1 648.1	1 451.5	221.0	152.3
Discontinued businesses	(0.4)	1.7	1.2	23.4	0.7	3.5
			1 649.3	1 474.9	221.7	155.8
Operating profit	143.2	139.1				
Realised stock holding gains	17.6	18.2				
Interest	(58.2)	(62.2)				
Profit before tax	102.6	95.1				

An analysis of employees by business is given in Note 10.

2 CHANGES IN ACCOUNTING POLICIES

During 1982 the Group changed certain of its accounting policies as outlined below. The effect of the changes has been applied retrospectively for the full year, and the comparative financial data for 1981 restated accordingly.
(a) The Group has adopted the policy of capitalising interest incurred during the construction period on major fixed asset additions. The effect of this change in 1982 is to increase profit before tax by £6.5 million and capital employed by £13.0 million.
(b) The carrying value of the Group's investments in related companies has been restated to reflect the Group's share of the net assets of the companies concerned. The Group has also reclassified the provision for unremittable funds in overseas subsidiaries from creditors falling due within one year to provisions for liabilities and charges. These changes have no effect on profit in 1982, and increase capital employed by £13.3 million.
(c) Two of the Group's subsidiary companies have changed the basis on which they account for cylinder rentals. This change has a negligible effect on profit, and reduces capital employed in 1982 by £6.5 million.

The above changes have been reflected in the following Notes:
Note 11 – Fixed assets – Tangible assets
Note 13 – Fixed assets – Investments (related companies and other investments)
Note 18 – Capital and reserves
The effect of the changes is the same in both the modified historical cost and the current cost accounts.

Note 2 continued overleaf

NOTES ON FINANCIAL STATEMENTS
(continued)

2 continued

The summary of the impact on the modified historical cost accounts for 1981 and 1982 is as follows:

	Before Accounting Policy Changes		After Accounting Policy Changes	
	1982	1981	1982	1981
	£ million	£ million	**£ million**	£ million
PROFIT AND LOSS ACCOUNT:				
Trading profit	**161.4**	158.4	**160.8**	157.3
Interest	**(65.3)**	(65.7)	**(58.2)**	(62.2)
Profit on ordinary activities before tax	**96.1**	92.7	**102.6**	95.1
Earnings	**59.7**	44.0	**64.5**	46.3
BALANCE SHEET:				
Fixed assets – Tangible assets	**1 263.4**	1 145.5	**1 277.6**	1 152.6
Investments	**72.1**	44.6	**71.4**	43.9
Creditors: Amounts falling due within one year	**(407.2)**	(372.0)	**(399.7)**	(365.2)
Provisions for liabilities and charges	**(43.0)**	(42.3)	**(58.2)**	(55.5)
Reserves – Profit and loss account	**(392.4)**	(259.1)	**(398.2)**	(259.7)
Related companies	**(19.3)**	(15.4)	**(18.6)**	(14.7)

3 INTEREST AND BORROWINGS

	1982	1981
(a) Interest	**£ million**	£ million
Interest payable and similar charges		
On bank overdrafts	**4.7**	4.4
On loans totally repayable within one year	**4.2**	7.7
On all other loans	**61.9**	57.2
On finance leases	**1.7**	1.8
	72.5	71.1
Less Interest receivable	**7.2**	5.4
Interest payable (net)	**65.3**	65.7
Less Interest capitalised	**7.1**	3.5
	58.2	62.2

(b) Borrowings and finance leases

	GROUP		PARENT	
	1982	1981	1982	1981
(i) Analysis of net borrowings and finance leases	**£ million**	£ million	**£ million**	£ million
United Kingdom				
5¾% to 6¼% Debenture Stocks 1981/90: secured	**4.9**	7.2	**4.9**	7.2
9% to 11¼% Tonnage Debenture Stocks 1988/92: secured	**16.6**	18.6	**16.6**	18.6
9% Convertible Unsecured Loan Stock 2001/06 (Note 18)	**82.0**	82.0	**82.0**	82.0
12¼% Unsecured Loan Stock 2012/17 (see (viii) below)	**25.0**	—	**25.0**	—
Sub-total carried forward	**128.5**	107.8	**128.5**	107.8

Note 3 continued on opposite page

3(b) *(i)* continued	GROUP		PARENT	
	1982 **£ million**	1981 £ million	**1982** **£ million**	1981 £ million
Sub-total brought forward	**128.5**	107.8	**128.5**	107.8
Revolving credit facilities				
Medium term	**9.5**	1.5	—	—
Long term	**48.0**	124.6	—	—
Other borrowings	**42.5**	18.2	**29.2**	14.3
Obligations under finance leases	**0.1**	0.3	—	—
Total United Kingdom	**228.6**	252.4	**157.7**	122.1
Overseas				
Airco, Inc., and other US companies				
Long term revolving credit facilities	**94.2**	27.3	—	—
4.85%–5% Promissory notes 1966/88: unsecured	**11.8**	16.9	—	—
$9\frac{3}{4}$% Sinking Fund Debentures 1986/2000: unsecured	**43.3**	40.7	—	—
$6\frac{3}{4}$%–$7\frac{3}{4}$% Industrial Revenue bonds 2005/10: secured	**9.4**	8.7	—	—
$11\frac{7}{8}$%–$13\frac{1}{2}$% Industrial Revenue bonds 2002/12: unsecured	**10.5**	—	—	—
$5\frac{3}{4}$%–7% Pollution Control notes 1984/2006: unsecured	**6.1**	5.7	—	—
6% Industrial Revenue Refunding bonds 1997/2007: unsecured	**6.6**	6.1	—	—
Other borrowings	**22.4**	18.4	—	—
Obligations under finance leases	**11.9**	13.2	—	—
African Oxygen Ltd				
$8\frac{3}{4}$% Debenture Stock 1981/95: unsecured	**3.5**	4.3	—	—
11.1% Debenture Stock 1991/98: unsecured	**5.1**	5.7	—	—
Other borrowings	**17.6**	19.3	—	—
Obligations under finance leases	**2.9**	3.5	—	—
British Oxygen Finance BV				
$10\frac{3}{4}$% Guaranteed bonds 1990: unsecured (US dollars)	**29.4**	27.3	—	—
The Commonwealth Industrial Gases Ltd				
Various debenture stocks: secured				
(Interest rates between 7.25% and 15.7%:				
repayment between 1982 and 1990)	**22.4**	17.3	—	—
Other borrowings	**49.2**	39.8	—	—
Other companies				
Borrowings and obligations under finance leases	**52.2**	36.1	—	—
Total Overseas	**398.5**	290.3	—	—
Total borrowings and finance leases	**627.1**	542.7	**157.7**	122.1
Less Cash and deposits	**37.8**	26.5	**10.6**	4.7
NET BORROWINGS AND FINANCE LEASES	**589.3**	516.2	**147.1**	117.4

Note 3 continued overleaf

NOTES ON
FINANCIAL
STATEMENTS
(continued)

3(b) continued	GROUP		PARENT	
	1982 £ million	1981 £ million	1982 £ million	1981 £ million
(ii) Analysis of net borrowings and finance leases by *major currency*				
Sterling	232.1	185.9	151.1	117.4
US dollar	251.8	235.4	(3.9)	—
Other	105.4	94.9	(0.1)	—
	589.3	516.2	147.1	117.4
(iii) Analysis of borrowings and finance leases between *fixed and variable interest rate*				
Fixed rate	324.7	285.7	128.5	107.8
Variable rate	302.4	257.0	29.2	14.3
	627.1	542.7	157.7	122.1
(iv) Analysis of net borrowing and finance leases by maturity				
Long term – amounts repayable beyond five years:				
Repayable by instalments	215.4	268.1	12.2	19.4
Other	196.3	120.4	108.5	82.0
Medium term – amounts repayable between one and five years:				
Repayable four to five years	27.7	25.7	7.9	8.0
Repayable three to four years	27.4	19.6	7.7	2.3
Repayable two to three years	36.0	18.5	2.2	1.1
Repayable one to two years	14.6	31.9	—	—
LOANS AND FINANCE LEASES (Note 16)	517.4	484.2	138.5	112.8
Short term – overdrafts and borrowings repayable within one year (Note 15)	109.7	58.5	19.2	9.3
Total borrowings and finance leases	627.1	542.7	157.7	122.1
Less Cash and deposits (Note 15)	37.8	26.5	10.6	4.7
NET BORROWINGS AND FINANCE LEASES	589.3	516.2	147.1	117.4
Obligations under finance leases included above amount to (see (vii) below)	15.0	17.1	—	—
Total amount due on long term loans which are repayable by instalments:	318.2	306.0	20.0	25.8
(v) Secured borrowings				
Secured borrowings included above are:				
Long term (repayable beyond five years)	33.9	44.5	13.6	19.4
Medium term (repayable between one and five years)	31.8	26.4	7.9	6.4
Short term (repayable within one year)	12.4	6.4	—	—
Total secured borrowings	78.1	77.3	21.5	25.8

Note 3 continued on opposite page

3(b) *(v)* continued
The Company's 5¾% and 6¾% Debenture Stocks are secured by a first floating charge on the undertaking and all the property and assets present and future wheresoever situate (including any uncalled capital) of the Company and certain of its United Kingdom subsidiaries (including BOC Ltd). The Debenture Stocks of The Commonwealth Industrial Gases Ltd are secured on that company's assets in Australia in a similar manner to the foregoing Debenture Stocks of the Company. The Company's Tonnage Debenture Stocks are secured by a charge on the revenues derived from certain long term contracts for the bulk supply of industrial gases to major customers in the United Kingdom and on the plants from which they are supplied.

(vi) Bank loans and overdrafts

	GROUP		PARENT	
	1982 **£ million**	1981 £ million	**1982** **£ million**	1981 £ million
The aggregate bank loans and overdrafts included in borrowings are:				
Unsecured	322.9	340.7	29.2	14.3
Secured	17.5	13.8	—	—
	340.4	354.5	29.2	14.3

	FINANCE LEASES £ million	OPERATING LEASES £ million
(vii) Leasing commitments		
Rentals are due under leases entered into in respect of fixed assets for the period 1st October 1982 to completion as follows:		
Year to 30th September 1983	3.6	12.8
Year to 30th September 1984	2.4	10.4
Year to 30th September 1985	2.1	6.7
Year to 30th September 1986	1.5	5.0
Year to 30th September 1987	1.4	3.5
Years after 1st October 1987	9.5	6.3
Total rentals due	20.5	44.7
Less: amount representing interest element	5.5	
Obligations under finance leases	15.0	

(viii) Unsecured Loan Stock
On 9th September 1982, £100 million 12¼% Unsecured Loan Stock 2012/17 was issued at £97.504 per cent. The Stock was payable as to £25 per cent on 14th September 1982 with the balance of £72.504 per cent being payable on or before 4th March 1983. Interest at the annual rate of 12¼% is payable on 2nd April and 2nd October in each year.

(ix) Redeemable securities
The total amount of uncancelled redeemable securities held by the Company on 15th December 1982 was:
£70 207 5¾% Debenture Stock 1981/86
£72 906 6¾% Debenture Stock 1985/90
£135 985 9% Tonnage Debenture Stock 1988
£250 000 9% Tonnage Debenture Stock 1990.

NOTES ON
FINANCIAL
STATEMENTS
(continued)

4 TAX

(a) General

The Group incurs tax liabilities in all national jurisdictions in which it operates. The amounts included in the tax charge relate to 'direct' taxes, i.e. those levied on profits earned; other taxes, for example those based on the employment of labour, the occupation of business premises and the importation of goods, are deducted in arriving at operating profits.

In the United Kingdom, the principal liability relates to Corporation Tax, currently levied at 52%. Because of reliefs available to the Group by way of accelerated depreciation (100% capital allowances), stock relief and double tax relief (on overseas income on which foreign tax has already been paid), the amount of the Corporation Tax liability is restricted to the minimum amounts payable (Advance Corporation Tax), calculated by reference to dividend payments.

In overseas territories, the Group is liable both to taxes assessed on profits earned and to withholding taxes deducted from dividends and certain other remittances to the United Kingdom. In the US and South Africa, substantial tax reliefs are available by way of investment incentives including accelerated depreciation, as a result of which the liabilities in those countries are minimal. In the US, the benefit of certain otherwise unused depreciation allowances were effectively sold for a cash sum during the year by means of leasing transactions entered into by Airco, Inc., under the United States Economic Recovery Tax Act of 1981. As a result the tax charge has been reduced by £8.3 million (1981: £2.2 million).

Deferred tax liabilities principally arising from the claiming of accelerated depreciation allowances are treated as described in accounting policy 10, page 20.

(b) Tax on profit on ordinary activities

	1982 £ million	1982 £ million	1981 £ million	1981 £ million
Payable in the United Kingdom:				
Advance Corporation Tax on dividends for the year	8.2		7.1	
Corporation Tax at 52% (1981: 52%) on profits after				
deducting all reliefs other than double tax relief	6.0		7.8	
Double tax relief	(6.0)		(7.8)	
Other provisions	0.9		—	
		9.1		7.1
Payable overseas:				
United States of America, at 46% (1981: 46%)	0.9		2.7	
Sale of tax benefits (United States)	(8.3)		(2.2)	
Australia, at 46% (1981: 46%)	8.7		10.8	
South Africa, at 46% (1981: 42%)	1.7		2.8	
Other countries	4.5		3.3	
		7.5		17.4
Total tax payable for the year (excluding				
related companies)		16.6		24.5
Provision for deferred tax				
United Kingdom	—		—	
Overseas	7.4		10.5	
		7.4		10.5
Tax charge arising in related companies		3.6		2.6
		27.6		37.6

Note 4 continued on opposite page

4 continued
(c) Deferred Tax
The amounts shown in the right hand column below represent the full potential liability of the Group in the event of the reversal of all timing differences in the UK and overseas, excluding any provision for tax that would have become payable in the event of the realisation of revalued assets (see (i) below). The amounts in the left hand column represent the amounts considered likely to become payable within the foreseeable future; these relate to certain overseas taxes. Any future liability in the UK is likely to be materially lower than 52% owing to the availability of relief for Advance Corporation Tax paid in prior years and available for offset against future liabilities.

	Provision for deferred tax in the accounts £ million	Full potential liability for deferred tax £ million
Arising from accelerated depreciation allowances	20.6	153.4
Other timing differences	3.9	29.2
Advance Corporation Tax available for offset	—	(33.3)
	24.5	**149.3**
Movement during the year:		
Balance at 1st October 1981	22.1	113.6
Exchange adjustments to opening balances	(1.4)	4.5
Arising during the year (see (ii) below)	7.4	28.6
Other movements	(3.6)	2.6
Balance at 30th September 1982	**24.5**	**149.3**

(i) In the event that revalued assets were to be entirely disposed of at their book value, additional potential deferred tax on such disposals would be approximately £138 million (1981: £128 million).
(ii) If provision for deferred tax were made on the basis of the full potential liability (excluding the amount in (i)), the tax charge for the year would be increased to £48.8 million (1981: £39.9 million).

5 EXTRAORDINARY ITEMS
Surpluses, net of losses and provisions, on disposals and closures of businesses.

	1982 £ million
Before tax	5.9
Tax	0.2
After tax	6.1

NOTES ON FINANCIAL STATEMENTS
(continued)

6 DIVIDENDS	1982		1981	
	pence per share	£ million	pence per share	£ million
Ordinary				
Interim, paid 5th October 1982	2.60	8.7	2.31	7.6
Proposed final, payable 5th April 1983	3.14	10.7	2.80	9.2
	5.74	19.4	5.11	16.8
Preference, paid 30th June and 31st December		0.1		0.1
		19.5		16.9

The amount payable on the proposed final dividend for 1982 has been based on the number of shares in issue at 30th September 1982, together with certain of the shares issued subsequent to the year end (see Note 22).

7 EARNINGS PER SHARE
The following amounts were used in computing the earnings per share shown in the Profit and Loss Account, page 12.

	Current Cost		Modified Historical Cost	
	1982 £ million	1981 £ million	1982 £ million	1981 £ million
(a) Earnings				
Group profit attributable to parent company				
(before extraordinary items)	67.0	47.3	64.5	46.3
Less Preference dividend	0.1	0.1	0.1	0.1
	66.9	47.2	64.4	46.2

			1982 million	1981 million
(b) Number of Ordinary shares				
undiluted			330.5	329.3
fully diluted			398.2	353.7

8 AUDIT FEES	1982 £ million	1981 £ million
Group	1.4	1.4
(Parent Company £52 000; 1981: £47 000)		

9 DIRECTORS

(a) Directors' Interests

The register kept by the Company for the purposes of Section 27 of the Companies Act 1967 shows that the directors of the Company and their families had the following interests (all beneficial) in the shares and debentures of the Company and its subsidiaries as at 1st October 1981 and 30th September 1982:

The BOC Group plc	at 30th September 1982 Ordinary		at 1st October 1981 Ordinary	
	Shares	**Other**	Shares	Other
Sir Leslie Smith	**60000**	**3268b**	60 000	3 268b
Paul Bosonnet	**19169**	**15000a**	15 465	15000a
		11488b		13945b
		171430c		
David J Craig	**31774**	**13327b**	31 400	13327b
		200000c		
		£875d		£875d
Jim Davidson	**500**		500	
Ian Fraser	**20312**		20 312	
Richard V Giordano	**64698**	**400000c**	69 318	
R C Hesketh-Jones	**51102**		54 052	
Robert Malpas	**13000**	**£250d**	13 000	£250d
Crocker Nevin	**500**		500	
David Pitts	**500**	**35000a**	500	35 000a
		60000c		
Donald Reich	**8448**		8 068	
Michael Shanks	**625**	**£156d**	625	£156d
Dick Taverne	**14000**	**£2500d**	10 000	£2 500d

Subsidiary companies:
The Commonwealth Industrial Gases Ltd

Jim Davidson	**53361**		53 361	

New Zealand Industrial Gases Ltd

Jim Davidson	**—**		236	
David Pitts	**165**		165	

All interests are in fully paid Ordinary Shares unless marked 'a' which are 5% paid or 'b' which are options under the Savings-Related Share Option Scheme or 'c' which are options under the Senior Executives' Share Option Scheme or 'd' which are 9% Convertible Unsecured Loan Stock 2001/06.

Between 1st October 1982 and 15th December 1982 the directors' interests as shown above remained unchanged. No director has a beneficial interest in any other debentures or preference shares of the Company or in any debentures or preference shares of any subsidiary company. No loans were made to the directors during the year nor were any such loans outstanding at any time during the year. Apart from the above and apart from service agreements which are dealt with in accordance with The Stock Exchange Listing Agreement, no director has had any material interest in any contract with the Company or its subsidiaries, requiring disclosure under Section 54 of the Companies Act 1980. The following information on certain related party transactions is given, although its disclosure falls outside the requirements of the Companies Acts 1948 to 1981 since the beneficial interests of the individuals concerned in the transactions are not material:

The Company has paid underwriting commissions and fees to Lazard Brothers & Co Limited ('Lazards') in connection with the issue in September 1982 of the 12¼% Unsecured Loan Stock 2012/17. Mr I J Fraser is Chairman of the Board of directors of Lazards.

Note 9 continued overleaf

THE BOC GROUP plc

NOTES ON FINANCIAL STATEMENTS
(continued)

9 (a) continued

Drexel Burnham Lambert Inc. ('Drexel'), investment bankers of New York, have received fees in connection with the acquisition of the Group's interests in Glasrock Medical Services Corp. and Mountain Medical Equipment Inc. Mr C Nevin is a managing director of Drexel.

Two directors, Mr R V Giordano and Mr D J Craig, who are US citizens, and an officer temporarily seconded to the UK occupy houses in London which are owned by the Group. In each case, the occupant pays to the Company a full market rent assessed by an independent firm of property valuers, and accordingly derives no financial benefit.

(b) Directors' Emoluments

	1982 £	1981 £
The emoluments of directors of the parent company (including payments to non-UK resident directors) were:		
Fees as directors	67 000	48 700
Management remuneration (including pension contributions)	1 898 700	1 664 200
Payment to past directors and their dependants	68 300	44 700
	2 034 000	1 757 600

	1982 £	1981 £
Fees, salaries and taxable benefits included in the above amounts of total emoluments were:		
Paid by parent company for duties in the UK	652 200	599 400
Paid by overseas subsidiaries for duties outside the UK	930 000	740 300
	1 582 200	1 339 700

	1982	1981
Fees, salaries and taxable benefits were divided between the Chairman and directors as follows:		
Chairman	122 000	121 000
Highest paid director (R V Giordano)	579 000	477 100
Other directors:	number	number
£5 001 to £10 000	–	1
£10 001 to £15 000	4	3
£15 001 to £20 000	1	2
£25 001 to £30 000	1	1
£40 001 to £45 000	1	1
£90 001 to £95 000	–	1
£100 001 to £105 000	1	1
£105 001 to £110 000	1	–
£185 001 to £190 000	–	1
£215 001 to £220 000	–	1
£225 001 to £230 000	1	–
£300 001 to £305 000	1	–

Directors' remuneration includes £242 800 (of which £118 700 relates to Mr R V Giordano) of benefits arising under the Airco Earnings Performance Unit Plan. The entitlement to these benefits was awarded in 1978 when Mr Giordano was president of Airco and had no executive office at the BOC Group Centre, and matured on 30th September 1982. Mr Giordano has no further participation in the Plan.

Other changes in remuneration of directors are attributable to bonus awards, based on the company's financial performance, determined in accordance with a plan administered by the Management Resources Committee of the Board (all of whose members are non-executive directors), increases in salary for the financial year, and exchange translation effects on remuneration payable in currencies other than sterling.

10 EMPLOYEES

(a) Average number of employees by business

	1982		1981	
	Year end	Average	Year end	Average
Industrial gases and cryogenic plant	15 290	15 750	15 950	15 980
Health care	6 540	6 540	6 390	6 700
Carbon, graphite and carbide	2 730	2 980	3 200	3 110
Welding	7 650	8 340	9 060	9 370
Other businesses	5 910	5 750	5 730	5 010
Corporate	240	240	230	200
Continuing businesses	38 360	39 600	40 560	40 370
Discontinued businesses	10	820	1 570	2 980
	38 370	40 420	42 130	43 350

	1982	1981
(b) Employment costs	**£ million**	£ million
Wages and salaries	381.9	366.7
Social security costs	39.6	37.3
Other pension costs	25.3	25.8
	446.8	429.8

	1982	1981
(c) Emoluments of UK Employees	**number**	number

The emoluments of senior Group employees of the Company
and its UK resident subsidiaries were:

£20 001 to £25 000	59	42
£25 001 to £30 000	20	15
£30 001 to £35 000	12	9
£35 001 to £40 000	8	4
£40 001 to £45 000	4	3
£45 001 to £50 000	6	4
£50 001 to £55 000	2	—
£55 001 to £60 000	1	—
£60 001 to £65 000	3	—
£85 001 to £90 000	1	—

(d) Loans to officers
At 30th September 1982 a loan of £26 600 was outstanding to a UK employee who is regarded as an officer of the Company.

THE BOC GROUP plc

NOTES ON FINANCIAL STATEMENTS
(continued)

11 **FIXED ASSETS** – Tangible assets

(a) Group	Total £ million	Land and buildings £ million	Plant machinery and vehicles £ million	Cylinders £ million	Construction in progress £ million
GROSS BOOK VALUE					
At 1st October 1981	2 121.0	331.2	1 334.5	385.0	70.3
Change in accounting policy	7.3	1.3	5.6	—	0.4
Amounts restated	2 128.3	332.5	1 340.1	385.0	70.7
Exchange adjustment	17.1	5.9	17.6	(8.3)	1.9
Owned by subsidiaries acquired (net)	2.8	—	0.6	1.1	1.1
Capital expenditure	221.7	18.8	123.3	21.2	58.4
Transfers between categories	—	2.2	5.9	0.6	(8.7)
Revaluations	52.3	(6.5)	48.6	10.7	(0.5)
Disposals	(45.3)	(7.2)	(32.8)	(5.3)	—
At 30th September 1982	**2 376.9**	**345.7**	**1 503.3**	**405.0**	**122.9**
DEPRECIATION					
At 1st October 1981	975.5	70.9	723.7	180.9	—
Change in accounting policy	0.2	—	0.2		—
Amounts restated	975.7	70.9	723.9	180.9	—
Exchange adjustment	8.3	3.0	10.4	(5.1)	—
Owned by subsidiaries acquired (net)	(1.1)	—	(1.2)	0.1	—
Provided during the year	122.6	10.5	95.0	17.1	—
Transfers between categories	—	(0.2)	(0.2)	0.4	—
Revaluations	29.0	(1.9)	26.2	4.7	—
Disposals	(35.2)	(1.0)	(30.6)	(3.6)	—
At 30th September 1982	**1 099.3**	**81.3**	**823.5**	**194.5**	**—**
NET BOOK VALUE 30th September 1982					
Owned assets	1 242.4	263.3	649.7	206.5	122.9
Leased assets	35.2	1.1	30.1	4.0	—
	1 277.6	**264.4**	**679.8**	**210.5**	**122.9**

Capital expenditure includes interest capitalised of £7.1 million (1981: £3.5 million). Depreciation provided during the year includes amortisation of capitalised interest amounting to £0.6 million (1981: £0.2 million). Net book value includes total interest capitalised (net of amounts amortised) of £14.2 million (1981: £7.1 million).

Note 11 continued on opposite page

11 (a) continued

Parent	Total £ million	Land and buildings £ million	Plant machinery and vehicles £ million	Construction in progress £ million
GROSS BOOK VALUE				
At 1st October 1981	60.3	14.2	46.1	—
Capital expenditure	4.0	1.2	0.7	2.1
Transfers from Group companies (net)	2.5	2.5	—	—
Revaluations	(4.1)	(4.3)	0.2	—
Disposals	(3.4)	(2.4)	(1.0)	—
At 30th September 1982	59.3	11.2	46.0	2.1
DEPRECIATION				
At 1st October 1981	19.6	0.8	18.8	—
Provided during the year	2.4	0.3	2.1	—
Transfers from Group companies (net)	0.1	—	0.1	—
Revaluations	(0.2)	(0.2)	—	—
Disposals	(0.7)	—	(0.7)	—
At 30th September 1982	21.2	0.9	20.3	—
NET BOOK VALUE 30th September 1982	38.1	10.3	25.7	2.1

(b) Land and buildings

	GROUP £ million	PARENT £ million
The net book value of land and buildings at 30th September 1982 comprised:		
Freehold property	230.9	2.1
Leasehold property - long term	26.1	8.2
- short term	7.4	—
	264.4	10.3

(c) Asset revaluations
During the year, most Group fixed assets were revalued on current cost principles. The amounts for plant and machinery were established either on a replacement cost basis (by the use of known replacement costs and/or appropriate price indices, with appropriate allowance for age and condition), or, if lower, by reference to economic value; in the case of tonnage supply schemes this is usually equivalent to existing book value based on historical costs. In the case of certain overseas territories it is not practicable to depart from historical cost figures. In the case of properties, the procedure varies according to the significance of individual sites. Major properties are revalued regularly, and adjusted between valuations, where appropriate, based on local property conditions. Minor properties are revalued less frequently, and some continue to be held at book values based on historical cost.

Note 11 continued overleaf

NOTES ON FINANCIAL STATEMENTS
(continued)

11(c) continued

Book values at 30th September 1982 were as follows:

	£ million
UK	
Major properties (and certain minor properties) revalued during 1982 by the Group Surveyor, Mr K R Pickett FRICS	55.3
Other minor properties	9.1
Overseas	
Major properties in US, stated at book values based on valuations in 1981 and indexed since	132.1
Other properties, stated at book values based on valuations	
– during 1982	10.8
– in earlier years	38.7
Minor properties	18.4
Total net book value of properties	264.4

The basis of valuations in 1982 was as follows:

(a) in the case of general purpose property, estimated purchase cost in the open market of similar property in existing use and condition;

(b) in the case of specialised properties, estimated current cost of site acquisition and erection less a depreciation deduction appropriate to age and condition.

	GROUP	
	1982	1981
(d) Analysis of depreciation charge	**£ million**	£ million
Depreciation on original cost	**80.6**	72.5
Additional depreciation on revaluations	**42.0**	39.4
Depreciation included in both modified historical cost and current cost accounts	**122.6**	111.9
Depreciation on leased assets included above	**5.6**	5.6
(e) Hire of plant, machinery and computers	**11.6**	10.4

(f) Capital commitments

At 30th September the directors had authorised capital expenditure on capital projects:

– against which orders had been placed	**68.9**	37.5
– authorised but not committed	**145.3**	179.1
	214.2	216.6

Note 11 continued on opposite page

11 continued

(g) Historical cost – Group	Total	Land and buildings	Plant machinery and vehicles	Cylinders	Construction in progress
GROSS BOOK VALUE	£ million	£ million	£ million	£ million	£ million
At 1st October 1981	1 307.4	205.5	831.7	199.9	70.3
Change in accounting policy	7.3	1.3	5.6	—	0.4
Amounts restated	1 314.7	206.8	837.3	199.9	70.7
At 30th September 1982	1 507.6	221.0	945.6	218.1	122.9
DEPRECIATION					
At 1st October 1981	517.4	53.2	390.5	73.7	—
Change in accounting policy	0.2	—	0.2	—	—
Amounts restated	517.6	53.2	390.7	73.7	—
At 30th September 1982	583.5	61.5	440.5	81.5	—
NET BOOK VALUE at 30th September 1982	924.1	159.5	505.1	136.6	122.9

12 FIXED ASSETS – Investments (subsidiary and related companies)	PARENT		
	Cost	Provision	Net
	£ million	£ million	£ million
At 1st October 1981	76.0	(1.3)	74.7
Acquisitions	0.5	—	0.5
Disposals	(7.9)	—	(7.9)
Utilised during the year	—	1.1	1.1
At 30th September 1982	68.6	(0.2)	68.4

	1982	1981
	£ million	£ million
Shares at cost, less amounts written off	68.4	74.7
Amounts owing to parent	301.6	210.4
	370.0	285.1
Less Amounts owing by parent	7.8	6.4
	362.2	278.7

NOTES ON FINANCIAL STATEMENTS
(continued)

13 FIXED ASSETS – Investments (related companies and other investments)
(a) The following companies are treated as related companies in accordance with accounting policy 1(b), page 17:

	Total issued share capital £ million	Group share of equity %
BOC-Nowsco International Ltd *Bermuda*	—	49
BOC-Nowsco Ltd *UK*	—	49
BOC-Nowsco Oilfield Services GmbH *Germany*	—	49
BOC-Nowsco (SE Asia) Pte Ltd *Singapore*	—	49
BOC-Nowsco Srl *Italy*	—	49
Consolidated Industrial Gases Inc *Philippines*	6.2	23
Datastream PLC *UK*	0.1	40
Hong Kong Oxygen & Acetylene Co Ltd *Hong Kong*	0.5	50
Indian Oxygen Ltd *India*	6.7	40
Industrial de Gases Hispano-Inglesa SA *Spain*	3.5	50
Industrial Gases Ltd *Nigeria*	4.6	30
Lien Hwa Commonwealth Corporation *Taiwan*	0.3	29
Malaysian Oxygen Bhd *Malaysia*	7.6	35
Nissan Edwards Shinku KK *Japan*	0.2	50
Singapore Oxygen Air Liquide Pte Ltd *Singapore*	11.3	50
Societa Vetri Speciali SpA *Italy*	1.2	50
Tanzania Oxygen Ltd *Tanzania*	0.4	40
Thai Industrial Gases Ltd *Thailand*	1.5	26
Thermit Welding (GB) Ltd *UK*	0.4	50
T.I.G. Trading Ltd *Thailand*	0.3	44
Zambia Oxygen Ltd *Zambia*	2.8	49

None of the above companies had any significant loan capital outstanding at 30th September 1982.

(b) The balance sheet value of related companies and other investments comprises:

	Related companies – Group share of net assets £ million	Other investments at cost £ million	Total £ million
At 1st October 1981	28.8	10.7	39.5
Change in accounting policy	4.7	—	4.7
Amounts restated	33.5	10.7	44.2
Exchange adjustment	(0.2)	(0.1)	(0.3)
Acquisitions	1.8	18.8	20.6
Disposals	—	(0.2)	(0.2)
Reclassification	—	2.6	2.6
Increase in net assets	6.8	—	6.8
At 30th September 1982	**41.9**	**31.8**	**73.7**

Note 13 continued on opposite page

13(b) continued Provisions against the above	Related companies £ million	Other investments £ million	Total £ million
At 1st October 1981	1.7	0.5	2.2
Change in accounting policy	5.4	—	5.4
Amounts restated	7.1	0.5	7.6
Provided during the year	1.5	—	1.5
Reclassification	—	(0.1)	(0.1)
Decrease in net assets	0.3	—	0.3
At 30th September 1982	8.9	0.4	9.3

	1982 £ million	1981 £ million
Total equity and other interests (net of provisions) *see analysis (c)*	64.4	36.6
Loans from Group companies (net)	7.0	7.3
	71.4	43.9

The cost of the investments in related companies amounted to £13.8 million (1981: £11.7 million).

(c) The total equity and other interests are analysed between listed and unlisted investments as follows:

Listed: The Stock Exchange, London	0.9	0.9
other stock exchanges	12.3	10.8
	13.2	11.7
Unlisted: equity at directors' valuation	42.7	18.7
others at directors' valuation	8.5	6.2
	64.4	36.6
Market value of listed investments	21.7	16.2

(d) Income from related companies and other fixed asset investments:

Listed securities	0.6	0.5
Unlisted securities	2.2	3.0
	2.8	3.5
Less Dividends received from related companies	1.6	2.5
Income from other fixed asset investments	1.2	1.0

14 SUBSIDIARY AND RELATED COMPANIES NOT CONSOLIDATED

In accordance with accounting policy 1(b), page 17, the directors consider it misleading to consolidate Uganda Oxygen Ltd (a subsidiary company). Also in accordance with accounting policy 1(b), Glasrock Medical Services Corp., and Mountain Medical Equipment Inc., have not been accounted for on an equity basis as significant commercial and financial influence did not exist at 30th September 1982.

In accordance with accounting policy 1(d), page 18, the profits of certain other subsidiary and related companies have been consolidated only to the extent that they are remittable.

	1982 £ million	1981 £ million
The book value of net tangible assets excluded at 30th September amounted to	24.7	14.6
Profits before tax not consolidated	5.4	4.1
Group share of retained profits not consolidated	2.6	2.3

THE BOC GROUP plc

NOTES ON FINANCIAL STATEMENTS
(continued)

15 NET CURRENT ASSETS	GROUP		PARENT	
	1982	1981	1982	1981
CURRENT ASSETS	£ million	£ million	£ million	£ million
Stocks				
raw materials	74.3	76.6	—	—
work in progress	110.4	95.2	—	—
gases and other finished goods for resale	139.3	131.1	—	—
payments on account	(21.9)	(28.1)	—	—
	302.1	274.8	—	—
Debtors				
trade debtors	230.3	238.2	—	—
current accounts with subsidiary companies	—	—	0.4	0.9
other debtors	40.6	61.3	0.6	2.4
prepayments and accrued income	17.3	10.8	1.1	0.3
	288.2	310.3	2.1	3.6
Deposits at short call	31.4	14.3	10.3	4.7
Cash at bank and in hand	6.4	12.2	0.3	—
	628.1	611.6	12.7	8.3
CREDITORS: Amounts falling due within one year				
Loans other than from banks	16.6	17.8	—	—
Bank loans and overdrafts	90.4	37.8	19.2	9.3
Obligations under finance leases	2.7	2.9	—	—
	109.7	58.5	19.2	9.3
Deposits and advance payments by customers	17.6	24.9	—	—
Trade creditors	97.8	110.8	—	—
Current accounts with subsidiary companies	—	—	2.5	1.1
Bills of exchange payable	3.3	7.9	—	—
Payroll and other taxes, including social security	11.7	13.4	0.1	—
Taxation – United Kingdom	7.3	7.6	9.5	7.6
– Overseas	21.6	22.8	—	—
Ordinary dividends – interim	8.7	7.6	8.7	7.6
– proposed final	10.7	9.2	10.7	9.2
Other creditors	69.8	74.9	1.8	2.7
Accruals and deferred income	41.5	27.6	4.1	3.5
	399.7	365.2	56.6	41.0
NET CURRENT ASSETS (LIABILITIES)	228.4	246.4	(43.9)	(32.7)
Stocks on a current cost basis	305.6	278.5	—	—
Stocks include the following amounts relating to long term contracts:				
work in progress	16.9	29.9	—	—
payments on account	(15.1)	(26.2)	—	—
Other debtors include amounts falling due after one year of	13.6	12.1	—	—
Trade debtors are net of provisions for doubtful debts of	12.4	8.5	—	—

Details of overdrafts, loans and finance leases are given in Note 3.

16 CREDITORS: Amounts falling due after more than one year	GROUP		PARENT	
	1982	1981	**1982**	1981
	£ million	£ million	**£ million**	£ million
Loans other than from banks	**255.1**	153.3	**128.5**	107.8
Bank loans and overdrafts	**250.0**	316.7	**10.0**	5.0
Obligations under finance leases	**12.3**	14.2	—	—
	517.4	484.2	**138.5**	112.8
Advance payments from customers under long-term supply contracts	**8.8**	7.2	—	—
Deferred income – Regional Development Grants	**7.0**	8.0	**3.8**	4.0
	533.2	499.4	**142.3**	116.8

Details of overdrafts, loans and finance leases are given in Note 3.

17 PROVISIONS FOR LIABILITIES AND CHARGES		Provided	Other	
	1982	in the year	movements	1981
	£ million	£ million	£ million	£ million
Pension and similar obligations	**7.6**	(0.4)	1.0	7.0
Deferred tax (Note 4)	**24.5**	7.4	(5.0)	22.1
Provision for unremittable profits in overseas subsidiaries (see accounting policy 1(d), page 18)	**14.0**	1.2	(0.4)	13.2
Other	**12.1**	(1.1)	—	13.2
	58.2	7.1	(4.4)	55.5

18 CAPITAL AND RESERVES
(a) Called up share capital

(i) Authorised and issued share capital	AUTHORISED		ALLOTTED AND ISSUED	
(a) Number of shares	**1982**	1981	**1982**	1981
	million	million	**million**	million
Ordinary shares of 25p each	**331.5**	329.4	**331.5**	329.4
Unclassified shares of 25p each	**218.5**	120.6	—	—
4.55% Cumulative preference shares of £1 each	**0.5**	0.5	**0.5**	0.5
3.5% Cumulative second preference shares of £1 each	**1.0**	1.0	**1.0**	1.0
2.8% Cumulative second preference shares of £1 each	**1.0**	1.0	**1.0**	1.0
(b) Nominal value of shares	**£ million**	£ million	**£ million**	£ million
ORDINARY				
Ordinary shares of 25p each	**82.9**	82.3	**82.9**	82.3
Unclassified shares of 25p each	**54.6**	30.2	—	—
	137.5	112.5	**82.9**	82.3
PREFERENCE				
4.55% Cumulative preference shares of £1 each	**0.5**	0.5	**0.5**	0.5
3.5% Cumulative second preference shares of £1 each	**1.0**	1.0	**1.0**	1.0
2.8% Cumulative second preference shares of £1 each	**1.0**	1.0	**1.0**	1.0
	2.5	2.5	**2.5**	2.5
Total	**140.0**	115.0	**85.4**	84.8

Note 18 continued overleaf

41

NOTES ON
FINANCIAL
STATEMENTS
(continued)

18(a)*(i)* continued
All Ordinary shares are fully paid except for 77 500 (1981: 97 500) shares which are 5% paid.
At 15th December 1982, Prudential Corporation plc had an interest in 18 077 887 Ordinary shares of 25p each representing 5.07% of the issued capital. The directors of The BOC Group plc are not aware of any other interests of 5% or more in the Ordinary share capital.

(ii) Issues of shares
During the year:
(a) 20 000 5% paid Ordinary shares of 25p each were fully paid up under the Share Incentive Scheme.
(b) 566 405 Ordinary shares of 25p each were issued under the Savings-Related Share Option Scheme.
(c) 1 564 371 Ordinary shares of 25p each were issued as the final consideration for the acquisition of shares in Software Sciences International Ltd.

Subsequent to the year end, 54 429 158 Ordinary shares have been issued or provisionally allotted in connection with three acquisitions, details of which are given in Note 22.

(iii) 9% Convertible Unsecured Loan Stock 2001/06
Each £100 of Stock will be convertible, during the month of March in any of the years 1985 to 2001, into 74 Ordinary shares of 25p each. Full conversion would require the issue of 60 682 370 Ordinary shares.

(iv) Savings-Related Share Option Scheme
Of the unissued shares, 14 130 404 Ordinary shares were, at 30th September 1982, reserved for the Savings-Related Share Option Scheme approved by shareholders in 1976. At 30th September 1982, options under that Scheme were outstanding in respect of a total of 6 767 159 Ordinary shares, and are exercisable at dates between 1st October 1982 and 31st October 1989 at prices ranging from 47½p to 148p per share.

(v) Senior Executives' Share Option Scheme
Of the unissued shares, 8 300 000 Ordinary shares were, at 30th September 1982, reserved for the Senior Executives' Share Option Scheme approved by shareholders on 30th July 1982. At 30th September 1982 options under that Scheme were outstanding in respect of a total of 2 262 790 Ordinary shares and are exercisable at dates between 8th September 1986 and 8th September 1989 at 200p per share.

(b) Reserves Movements on reserves during the year were as follows: *(i) Modified Historical Cost* GROUP	Share Premium Account £ million	Revaluation Reserve £ million	Other Capital Reserves £ million	Profit and Loss Account £ million	Related Companies' Reserves £ million
Balance at 1st October 1981	44.3	372.9	10.6	259.1	15.4
Changes in accounting policies	—	—	—	0.6	(0.7)
Amounts restated	44.3	372.9	10.6	259.7	14.7
Exchange adjustment	—	10.5	0.3	13.3	0.1
Retained earnings	—	—	—	48.5	2.6
Transfer in respect of additional depreciation – current year	—	(39.0)	—	39.0	—
– prior years	—	(41.5)	—	41.5	—
Asset revaluation surplus (net of minorities)	—	17.6	—	—	1.2
Reserves reclassified	—	3.1	0.7	(3.8)	—
Premium on share issue	1.3	—	—	—	—
Balance at 30th September 1982	**45.6**	**323.6**	**11.6**	**398.2**	**18.6**

Note 18 continued on opposite page

18(b) *(i)* continued	Share Premium Account £ million	Revaluation Reserve £ million	Other Capital Reserves £ million	Profit and Loss Account £ million
PARENT				
Balance at 1st October 1981	44.3	1.4	15.5	23.9
Retained earnings	—	—	—	46.2
Asset revaluation deficit	—	(3.9)	—	—
Reserves reclassified	—	2.5	—	(2.5)
Premium on share issue	1.3	—	—	—
Balance at 30th September 1982	**45.6**	**—**	**15.5**	**67.6**

	Share Premium Account £ million	Revaluation Reserve £ million	Other Reserves		Profit and Loss Account £ million	Related Companies' Reserves £ million
			Current Cost Reserve £ million	Other Capital Reserves £ million		
(ii) Current Cost						
GROUP						
Balance at 1st October 1981	44.3	376.4	45.9	7.1	216.7	15.4
Changes in accounting policies	—	—	—	—	0.6	(0.7)
Amounts restated	44.3	376.4	45.9	7.1	217.3	14.7
Exchange adjustment	—	10.5	1.1	0.3	12.0	0.1
Retained earnings	—	—	—	—	50.9	2.6
Transfer in respect of additional depreciation – current year	—	(39.0)	39.0	—	—	—
– prior years	—	(41.5)	41.5	—	—	—
Realised stock holding gains	—	—	16.5	—	—	—
Monetary working capital adjustment	—	—	5.5	—	—	—
Gearing adjustment	—	—	(24.4)	—	—	—
Asset revaluation surplus (including stocks)	—	17.6	—	—	—	1.2
Reserves reclassified	—	2.9	(1.6)	4.2	(5.5)	—
Premium on share issue	1.3	—	—	—	—	—
Balance at 30th September 1982	**45.6**	**326.9**	**123.5**	**11.6**	**274.7**	**18.6**

The undistributed profits of Group companies overseas may be liable to overseas taxes and/or UK taxation (after allowing for double tax relief) if distributed as dividends. There are exchange control restrictions in certain countries on the remittance of funds to the UK. Provision has been made against those dividends declared by overseas companies currently 'blocked'.

NOTES ON
FINANCIAL
STATEMENTS
(continued)

19 CONTINGENT LIABILITIES AND BANK GUARANTEES

	GROUP £ million	PARENT £ million
Guarantees in respect of related companies' borrowings	3.9	3.9
Other guarantees and contingent liabilities	8.1	0.1
	12.0	4.0

The parent company has guaranteed bank borrowings of certain wholly-owned subsidiaries amounting to £188.7 million and a further £9.6 million in respect of partly-owned subsidiaries.

Various Group companies are parties to legal actions and claims which arise in the ordinary course of business, some of which are for substantial amounts. While the outcome of some of these matters cannot readily be foreseen, the directors believe that they will be disposed of without material effect on the net asset position as shown in these accounts.

20 PENSION OBLIGATIONS

The Group's pension schemes, referred to in accounting policy 13, page 21, cover all of the Group's material obligations to provide pensions to its retired employees and the current workforce. Accounts for these schemes are prepared separately by the trustees and circulated in accordance with local requirements.

Based on the most recent actuarial valuations of the Airco pension funds (primarily January 1981) the total unfunded actuarial liability was approximately US$41 million; the liability is being funded out of annual profits on an actuarial basis calculated over a period of 30 years. At the time of the acquisition of Airco a provision of US$27 million was made (following US accounting practice) in respect of the unfunded vested obligations of the Airco pension funds at that date; this amount is being released to profit and loss account over a period of 15 years, and the remaining balance of the provision is included in Provisions for Liabilities and Charges (Note 17).

Based on the latest actuarial valuation of the UK pension funds (completed in January 1981, with respect to the position at April 1978) and the actuarial valuations of the Australian and South African pension funds (with respect to the positions at June 1980 and June 1981 respectively), the present funding arrangements are considered satisfactory, and adequate to meet the future liabilities of these funds.

21 AMOUNTS INCLUDED IN CONSOLIDATED STATEMENT OF SOURCES AND APPLICATIONS OF FUNDS – supplementary information

	1982		1981	
(a) Acquisitions and disposals of businesses	Acquisitions £ million	Disposals £ million	Acquisitions £ million	Disposals £ million

The outflow of funds arising on the acquisitions of businesses and the inflow of funds arising on the disposals of businesses were applied to:

	Acquisitions	Disposals	Acquisitions	Disposals
Tangible fixed assets	(8.6)	6.3	(6.1)	1.2
Goodwill	—	6.0	(1.0)	—
Related companies and other fixed asset investments	(22.3)	1.1	(4.0)	1.2
Stocks	(0.2)	6.4	(3.9)	1.5
Debtors	(0.1)	11.2	(1.8)	2.4
Creditors (including taxation)	0.1	(5.6)	2.2	(2.9)
Other	(0.1)	0.1	(0.2)	(0.4)
	(31.2)	25.5	(14.8)	3.0

Note 21 continued on opposite page

21 continued		1982	1981
(b) Net change in borrowings		£ million	£ million
Long and medium term borrowings		(27.1)	18.9
Short term borrowings		(59.3)	1.4
Cash and deposits		10.7	13.2
		(75.7)	33.5

22 SUBSEQUENT EVENTS

Since the year end the Group has entered into three separate transactions for the acquisitions of businesses, all of which have involved the issue of Ordinary shares as part or full payment of the consideration.

On 1st October 1982 the Group acquired three industrial gas businesses in South America for £20.3 million. The consideration, which has still to be finally determined, consists primarily of the issue of 7 929 158 Ordinary shares which will rank for the final dividend for 1982.

On 19th October 1982 the Group agreed to acquire the home medical business of Glasrock Medical Services Corp., and its 26% stake in Mountain Medical Equipment Inc., for US$76 million, the surrender of the Glasrock shares already held by the Group and the assumption of certain liabilities. The consideration has not yet been finally determined, but a provisional allotment of 29 000 000 Ordinary shares has been made. These shares will not rank for the final dividend for 1982.

On 15th November 1982 the Group increased its stake in Osaka Sanso Kogyo KK, a major Japanese industrial gases company. The investment by the Group involved the subscription for new shares and for a convertible bond, and has been covered by the issue of 17 500 000 Ordinary shares which will not rank for the final dividend for 1982.

23 PROFIT AND LOSS ACCOUNT OF THE PARENT COMPANY

In accordance with the concession granted under section 149 (6) of the Companies Act 1948 (as amended), the profit and loss account of The BOC Group plc has not been separately presented in these financial statements. The amount of the consolidated profit for the financial year is attributable as follows:

Current Cost			Modified Historical Cost	
1981	1982		1982	1981
£ million	£ million		£ million	£ million
20.0	65.7	parent company	65.7	20.0
23.1	3.1	subsidiary companies	0.7	22.1
4.8	4.2	related companies	4.2	4.8
47.9	73.0		70.6	46.9

GROUP COMPANIES

The following subsidiaries carry on businesses, the results of which, in the opinion of the directors, principally affect the amount of the profit or the amount of the assets of the Group:
African Oxygen Ltd
Airco, Inc.
BOC Ltd
The Commonwealth Industrial Gases Ltd

A comprehensive list of the Group operating companies and certain financing companies is detailed below. All shares held are ordinary shares. Companies are held either by The BOC Group plc or through other operating companies or through wholly-owned companies formed for the convenient holding of shares in certain subsidiary or related companies.

The percentage Group Holdings shown below represent the ultimate interest of The BOC Group plc.

The auditors of The BOC Group plc are Coopers & Lybrand.
Certain subsidiary and related companies, accounting for approximately 46% of the Group's turnover and 48% of Group's gross assets, are audited by firms other than Coopers & Lybrand (principally Deloitte, Haskins & Sells) and are indicated by an asterisk.

	Group Holding %		Group Holding %
AUSTRALIA		GERMANY	
The Commonwealth Industrial Gases Ltd	57	*BOC-Nowsco Oilfield Services GmbH	49
		*Edwards Kniese & Co Hochvakuum GmbH	88
BANGLADESH		*Heimsyphon GmbH	100
*Bangladesh Oxygen Ltd	60		
		HONG KONG	
BERMUDA		Hong Kong Oxygen & Acetylene Co Ltd	50
*BOC-Nowsco International Ltd	49		
Priestley Insurance Company Ltd	100	INDIA	
		*Indian Oxygen Ltd	40
BRAZIL			
*Brasox Industria e Comercio Ltda	100	INDONESIA	
*Edwards do Brasil Ltda	100	*P.T. Industrial Gases Indonesia	29
		*P.T. Krama Yudha Commonwealth	40
CANADA			
Canadian Oxygen Ltd	100	IRELAND	
		Irish Industrial Gases Ltd	100
COLOMBIA			
Gases Industriales de Colombia SA		ITALY	
(acquired October 1982)	100	*BOC-Nowsco Srl	49
		Edwards Alto Vuoto SpA	100
DENMARK		Saccab SpA	100
A/S Kulsyre & Tørisfabriken 'Union'	100	*Societa Vetri Speciali SpA	50
FIJI		JAPAN	
CIG Fiji Ltd	50	*Daisan – BOC Ltd	51
		*KK Japan Helium Center	40
FINLAND		*Kokusai Tansan KK	45
Suomen Viggo Oy	100	Nippon BOC KK	100
		Nissan Edwards Shinku KK	50
FRANCE		*Osaka Sanso Kogyo KK (acquired November 1982)	43
Assistance Technique Médicale SA	100		
*Cryostar-France SA	100	KENYA	
SBS SA	100	East African Oxygen Ltd	66
Viggo France Sarl	100		

	Group Holding %		Group Holding %
MALAWI		SWITZERLAND	
Industrial Gases Ltd	45	*Airco Helex AG	100
		*Cryostar AG	100
MALAYSIA			
Malaysian Oxygen Bhd	35	TAIWAN	
		Lien Hwa Commonwealth Corporation	29
MAURITIUS			
*Les Gaz Industriels Ltee	21	TANZANIA	
		Tanzania Oxygen Ltd	40
NETHERLANDS			
*Airco Temescal BV	100	THAILAND	
British Oxygen Finance BV	100	*Thai Industrial Gases Ltd	26
		*T.I.G. Trading Ltd	44
NETHERLANDS ANTILLES (ARUBA)			
Antilles Industrial Gases NV *(acquired October 1982)*	50	UGANDA	
		Uganda Oxygen Ltd	66
NEW ZEALAND			
New Zealand Industrial Gases Ltd	61	UNITED KINGDOM	
		BOC Investments Ltd	100
NIGERIA		BOC Ltd	100
*Industrial Gases Ltd	30	BOC-Linde Refrigeration Ltd	25
		*BOC-Nowsco Ltd	49
NORWAY		BOC Overseas Finance Ltd	100
Odda Smelteverk A/S	100	BOC Technologies Ltd	100
		BOC Transhield Ltd	100
PAKISTAN		British Medical Data Systems Ltd	51
*Pakistan Oxygen Ltd	60	Cryoplants Ltd	100
		*Datastream PLC	40
PAPUA NEW GUINEA		G L Baker (Transport) Ltd	100
CIG Bougainville Pty Ltd	42	The Medishield Corporation Ltd	100
CIG Papua New Guinea Pty Ltd	42	*The Oxford Instruments Group Ltd	16
		Thermit Welding (GB) Ltd	50
PHILIPPINES			
Consolidated Industrial Gases Inc	23	USA	
Philippine Welding Equipment Inc	57	*Airco, Inc.	100
		*Airco Energy Company Inc.	100
SINGAPORE		*Airco Superconductors Inc.	100
*BOC-Nowsco (SE Asia) Pte Ltd	49	*BOC Financial Corporation	100
Singapore Oxygen Air Liquide Pte Ltd	50	*Edwards High Vacuum Inc.	100
		*Fraser Harlake Inc.	100
SOUTH AFRICA		*Pioneer Viggo Inc.	100
African Oxygen Ltd	60		
Afrox Ltd	60	VENEZUELA	
*Dowson & Dobson Ltd	60	CA Gases Industriales de Venezuela	
Medishield (SA) Ltd	100	*(acquired October 1982)*	100
SOUTH WEST AFRICA (NAMIBIA)		WESTERN SAMOA	
South West African Oxygen (Pty) Ltd	60	*Samoa Industrial Gases Ltd	39
SPAIN		ZAMBIA	
BOC Medishield SA	100	Zambia Oxygen Ltd	49
Industrial de Gases Hispano-Inglesa SA	50		
		ZIMBABWE	
SWEDEN		Oxygen Industries (Pvt) Ltd	100
Mediada AB	100		
Viggo AB	100		

FIVE YEAR RECORD

All amounts are stated on the modified historical cost convention, as described in accounting policy 1(a), page 17. Summary financial information based on alternative accounting conventions to those used for the preparation of the financial statements is contained on pages 50 and 51. The 1980 and 1981 figures have been restated as a result of changes in accounting policies (see Note 2 of the Notes on financial statements).

	1978 £ million	1979 £ million	1980 £ million	1981 £ million	**1982 £ million**
Turnover					
continuing businesses	925.9	960.8	1 062.8	1 443.7	**1 506.6**
discontinued businesses	270.2	268.2	131.7	78.0	**27.6**
	1 196.1	1 229.0	1 194.5	1 521.7	**1 534.2**
Operating profit (see note 1 below)					
continuing businesses	94.2	91.7	102.8	137.4	**143.6**
discontinued businesses	3.8	12.3	(2.8)	1.7	**(0.4)**
	98.0	104.0	100.0	139.1	**143.2**
Trading profit	115.8	124.6	118.2	157.3	**160.8**
Airco adjustment (see note 2 below)	(18.4)	—	—	—	
Interest	(30.9)	(51.9)	(53.8)	(62.2)	**(58.2)**
Profit on ordinary activities before tax	66.5	72.7	64.4	95.1	**102.6**
Tax on profit on ordinary activities	(30.8)	(28.1)	(17.3)	(37.6)	**(27.6)**
Attributable to minority shareholders	(8.5)	(7.6)	(7.3)	(11.2)	**(10.5)**
Earnings	27.2	37.0	39.8	46.3	**64.5**
Extraordinary items	(2.9)	(2.0)	(10.6)	0.6	**6.1**
Profit for the financial year	24.3	35.0	29.2	46.9	**70.6**
Earnings per Ordinary share					
nil distribution basis	9.40p	13.21p	14.21p	16.17p	**21.91p**
net basis	8.45p	11.39p	12.18p	14.02p	**19.50p**
Ordinary Dividend per Share					
(including tax credit)	5.225p	6.0p	6.6p	7.3p	**8.2p**
Number of fully paid Ordinary shares in issue at the year end (millions)	321.2	324.3	326.1	329.3	**331.4**

1 Figures reflect the progressive revaluation of fixed assets undertaken since 1973 and the consequent charging of additional depreciation. The figures of profit and capital employed before 1980 are therefore not fully comparable from year to year. Operating profit is after charging depreciation on a current cost basis and excludes realised stock holding gains due to inflation.
2 Turnover, operating profit, trading profit and capital expenditure for 1978 included 100 per cent of Airco, Inc., for the full twelve months to 30th September 1978. The Airco adjustment then eliminated that part of Airco's trading profit attributable to outside shareholders in the period before Airco became a subsidiary.

	1978 £ million	1979 £ million	1980 £ million	1981 £ million	**1982 £ million**
Employment of Capital					
Fixed assets					
Tangible assets	820.4	808.0	899.7	1 152.6	**1 277.6**
Related companies and other investments	18.3	25.4	29.5	43.9	**71.4**
Working capital (excluding bank balances and short term loans)	274.3	234.4	244.0	278.4	**300.3**
	1 113.0	1 067.8	1 173.2	1 474.9	**1 649.3**
Capital employed					
Shareholders' capital and reserves	499.1	516.3	585.9	787.0	**883.0**
Minority shareholders' interests	68.6	64.0	79.4	101.0	**103.0**
	567.7	580.3	665.3	888.0	**986.0**
Non current liabilities and provisions	48.3	36.2	34.5	70.7	**74.0**
Net borrowings and finance leases (see Note 3, page 25 of the Notes on financial statements)	497.0	451.3	473.4	516.2	**589.3**
	1 113.0	1 067.8	1 173.2	1 474.9	**1 649.3**
Capital expenditure	133.5	132.2	137.3	155.8	**221.7**
Depreciation					
Historical cost basis	50.5	55.1	57.0	72.5	**80.6**
Additional	13.9	22.2	30.0	39.4	**42.0**
Charged against profit	64.4	77.3	87.0	111.9	**122.6**
Return on average capital employed (based on trading profit before Airco adjustment, interest and taxation)	10.4%*	11.4%	10.6%	11.9%	**10.3%**
Return on equity on a CCA basis (CCA earnings as a per cent of average shareholders' capital and reserves)	3.4%*	5.3%	6.5%	6.8%	**8.0%**
Net borrowings and finance leases as a per cent of capital employed	44.7%	42.3%	40.4%	35.0%	**35.7%**

*Based on year-end capital employed

Employee statistics (excluding related companies) numbers employed at 30th September					
United Kingdom	20 500	19 800	16 600	13 450	**11 100**
Overseas	35 000	28 800	28 100	28 680	**27 270**
	55 500	48 600	44 700	42 130	**38 370**

ALTERNATIVE ACCOUNTING CONVENTIONS

As explained in accounting policy 1(a), page 17, the financial statements present information on both the modified historical cost and the current cost accounting bases. For the convenience of readers accustomed to other accounting conventions, information is given below on the following bases:
(i) the historical cost convention (which differs from the modified historical cost

convention in that assets are stated by reference to their original cost)
(ii) the accounting conventions as applied in the United States of America (US Generally Accepted Accounting Principles).
Information presented under US GAAP deals, except where otherwise stated, with continuing operations only; profits and losses resulting from discontinued businesses are shown separately. Information presented on the UK historical cost basis follows the treatment described in accounting policy 1(c), page 18.

Consolidated Profit and loss accounts for the years ended 30th September

	Historical cost		US GAAP	
	1982	1981	1982	1981
	£ million	£ million	£ million	£ million
Turnover	1 534.2	1 521.7	1 476.2	1 308.8
Cost of sales	(860.8)	(825.0)	(827.0)	(697.9)
Gross profit	673.4	696.7	649.2	610.9
Operating expenses	(481.5)	(508.6)	(462.1)	(435.2)
Share of profits of related companies	9.7	7.6	9.7	7.3
Income from other fixed asset investments	1.2	1.0	1.2	1.0
Trading profit	202.8	196.7	198.0	184.0
Interest (net)	(58.2)	(62.2)	(57.8)	(59.1)
Profit on ordinary activities before tax	144.6	134.5	140.2	124.9
Tax on profit on ordinary activities	(27.6)	(37.6)	(57.8)	(32.7)
Minority interests	(13.4)	(14.2)	(13.4)	(13.6)
Income from continuing businesses			69.0	78.6
Discontinued businesses:				
Income from businesses up to dates of discontinuance			(0.7)	1.3
Profits (losses) on sale or closure			6.1	(2.5)
Earnings	103.6	82.7	74.4	77.4
Extraordinary items	6.1	0.6	—	—
Profit for the financial year (Net income)	109.7	83.3	74.4	77.4

Note: The profit and loss accounts presented on a US GAAP basis have been prepared by translating the profit and loss accounts of foreign subsidiaries at average exchange rates for the periods concerned. The difference between the consolidated profit for the financial year computed at average as opposed to closing rates has been taken directly to reserves.

Consolidated Balance sheets at 30th September

	Historical cost		US GAAP	
	1982	1981	1982	1981
	£ million	£ million	£ million	£ million
Fixed assets:				
Intangible assets (see Note below)	—	—	**33.7**	33.8
Tangible assets	**924.1**	797.1	**951.8**	823.8
Investments	**71.4**	43.9	**71.4**	43.9
Long term receivables	**13.6**	12.1	**13.6**	12.1
	1 009.1	853.1	**1 070.5**	913.6
Net current assets	**214.8**	234.3	**230.1**	247.5
Long term liabilities and provisions	**(591.4)**	(554.9)	**(690.4)**	(619.2)
	632.5	532.5	**610.2**	541.9
Capital and reserves:				
Called up share capital	**85.4**	84.8	**85.4**	84.8
Reserves	**474.0**	370.8	**452.0**	380.4
	559.4	455.6	**537.4**	465.2
Minority interests	**73.1**	76.9	**72.8**	76.7
	632.5	532.5	**610.2**	541.9

Note: Intangible fixed assets represent goodwill, which on a US GAAP basis is capitalised and amortised over 40 years.

Earnings per Ordinary share:				
undiluted				
nil distribution basis	**33.74p**	27.22p	**24.91p**	25.62p
net basis (after ACT written off)	**31.33p**	25.07p	**24.91p**	25.62p
fully diluted				
nil distribution basis	**30.01p**	26.07p	**22.68p**	24.57p
net basis (after ACT written off)	**27.60p**	23.91p	**22.68p**	24.57p
Depreciation (£ million)	**80.6**	72.5	**81.4**	61.0
Return on average capital employed (based on trading profit)	**16.8%**	19.5%	**15.5%**	17.3%
Return on equity	**20.8%**	21.1%	**14.9%**	19.2%
Net borrowings and finance leases as a per cent of capital employed	**45.5%**	46.1%	**42.9%**	43.3%

THE BOC GROUP plc

GENERAL INFORMATION

Analysis of Ordinary shareholdings at 30th September 1982

Size of holding 25p shares	Number of accounts	Per cent of total number of accounts	Number of 25p shares	Per cent of ordinary capital	Average holding 25p shares
1–500	17 300	36	4 419 395	1	255
501–1 000	10 631	22	8 030 196	3	755
1 001–5 000	17 551	37	37 451 405	11	2 134
5 001–50 000	2 012	4	23 099 584	7	11 481
50 001–1 000 000	427	1	97 431 797	29	228 178
Over 1 000 000	63	—	160 985 070	49	2 555 319
	47 984	100	331 417 447	100	

Capital Gains Tax

For capital gains tax purposes the market values of The BOC Group plc ordinary shares, preference shares and loan stocks at 6th April 1965 were:

Ordinary shares of 25p	45.3125p	
4.55% Cum pref shares (formerly 6¼%)	98.75p	(£1 units)
3.5% Cum 2nd pref shares (formerly 5%)	72.5p	(£1 units)
2.8% Cum 2nd pref shares (formerly 4%)	56.25p	(£1 units)
5¾% Debenture stock 1981/86:	£87	
6¾% Debenture stock 1985/90:		
fully paid	£99½	
£50 paid	£51½	

The Company is not a close company within the meaning of the Income and Corporation Taxes Act 1970 and subsequent legislation. There has been no change in that status since 30th September 1982.

FINANCIAL CALENDAR

Dividend and interest payments

Ordinary shares
Interim announced May, paid October
Final proposed December, paid April

Preference shares
Paid half yearly, 30th June and 31st December

Debenture stocks
5¾% and 6¾% Debenture Stocks:
Paid half yearly, 15th May and 15th November
9% and 11½% Tonnage Debenture Stocks:
Paid half yearly, 15th June and 15th December

9% *Convertible Unsecured Loan Stock*
Paid half yearly, 2nd January and 2nd July

12¼% *Unsecured Loan Stock*
Paid half yearly, 2nd April and 2nd October

Announcement of Group results

Three months' results, February
Half year's results, May
Nine months' results, August
Year's results, December
Report and Accounts, January

Appendix B

Sources of Comparative Statistics and Data

The leading organization producing comparative statistics and data is the Centre for Interfirm Comparison (a non-profit undertaking jointly established by the British Institute of Management and the British Productivity Council). The Centre's main activity is the conduct of inter-firm comparisons as a service to management; it also advises on the use of management ratios within companies. It carries out comparative surveys and research activities in the field of performance assessment. For further information: Centre for Interfirm Comparison, 8 West Stockwell Street, Colchester, Essex CO1 1HN (telephone: 0206 62274), or 25 Bloomsbury Square, London WC1A 2PJ (telephone: 01-637 8406).

One of the principal commercial organizations producing individual business ratio reports for each of a wide range of industrial sectors is Inter Company Comparisons Ltd. The reports present details of profitability, liquidity and efficiency ratios for the principal companies operating in each industry. For further information: Inter Company Comparisons Ltd, ICC House, 81 City Road, London EC1Y 1BD (telephone: 01-253 0063).

Other companies active in the field of comparative information provision include the following: Datastream International PLC, Atlas House, 1 King Street, London EC2V 8DU (telephone: 01-600 6411); Extel Statistical Services Ltd, 37-45 Paul Street, London EC2A 4PB (telephone: 01-253 3400); Jordan & Sons Ltd, 47 Brunswick Place, London N1 6EE (telephone: 01-253 3030).

In addition to these services, there are several annual or regular directories and yearbooks that contain valuable financial, organizational and statistical data on relevant companies. *The Times 1000* is an annual publication giving details of the turnover and capital employed, profit margin and return on total capital employed ratios (in addition to a considerable amount of other information) for each of the 1,000 largest British industrial and commercial companies, and for a wide range of financial institutions. *The Stock Exchange Official Year Book* is an annual publication giving full corporate and financial information on all companies listed on the Stock Exchange, including a summarized balance sheet and capital formation details for each company. The Institute of Chartered Accountants in England and Wales issues an annual survey of published accounts, recently re-titled *Financial Reporting*, which reports the results of detailed analyses of the reporting practices of a sample of 300 large industrial and commercial companies.

Government statistical bulletins and digests are useful sources of aggregated financial and performance data. The *Business Monitor* series provides information on a wide range of financial and industrial sectors, while the monthly *Financial Statistics* and the annual *Company Finance* digests provide aggregate balance sheet, profit and loss account, funds statement, and capital formation data for industrial and commercial companies.

Finally, the directories, yearbooks and member publications of professional associations and trade bodies frequently provide financial and organizational information on their members and their activities. There are a considerable number of national and international directories and guides listing 'key' or sizeable enterprises; these entries are usually restricted to basic organizational and product information, but they form useful starting points for identifying appropriate companies and their activities.

In terms of examining the actual published annual reports and accounts of individual companies, a number of the larger municipal libraries throughout the United Kingdom maintain up-to-date collections of annual reports and accounts. The Guildhall Library in London has perhaps the largest accessible collection of such reports and accounts, while many university and business school libraries possess selective collections. For a considerable number of companies, key financial and operational data are available on a variety of computer tapes and information systems; as, for example, the London Business School's or the Manchester Business School's computerized company records. The London Business School issues the quarterly *Risk Measurement Service* report, which details selected investment data for all quoted companies and provides risk measures for each company.

Further Reading

Accounting Standards Committee, *Setting Accounting Standards*, London: ASC, 1978.

Accounting Standards Committee, *The Corporate Report*, London: ASC, 1975.

Altman, E. I., 'Financial ratios, discriminant analysis and the prediction of corporate bankruptcy', *Journal of Finance*, September 1968.

Altman, E. I., Haldeman, R. G. and Narayanan, P., 'Zeta analysis: a new model to identify bankruptcy risk of corporations', *Journal of Banking and Finance*, June 1977.

Anderson, O. D., *Time Series Analysis and Forecasting*, London: Butterworth, 1976.

Argenti, J., *Corporate Collapse*, New York: McGraw-Hill, 1976.

Ashton, R. K., 'Taxation of corporations in the UK' in J. E. Broyles, I. A. Cooper and S. Archer (eds), *Financial Management Handbook*, 2nd edn, Aldershot: Gower, 1983.

Beaver, W. H., 'Financial ratios as predictors of failure', *Empirical Research in Accounting*, supplement to *Journal of Accounting Research*, 1966.

Beaver, W. H., *Financial Reporting: an Accounting Revolution*, Englewood Cliffs, NJ: Prentice-Hall, 1981.

Bernstein, L. A., *The Analysis of Financial Statements*, Homewood, Ill.: Dow-Jones/Irwin, 1978.

Bird, P., *Understanding Company Accounts*, London: Pitman, 1979.

Cox, B., *Value Added*, London: Heinemann, 1979.

Cox, B., 'Value added and the management accountant', in D. Fanning (ed.), *Handbook of Management Accounting*, Aldershot: Gower, 1983.

de Paula, F. C. and Attwood, F. A., *Auditing: Principles and Practice*, 16th edn, London: Pitman, 1982.

Dobbins, R. and Fanning, D., 'Social accounting', in M. A. Pocock and A. H. Taylor (eds), *Handbook of Financial Planning and Control*, Farnborough: Gower, 1981.

Fanning, D., 'Employment reports – an appraisal', *Employee Relations*, vol. 1, no. 4, 1979.

Foster, G., *Financial Statement Analysis*, Englewood Cliffs, NJ: Prentice-Hall, 1978.

Gibson, C. H. and Boyes, P. A., *Financial Statement Analysis*, Boston, Mass.: CBI Publishing, 1979.

Ingham, H. and Harrington, L. T., *Interfirm Comparison*, London: Heinemann, 1980.

Lee, T. A., *Company Financial Reporting: Issues and Analysis*, 2nd edn, Wokingham, Berks.: Van Nostrand Reinhold, 1982.

Lee, T. A. (ed.), *Developments in Financial Reporting*, Oxford: Allan, 1981.

Lee, T. A. and Tweedie, D. P., *The Institutional Investor and Financial Information*, London: Institute of Chartered Accountants in England and Wales, 1981.

Lee, T. A. and Tweedie, D. P., *The Private Shareholder and the Corporate Report*, London: Institute of Chartered Accountants in England and Wales, 1977.

Lev, B., *Financial Statement Analysis: a New Approach*, Englewood Cliffs, NJ: Prentice-Hall, 1974.

Lewis, R., Pendrill, D. and Simon, D. S., *Advanced Financial Accounting*, London: Pitman, 1981.

McMonnies, P. N., *The Companies Act 1981: a Practical Guide*, London: Oyez Publishing, 1982.

Mepham, M. J., *Accounting Models*, Stockport: Polytech, 1980.

Morley, M. F., *The Value Added Statement*, London: Gee, 1978.

Parker, R. H., *Understanding Company Financial Statements*, 2nd edn, Harmondsworth, Middx.: Pelican, 1982.

Pendlebury, M. W., 'The application of information theory to accounting for groups of companies', *Journal of Business Finance and Accounting*, vol. 7, no. 1, 1980.

Samuels, J., Rickwood, C. R. and Piper, J., *Advanced Financial Accounting*, Maidenhead, Berks.: McGraw-Hill, 1982.

Seidler, L. J. and Seidler, L. (eds), *Social Accounting: Theory, Issues and Cases*, New York: Melville, 1975.

Stock Exchange, *Admission of Securities to Listing*, latest edn, London: Stock Exchange, 1979 *et seq.*

Taffler, R. J., 'The Z-score approach to measuring company solvency', *The Accountant's Magazine*, March 1983.

Taffler, R. J. and Tisshaw, H., 'Going, going, gone – four factors which predict', *Accountancy*, March 1977.

Tamari, M., *Financial Ratios: Analysis and Prediction*, London: Elek, 1978.

Tolley's Corporation Tax, Croydon: Tolley, annually.

Woolf, E., *Auditing Today*, London: Prentice-Hall, 1979.

Index

accountability 1-3
accounting principles 5; *see also* standards
Addo plc
    balance sheets 63, 64
    funds flow statement 66
administrative expenses 24-5
Altman, E., multiple discriminant analysis
    technique 157-8
Argyll Foods plc 29
assets, *see* current assets, fixed assets,
    revaluation (of assets), total assets
audit 3
    certificate 3
    and directors' reports 4
auditors
    and director's report 76
    fees disclosure 35
    opinion 95

bankruptcy, predicting 156-9
banks, social and community activities 87-8
British Institute of Management 217
British Oxygen Company plc 26, 29, 33
    accounting policies and definitions 35,
        181-5
    additional financial reports 210-16
    auditor's report 93, 175
    balance sheet 39-40, 49-50, 51, 177, 180
    chairman's statement 78-80
    corporation tax 31, 32
    director's report 72, 165-74
    earnings per share 36
    employee statistics 35, 132
    financial reporting standards 9
    financial review 108-9, 110-14
    funds flow statement 58, 177
    gearing position 143-50
    notes on financial statements 186-209
    profit and loss account 20, 176
    segmental analysis 124-5
    time-series analysis 153
    value added statement 68, 179
British Productivity Council 217

capital
    return and profitability 107-113
    see also share capital
capital structure ratios, and analysing gear-
    ing 143-8
cash flow statement 65
Centre for Interfirm Comparison 156, 217
chairman's statement 2, 77-8
Companies Act 1948 3, 54
Companies Act 1967 36
Companies Act 1981 3-5, 15, 26, 27, 30, 33,
    34-5, 36, 38-9, 43, 54, 55, 56, 72
company comparison 155-6
    problems of 155-6
    and segmental reporting 125-6

company holdings 75
company reports
    and accountability 2-3
    on corporate objectives 90
    format of 9-10
    purpose of 10-11
    reduced disclosure 36-7
    statutory requirements 3-6
Consultative Committee of Accountancy
    Bodies
    Accounting Standards Committee 6
    Auditing Practices Committee 6, 94
contingencies 55
Council of the Stock Exchange 6, 7
creditors 52-3
    turnover and payment 128-9
cross-sectional analysis 154-5
    problems of 155-6
current assets
    cash 52
    and current ratio 135
    debtors 51-2
    and investments 49
    stocks 50-1
current cost accounting 42-5
    gearing adjustment 147-8

debt 142
    in gearing ratios 145, 146
debtors 51-2
    turnover and collection 127-8
decision-making, and use of financial ratios
    151-2
defensive interval 139-41
Department of Trade 5, 29
depreciation charges 25, 46
directors 2, 34-5
    disclosure of information on 74-5
directors' report 2, 4
    contents 72-6
disabled people, employment of 75-6
distribution costs 23-4
dividend cover ratio 149-50
dividends 62
    disclosure of 33-4
    from group company shares 26-7
donations 76

employee ratios 131-3
employee report 10
employees
    information disclosure 34, 35
    and value added 70
employment information 75-6, 81-5
environmental issues, and company reports
    7-8, 86
equity 142
    return calculation 117-18

European Economic Community
 code on trade with South Africa 86-7
 and company law 1, 4
exceptional items, in profit and loss accounts 30
executives *see* stewardship
exemptions, from current cost accounting statements 43
 from full public disclosure 36-7
extraordinary items
 in funds statements 62
 in profit and loss accounts 33

financial commitments 55-6
financial ratios
 calculation 103-4
 comparison 102-3
 indicating performance 127-31, 134
 indicating profitability 107-9, 114-25
 to assess gearing 143-50
 to assess liquidity 135-8
see also ratio analysis
financial statements
 and accounting standards 11
 additional 81-91
 analysis 101
 content and structure 2, 8-9
fixed assets
 intangible 46-8
 investments 48-50
 loans 50
 shares 50
 tangible 48
 transactions 75
Fleet Holdings plc 21, 32, 33, 36
 auditor's report 93
 balance sheet 39, 41
 employee information 35
 funds flow statement 59
forecasting 74
 and use of financial ratios 151-2
foreign currency transactions 35, 89-90
format
 of auditor's reports 92-3
 of balance sheets 38-42
 of company reports 9-10
 of financial statements 8-9
 of funds flow statements 58
 of profit and loss accounts 15-21
 of value added statements 68-9
funds, definition 60
funds flow statement 2
 construction 62
 contents 58-62
 format 58
 usefulness 66-7

gearing 142
 analysis by financial ratios 143-50
goodwill, accounting for 47-8
government, money exchanges with 88-9

Health and Safety at Work Act 1974/75

income
 investment 29
 operating 26
 shares 26-9

income statement *see* profit and loss account
interest, disclosures 29-30
interest cover ratio 148-9
investments
 as assets 48-9
 income 29

Law Commission 6
legislation 1
 see also Companies Acts
liabilities and charges 53
limited liability 1-2
liquidity assessment
 and defensive interval 139-41
 and financial ratios 135-8
 and funds flow analysis 138-9
Lloyds, ruling council 6
loans 50, 142

Macarthys Pharmaceuticals plc, value added statement 70
management performance, financial ratios indicating 127-31, 134
Marks & Spencer plc
 employment report 82, 86
 financial relationship with government 89
Marley plc
 auditor's report 93-4
 value added statement 69
minority interests 55
"modified" accounts 4
multiple discriminant analysis, and prediction of bankruptcy 157-9

National Westminster Bank plc, social and community activities 87-8

"over-trading" 135
"position" statement *see* balance sheet
prior year items 33
profit and loss account 2, 4, 15
 contents 22-36
 formats 15-21
profitability, indicators of 107-26

quick ratio 137-8

Rank Organisation plc, funds flow statement 61
ratio analysis
 of financial statements 101-2
 problems of 104-6
 purpose of 151
Registrar of Companies 4, 9, 36
"related" company 27-8, 62
research and development 74
reserves 54
revaluation (of assets) 25-6, 45-6
risk, and company gearing 142-3
Rowntree Mackintosh plc, social responsibility report 87

sales, and profitability 121-4
sales costs 23
Scottish & Newcastle Breweries plc, employment report 83-5

segmental analysis
  and profitability 124-6
  and ratio analysis 106
share capital 54
shares
  earnings per share 35-6, 118-21
  group company 26-7
  own 50
  price/earnings ratio 121
  related company 27-9
social accounting 7-8, 85-8
social reporting *see* social accounting
sources and applications of funds statements
  see funds flow statement
South Africa, and company interests 86-7
standards
  of accounting 5-7, 11-12, 29, 76, 90-1
  of auditing 94
Statements of Standard Accounting Practice
  5, 6-7, 27, 28, 29, 30-1, 33, 35, 47, 55,
  56, 58
  on current cost accounting statements
  42-5

stewardship 2
Stock Exchange 49
  Listing Agreement 29, 30, 72
  see also Council of the Stock Exchange
stock turnover ratio 129-31
stocks, and the balance sheet 50-1

Taffler, R. J., multiple discriminant analysis
  technique 158-9
taxation 60-1
  disclosure in profit and loss accounts
  30-3
time series analysis 152-4
total assets, returns calculations 114-17
turnover 22-3

value added statement 2
  contents 69-71
  format 68-9
  usefulness 71

working capital ratio 135-7